Greatness & Limits of Common Priesthood in
16th Century Reformation Theology

Classic Theology and Contemporary Issues
Series editor:
Gijsbert van den Brink (VU Amsterdam)
Volume II

I. Cornelis van der Knijff, *Between Providence and Choice Biography*

Martijn S. Pouw

Greatness & Limits of Common Priesthood
in 16th Century Reformation Theology

A Realist Phenomenological Study
of the Common Priesthood in Luther and
Calvin from a Roman Catholic Perspective

Summum

This publication is made possible by the generous support of the J.E. Jurriaanse Stichting, C.J. de Vogel Stichting, Sormani Fonds, Stichting Zonneweelde and Jan Louis Burggraaf.

J.E. Jurriaanse Stichting Ⓥ

Cover design: Brainstorm
Typesetting: Gewoon Geertje

ISSN 2666-2434
ISBN 9789492701138

Copyright © Summum Academic Publications, Kampen, The Netherlands.
www.summumacademic.com

All rights reserved. No part of this publication may be reproduced, translated, stored in aretrieval system, or transmitted in any form by any means, electronic, mechanical, photocopying, recording or otherwise, without prior written permission from the publisher.

Table of Contents

ABBREVIATIONS	IX
FOREWORD	11
INTRODUCTION	15
1. Existential theology: existential approach	17
2. Prolegomena	19
3. Structure of the book	21
CHAPTER 1 – COMMON PRIESTHOOD IN LUTHER	**23**
1. Relevant elements of luther's life and person	23
1.1 Historical context	23
1.1.1 Society divided into estates	23
1.1.2 Luther's ecclesial world	25
1.1.3 The poor spiritual state of the spiritual estate	28
1.2 Luther's experience of salvation	29
1.3 Luther's objections to the Catholic Church	31
	35
2. Luther's relationship with God	35
2.1 Widening the gap	35
2.1.1 God's glory versus human sin	35
2.1.2 The role of the law	36
2.2 Bridging the gap	37
2.2.1 God's saving action	37
2.2.2 Personal encounter: despair and faith	38
2.2.3 Identification and free benefits	39
2.3 Leaping the gap	41
	45
3. Luther's theological framework	45
3.1 Main features	45
3.1.1 Dialectical, exclusive and dualistic	46
3.1.2 Subjective act of faith	46
3.1.3 Passivity towards God	47
3.1.4 Impossibility of communion in the temporal-earthly sphere	47
3.2 Back in the world	48
3.2.1 On the individual level	48
3.2.2 Community level	55
3.3 Preliminary conclusion	60

4. The common priesthood in Luther 63
   4.1 Fundament of the priesthood 63
   4.2 The believers' participation in Christ's priesthood 65
   4.3 Finality of priesthood 68
   4.4 The exercise of the priesthood: functions 69
       4.4.1 Preaching and teaching 70
       4.4.2 Prayer 71
       4.4.3 Sacrifice 72
       4.4.4 Other functions 80
   4.5 Relation between Priesthood and ministries 81
   4.6 Mediation 82
   4.7 Conclusion 84

CHAPTER II – COMMON PRIESTHOOD IN CALVIN **87**
1. Relevant elements of Calvin's life, person and theology 87
   1.1 Life and person 87
   1.2 Calvin's theological framework and key insights 89

2. The relationship between God and humans 95
   1.1 Widening the gap 95
   2.1 Bridging the gap 98
       2.2.1 True knowledge and faith 98
       2.2.2 The role of the law and the gospel 100
   2.3 Leaping the gap 101
       2.3.1 Wondrous exchange and benefits 102
       2.3.2 Mystical union 102
       2.3.3 Direct eschatological access 107
   2.4 Back in the world 108
       2.4.1 A process of regeneration 108
       2.4.2 Emphasis on the external and visible Church 110
       2.4.4 Without human cooperation 113
       2.4.5 Human freedom and obedience 114
       2.4.6 The believers' identification with Christ by external cross-bearing 116
       2.4.7 The value of human works and service to God . . . 118
       2.4.8 Double predestination 119
       2.4.9 Secularisation 119
   2.5 Preliminary conclusion 120

3. The common priesthood in Jean Calvin ... 123
   3.1 Fundament of the priesthood ... 124
   3.3 Finality of priesthood ... 128
   3.4 The exercise of the priesthood ... 128
      3.4.1 Intercessory prayer ... 130
      3.4.2 Spiritual sacrifices ... 131
   3.5 Relation between priesthood and ministries ... 135
   3.6 Mediation ... 137
   3.7 Conclusion ... 138

CHAPTER III – Reformed common priesthood revisited ... **141**
1. Luther and Calvin compared ... 141
   1.1 Personalities and main motivation ... 141
   1.2 Mitigating the common priesthood ... 142
   1.3 Reframing the relationship between God and humans ... 144
   1.4 Preliminary conclusion ... 147

2. Evaluation ... 149
   2.1 Points of connection with the Catholic understanding of common priesthood ... 149
      2.1.1 Christ is the only and true eternal High Priest and Redeemer ... 149
      2.1.2 Greatness of the Christian life in the world ... 149
      2.1.3 The believer's personal encounter with Christ ... 150
      2.1.4 The importance of humility ... 150
      2.1.5 Unconditional love and free gift ... 151
      2.1.6 Certainty, freedom and love of neighbour ... 151
   2.2 Points of divergence with a Catholic understanding of common priesthood ... 152
      2.2.1 Limitation of Christ's priesthood and sacrifice ... 153
      2.2.2 Separation between Christ's sacrifice and the believers' offerings ... 153
      2.2.3 A shift from self-giving to self-denial ... 154
      2.2.4 Exclusive focus on the world ... 156
      2.2.5 Oblivion of the task to bring back the world to God ... 156

3. Some theological implications of reformed understanding of common priesthood ... 159
   3.1 Greatness, but also confusion ... 159
   3.2 Gnostic, situational and relational redemption and priesthood ... 161

   3.2.1 Gnostic redemption   161
   3.2.2 Situational redemption   161
   3.2.3 Relational redemption   162
  3.3 Paradoxical anthropology   163
  3.4 Weak ecclesiology   166
   3.4.1 No real communion in the intermediate time   166
   3.4.2 No human mediation of divine realities   166
  3.5 Preliminary conclusion   168

4. Key elements of a catholic understanding and exercise of common priesthood   171
  4.1 Some epistemological and anthropological principles   171
   4.1.1 Open, inclusive and fruitful   171
   4.1.2 Principle of continuity and unity   172
   4.1.3 Moderate paradox   172
   4.1.4 Christ's Incarnation as a positive and effective event   173
   4.1.5 God respects and assists humans   174
  4.2 The intermediary time and space   177
   4.2.1 God's salvific plan   177
   4.2.2 Already, but not yet   178
   4.2.3 Layered structure   178
   4.2.4 The access to God   179
  4.3 A family community   180
   4.3.1 Real spiritual communion   181
   4.3.2 Stable community   182
   4.3.3 Dynamic communication   187
  4.4 The exercise of the priesthood in the temporal earthly sphere   192
   4.4.1 Christ eternal priesthood and sacrifice   192
   4.4.2 Continuity of Christ's heavenly priesthood and sacrifice on earth   193
   4.4.3 Sacramental union and double participation   193
   4.4.4 A real human role   194
  4.5 Conclusion   196

CONCLUSION   199
BIBLIOGRAPHY   207

ABBREVIATIONS

c.	canon
CCC	Catechism of the Catholic Church
CIC	*Codex Iuris Canonici* (Code of Canon law)
CN	*Communionis Notio*
FC	*Familiaris Consortio*
GS	*Gaudium et Spes*
Instit.	Institutes of the Christian Religion (by J. Calvin)
LG	*Lumen Gentium*
LW	Luther's Works, Jaroslav Pelikan and Helmut T. Lehmann (eds.), 56 vols., Concordia, St. Louis and Fortress, Philadelphia 1955–1986,
UR	*Unitatis Redintegratio*
WA	Weimarer Ausgabe
PO	*Presbyterorum Ordinis*
SC	*Sacrosanctum Concilium*
SJT	Scottish Journal of Theology
Tischr.	Tischreden (Table Talk)

FOREWORD

You may be wondering why a Catholic priest is so interested in re-discovering the teachings of Protestant reformers on the common priesthood. Let me relate to you the genesis and development of this book.

I come from the Netherlands, a country where Protestant reformation was very much at home, while at the same time keeping a stable Catholic population over the years. I myself went to Protestant schools both for my primary and secondary education. In spite of that, I have to admit that I had never really immersed myself into the ideas of Luther and Calvin, and only knew the usual clichés: *sola fide*, *sola gratia* and *sola scriptura*, zero devotion to the saints, including Mary, no purgatory, among others. I still remember that one day at high school—I was then 15 years old—a protestant friend asked me, "Why don't Catholics go directly to the Lord, but take all kinds of detours?" I was speechless.

Fast-forward to 2017. I was in Rome pursuing my graduate studies in theology. While searching for a topic for my doctoral dissertation, I bumped into some of the writings of two key Protestant reformers, Martin Luther and John Calvin. Given my background, I toyed with the idea of writing a dissertation about a topic that may help bring about a more reasoned dialogue in present-day ecumenism. And so, I began to immerse myself into the writings of Luther and Calvin. As I poured into their theology, one idea stood out: the priesthood of all believers. I felt like one of the kids in the Chronicles of Narnia discovering a whole new world through my own wardrobe.

Admittedly, It was by no means easy to become fully acquainted with the theology and spirituality of the 16th-century Reformers. I am well aware of the fact that I may not have fully succeeded in understanding every nook and cranny of their teachings. Nevertheless, I am confident that this research has yielded some very interesting insights that are worth sharing, discussing and reflecting upon further. Rest assured, I made considerable effort in trying to grasp and reflect upon their extant writings. I believe that, on the whole, a true and fair view of their ideas and points of view have been presented in this book. I am aware that it is possible that here and there I would have missed a point, have not been as exhaustive or have gone wrong. I would therefore be grateful to receive your inputs to help me improve my understanding and insights. I see this book as a start for dialogue in a spirit of Christian fraternity and charity.

You may be wondering about the theoretical framework upon which this book is built and its corresponding methodology. This book exposes the visions and insights of the 16th century Reformers vis-a-vis Catholic doctrine as formulated in the Second Vatican Council (second half of the 20th century). Would it be fair to compare and contrast theological concepts that were developed four centuries apart? Had it not been more accurate to compare Luther and Calvin with their contemporaries, such as a Robert Bellarmine? And the Second Vatican Council with the views of Karl Barth or Wolfhart Pannenberg? It is true that there is merit in doing so. However, they fall beyond the main purpose of the book, which is to identify the conditions for a proper understanding and exercise of the common priesthood of all believers, and not so much an historical overview of the development of this doctrine. Above all, this work aims to provide points of departure for the promotion of ecumenical dialogue, starting with the reformers themselves.

Luther and Calvin are pioneers of the 'common priesthood' doctrine— the former by providing its theoretical framework and the latter through its practical application. It is therefore, worth spending time trying to fathom and reflect on their writings on this point. It is well known that in the centuries following the Reformation and the Council of Trent, theological discourse was characterized by polarization. Catholic theologians concentrated on defending the ministerial (sacramental) priesthood over and against the common priesthood, though without denying it, as it was considered primarily a Protestant affair. At the same time, it is striking to note that even in Protestant theology after the Reformation relatively little attention was paid to this doctrine. It appears to have been taken for granted. On the other hand, the Catholic understanding of common priesthood only regained full prominence in the 20th Century during Second Vatican Council. In this light, it is not inconsistent to study the original positions of the Reformers (16th Century) vis-a-vis the developments in Catholic theology in the 20th century. Hence, the present study should never be seen as an anachronistic way of 'lecturing' the reformers, but rather an attempt to organise an encounter of different views for a fruitful dialogue, hopefully leading to harmonisation.

This book is based on a doctoral research conducted between January 2017 and October 2018 under guidance of prof. Miguel de Salis Amaral. I would like to thank J.E. Jurriaanse Stichting, C.J. de Vogel Stichting, Sormani Fonds, Stichting Zonneweelde and Jan Louis Burggraaf for their financial contribution, and prof. Gijsbert van den Brink for accepting this study in the series *Classical Theology and Contemporary Challenges.* Furthermore, for helpful critical reading and English language editing, I am grateful to Oliver Tuazon.

M. Pouw
Utrecht, 26 June 2020

INTRODUCTION

In 2017, the Lutheran community and the Catholic Church jointly commemorated 500 years of the Protestant reformation.¹ This reformation in the 16th century had a great impact, causing deep divisions and conflicts in the life of both Church and society of late medieval Europe, and which is still felt until the present day.

Ecclesiology is of key importance to ecumenical dialogue² and, for many theologians, an essential aspect of it lies at the very core of Protestant ecclesiology: the concept of common or universal priesthood.³ Luther affirmed, in the context of the 16th century, the radical equality of all believers by explicitly referring to the priesthood common to everyone. In doing so, he blurred the essential distinction between ordinary Christians—laymen—⁴ and the ordained clergy. The priesthood of all believers became a fundamental principle and feature of the whole Protestant reformation movement.

In Protestant communities, common priesthood is being exercised without the ministerial priesthood—understood as being essentially distinct from the common priesthood, though both forms of priesthood are mutually ordained to each other—⁵ for five centuries. However, there are indications that even the common priesthood within Protestantism nowadays is in crisis.⁶ The hypothesis is that this crisis and loss of meaning

---

1 LUTHERAN–ROMAN CATHOLIC COMMISSION, Report *From Conflict to Communion*, Joint Lutheran–Roman Catholic Commemoration of the reformation in 2017, published in 2013.
2 *Ibidem*, no 96, where the joint commission stated: «An important topic for further discussion is how we can deepen our convergence on those issues where we still have different emphases, especially with respect to the doctrine of the Church».
3 According to the Lutheran theologian Hans Martin Barth, the Evangelical Church is «the church of the universal priesthood—or it is nothing», in: H.M. BARTH, *Einander Priester sein. Allgemeines Priestertum in ökumenischer Perspektive*, Vandenhoeck & Ruprecht, Göttingen 1990, 103.
4 The term "lay" or "laity" has in common use of language the meaning of "non-professionals", however, in the context of this book, it expresses the phenomenon of "non-ordained" Christians.
5 Cfr. VATICAN COUNCIL II, Dogm. const. *Lumen Gentium*, no 10.
6 Wolfgang Hering, a protestant pastor, asserted in 2009 «in the Evangelical Church the phrase "priesthood of all believers" is merely used as a standard expression, and most of the time without understanding its meaning», in: W. HERING, *Zwischen Gott und Welt*.

might be due, among other causes, to the fact that within Protestant communities, ministerial priesthood is lacking.

This book aims to clarify the importance of the relationship between the common and ministerial priesthoods, in order to develop a good understanding and exercise of the common priesthood, by studying the notion of the "priesthood of all believers" in Luther and Calvin. It is an attempt to thoroughly grasp and re-think Luther's and Calvin's notions of common priesthood without the ministerial, to understand better and to shed light upon the necessary mutual relationship between both ministerial and common priesthoods as maintained in Roman Catholic doctrine. Reformation theology is a kind of case study to resolve the underlying question: which are the necessary conditions for a good understanding and exercise of a meaningful Christian common priesthood in the world? At the same time, this study may contribute to the ongoing discussion on the topic by bringing in elements that could be relevant, and may even open horizons in contemporary ecumenical dialogue on a common understanding of this particular doctrine of the Church.[7]

The study is conducted from a Catholic point of view. The Catholic doctrine—especially since the Second Vatican Council[8]—on common and ministerial priesthoods is the point of reference, but with an open attitude, by evaluating points of connection among Evangelical,[9] Reformed and Catholic doctrine and spirituality, which could mutually enrich their understanding of the same. The study also attempts to detect elements of divergence in the various ways of reasoning of the said faith traditions, while proposing possible new ways of understanding the concept and role of the common priesthood.

Given the diversity of the Protestant movement, the present study is limited to the original views of two main reformers of the 16th century:

Anmerkungen zum Priestertum aller Gläubigen, «Deutschen Pfarrerblatt», 1 (2009) 1 (my translation); See also BARTH, *Einander Priester sein*, 29 and R. MUTHIAH, *Christian Practices, Congregational Leadership and the Priesthood*, «Journal of Religious Leadership» 2 (2003), 167-203.

7 Cfr. LUTHERAN–ROMAN CATHOLIC COMMISSION, Report *From Conflict to Communion* (2013), no 211.

8 *Ibidem*, no 90, «While the Council of Trent largely defined Catholic relations with Lutherans for several centuries, its legacy must now be viewed through the lens of the actions of the Second Vatican Council (1963-1965). This Council made it possible for the Catholic Church to enter the ecumenical movement and leave behind the charged polemic atmosphere of the post-Reformation era. (…)».

9 Hereafter I will not always make the distinction between "Evangelical" and "Reformed" doctrine and spirituality, but rather use the term "Reformed" to indicate both Evangelical (Luther) and Reformed (Calvin) views.

Martin Luther and John Calvin. On one hand, Luther is undoubtedly considered the leading figure of the Protestant reformation movement in the 16th century.[10] On the other hand, Calvin is regarded to be a highly influential reformer—both due to his theology and his practical application of his ideas in the local Church of Geneva—who already enjoyed, during his lifetime, an international reputation as a reformer distinct from Luther.[11]

1. Existential theology: existential approach

Reformation theology—especially Luther's, but to a large extent the same holds true for Calvin—[12] is profoundly existential, where the point of departure for doing theology is human experience,[13] i.e., that of the forgiveness of sins and salvation, in a personal encounter with the triune God, which is confronted with data of the Scripture. In this experience, Luther discovered that faith alone in Jesus Christ and personal adherence to him makes a human being just before God; human works are of no avail. Luther firmly grounded this existential discovery in Scripture, especially in the letters of St. Paul, the Gospel of St. John and the Psalter. This profound personal conviction provided him with a hermeneutical key to the whole Scripture, thoroughly scrutinising it for its affirmation.[14]

In part as a reaction to late scholasticism, Luther took his own spiritual experience and conviction as a firm basis for the interpretation of his relationship with God, making it paradigmatic and normative for each authentic religious experience. In fact, Luther held and preached his particular religious experience as the only valid one.[15] This personal experience with God caused Luther to reframe the relationship between God and humans in its very essence. The doctrine of justification by faith

---

10 Cfr. J. LORTZ, Geschichte der Kirche in ideengeschichtlicher Betrachtung / Bd. II, Die Neuzeit, Aschendorff, Münster 1964, 72.
11 Cfr. B. COTTRET, Calvin: A Biography, Eerdmans Grand Rapids, Michigan 2000, 235.
12 Though Calvin is different from Luther, it can hardly be denied that he moves within Luther's framework. It is, therefore, crucial to first understand Luther's frame before discussing Calvin's specific approach in Chapter 2.
13 Cfr. C. EASTWOOD, The Priesthood of All Believers. An Examination of the Doctrine of All Believers from the Reformation to the Present Day, Epworth, London 1960, 10.
14 Cfr. R. GARCÍA VILLOSLADA, Martin Lutero, Vol. 1, Biblioteca de Autores Cristianos, Madrid 1976, 228.
15 LW 39:249, «(...) whoever does not accept my teaching may not be saved—for it is God's and not mine. Therefore, my judgement is also not mine but God's». Also LW 45:347-348, «I wish to assure you and declare to you frankly and openly that he who heeds me in this matter is most certainly not heeding me but Christ; and he who gives me no heed is despising not me, but Christ (Luke 10:16)».

alone is to be regarded as fundamental in Luther's doctrine and spirituality; it shapes his thought on all other issues.[16]

Due to the fact that Luther's approach to theology was thoroughly existential, our way of proceeding in this book should also be "existential". This means, firstly, that in order to understand Luther's experience with God and to grasp his *forma mentis*, it is not enough to listen and read what Luther says, how he says it and why he says it. It is necessary to live—as it were—his personal experience of redemption in Christ and his encounter with God the Father through the Holy Spirit. One should try to share his feelings, his way of seeing and perceiving reality, and endeavour to make them one's own, for this is the best—or perhaps even the only—way to establish a dialogue with him.

Secondly, Dr. Fr. Martin Luther's theological views are to be properly interpreted, above all, in the light of the life and experiences of Luther himself, while the contrary is valid as well: the internal mutual relationships between Luther's theological positions and views, shed light upon his experiences, motivations and intentions.

Due to the existential character of his theology, it is not surprising that Luther has never written a systematic account of his theology. Some of his works are more scholarly, like his commentaries on the Psalms or the books of the Old and New Testament, while others are more polemical, such as his letters against his adversaries or his famous informal table talks. Luther is fond of using hyperboles, paradoxes and dialectical oppositions. Furthermore, it should be taken into account that he has developed his insights over time: from his initial views, which were in conformity with Catholic teachings, to increasingly divergent views. Finally, it should be observed that "Catholic teaching" in the 16th century was not—and still is not—a univocal concept, and so it appears that Luther partly opposed theological views of his days, which could not be properly considered as "Catholic".

These factors do not improve the doctrinal clarity of the issue under discussion, and it is sometimes difficult to grasp the true meaning of Luther's words. More than trying to lift "the veil of language" in order to discover what Luther really wanted to say or to give an historical overview

---

16 Cfr. A. GARUTI, *Primacy of the Bishop of Rome and Ecumenical Dialogue*, Ignatius press, San Francisco 2004, 87. Voss points out that Luther at the beginning held the traditional Catholic view on priesthood, but that he modified his view after having discovered the doctrine of justification by faith alone and the sharing by the believer of Christ's benefits obtained on the cross. Cfr. H.J. VOSS, *The priesthood of all believers and the mission Dei: A canonical, catholic and contextual perspective*, Wheaton, Illinois 2013, 190.

of the development of his thought, I will rather in this book try to indicate some lines of Reformed reasoning, their implications, and the internal mutual relations between the theological positions, which are relevant for the Reformed understanding and exercise of the common priesthood.

2. Prolegomena

It seems, therefore, that the most adequate approach to Luther's theology and spirituality is realist phenomenology,[17] the study of (Christian) phenomena such as they are given to us in reality and to try to discover their essences by confronting these experiences with—and in that same—reality, comparing them to, and distinguishing them from, similar phenomena. The realist phenomenological method proposes to investigate thoroughly, by rational inquiry, the content of these phenomena, like sin, faith, contrition, mercy, forgiveness, salvation, sanctification, love, sacrifice, church, communion of saints, solidarity, priesthood, etc., as experienced by humans in relation to God and others.

However, Luther himself excluded from the very start this way of proceeding. After all, human reason, since it is part of what he considered as corrupted human nature, cannot know reality as it is and can, therefore, never be trusted.[18] Dr. Luther allowed only one possible path for true knowledge of God's Revelation: the experience of the paradox of Christ on the cross, *theologia crucis*.[19] Luther established as a hermeneutical and gnostic principle that God shows himself only and always as the exact

---

17 Realist phenomenology was developed in Germany at the beginning of the 20th century by young philosophers who gathered around Edmund Husserl. Inspired by the publication of his *Logical Investigations* (1900-01), where he sought to refute the errors of Anglo-Saxon empiricism and Kantian transcendentalism by arguing that the essences of phenomena are given in experience and open to rational inquiry, these young men and women adopted the slogan *"Zurück nach die Sachen selbst"* ("Back to the things themselves"). Among these young realist phenomenologists were Max Scheler, Adolf Reinach, Alexander Pfänder, Dietrich von Hildebrand, Edith Stein, Hedwig Conrad-Martius and Roman Imgarden. Cfr. A. A. M. KINNEGING, *Realist Phenomenology and the foundations of natural law: the vindication of the moral order in the works of Scheler, Hartmann and Hildebrand*, «American Journal of Jurisprudence» 46 (2001), 257-276 and A. MACINTYRE, *Edith Stein, A philosophical Prologue*, Continuum, London, New York 2006, 19-28.

18 See for Luther's complex relationship with "reality" the work of H. BLAUMEISER, *Martin Luthers Kreuzestheologie: Schlüssel zu einer Deutung von Mensch und Wirklichkeit; eine Untersuchung anhand der Operationes in Psalmos (1519-1521)*, Bonifatius, Paderborn 1995.

19 «Ergo in Christo crucifix est vera theologia et cognitio Dei» (Thesis 20 Heidelberg Dispute of 1518). It was Walther von Loewenich, who first showed the importance of this hermeneutical principle in Luther's theological framework (*Luthers teologia crucis*, 1929). Cfr. BLAUMEISER, *Martin Luther's Kreuzestheologie*, 73.

opposite of reality, as that what he seems to us (*sub contraria specie*).[20] He exclusively shows himself and his most intimate reality to us where we least expect it, which, according to human parameters appear as not divine or even contrary to the divine: in weakness, fragility, suffering and the scandal of the cross.[21] For him, true theology can only be practised by a theologian "who hangs on the cross" and has thus purified his human vision, and can properly understand and live the Gospel. The same holds true for each believer.[22] Radical paradox, and thus dialectics, is essential to Luther's way of thinking about God and humans. We can grasp God and true reality only "in faith" and—as a matter of principle—not "in reality", for in the temporal sphere of common experience, humans—due to their sinfulness—are always deceived. "True spiritual supernatural reality" grasped in faith is *always* the exact opposite of the reality as it appears to us in the temporal-empirical sphere: the "false or apparent reality", as grasped by human reason.[23] Faith not only transcends reason,

---

20 P. ALTHAUS, *The Theology of Martin Luther*, Fortress Press, Philadelphia 1966, 34: «The theology of the cross means that God hides himself in his work of salvation and that he acts and creates paradoxically while camouflaging his work to make it look as though he were doing the opposite. This is precisely what God characterises».

21 BLAUMEISER, *Martin Luther's Kreuzestheologie*, 469, «Für Luther besteht kein Zweifel: Von Gott verlassen und Tod und Hölle ausgeliefert, hat Christus die unterscheidende Form des neuen Bundes geoffenbart und die neue Gestalt aller Dinge erschlossen. An seiner Doppelexistenz—gekreuzigte und verlassene Menschheit und gleichzeitiges verborgenes Gott sein—scheint darum exemplarisch das Deutungskriterium aller Wirklichkeit auf». Cfr. GARCÍA VILLOSLADA, *Martín Lutero*, Vol. 1, 363 ss; ALTHAUS, *The Theology of Martin Luther*, 25.

22 This way of framing has two major effects. Besides distrusting one's natural capacities to know God "from below", i.e., from the created world towards the Creator by way of natural theology, this principle also establishes a fundamental distrust in Revelation itself, i.e., in the way God reveals himself to humans. After all, it presupposes that God *never* shows himself in normal ordinary circumstances in a form adequate to human understanding, but *always*—apparently to tempt humans—under an opposite form to provoke an act of faith. The normality of the life of Jesus on earth and his humanity is lost out of sight. I will come back to this in Chapter 3, section 4.1.

23 ALTHAUS, *The Theology of Martin Luther*, 32-33, «Judged by the standards of reason and experience of the world, true reality is unreal, and its exact opposite is real. Only faith can apprehend that true and paradoxical reality. (…). To believe means to live in constant contradiction of empirical reality and to trust one's self to that which is hidden. Faith must endure being contradicted by reason and experience; and it must break through the reality of this world by fixing its sights on the world of the promise». See also BLAUMEISER, *Martin Luther's Kreuzestheologie*, 449, «Alles scheint damit auf eine spiegelbildlich entgegengesetzte Urteilsweise hinauszulaufen und ließe sich sehr schnell zu einer abstrakten Hermeneutik der Verborgenheit unter dem Gegenteil formalisieren, in der sich die wahre Wirklichkeit und das, was uns Menschen von ihr

but faith also believes *against* reason.[24] Therefore, the act of faith *in itself* seems to include the rejection of human reason, and the "reality" as perceived by human reason, disqualifying it as mere false appearances.[25]

The realist-phenomenological method supposes that human reasoning is capable to discover the essences of phenomena, such as they are given to us in experience. The basic attitude towards phenomena is of trust and confidence in the goodness of God, who wants to be discovered by humans, also in a rational way. At the same time, however, it is true that humans are hurt by original and personal sin, a datum that undoubtedly must be taken into account while exercising (realist-phenomenological) theology. Humans can err and they have to rely on God's grace to ascertain true knowledge of God and humans. However, a positive valuation of the capabilities of humans to grasp these realities should not exclude human reason, but be open to its real purification and elevation, also in the temporal-earthly sphere of common experiences.

There are two other arguments for allowing this approach. Firstly, Luther's point of departure for doing theology is his own religious experience. A theological framework based on a particular experience should be open to a rational investigation of that experience and cannot be denied by arguing that the other "lacks faith" and that "his reason is corrupted". Moreover, as we have seen, Luther made his own religious experience normative for each authentic religious experience. One thing is to acknowledge the authenticity of Luther's own religious experience, but quite another is to hold and preach that that particular religious experience is the only valid one.

3. Structure of the book

This book consists of three chapters. Chapters I and II deal with the common priesthood in Luther and Calvin respectively. Chapter I starts with a brief outline of two historical issues, which are particularly relevant for the understanding of universal priesthood as radically equal to all believers. Then, I will provide a short sketch of Luther's life and personality, to be continued by the specific way Luther experienced and conceived his

---

erscheint, sozusagen wie das Positiv und das Negativ einer Fotografie gegenüberstehen».

24 Cfr. ALTHAUS, *The Theology of Martin Luther*, 67.

25 One could argue that Luther does not reject reason as such, but required that it should be illuminated by faith. However, Luther's concept of faith appears not very helpful, because it seems not to illuminate, but rather the contrary, it "makes clear" that humans are capable of nothing in their relationship with God and only have to rely on Christ and trust in God's promises.

relationship with God. Thirdly, I will give an overview of the key elements of Luther's theological framework, after which follows a systematic outline of his doctrine on the common priesthood.

Chapter II which pertains to the common priesthood in Calvin, has the same structure with a slight difference. After the short sketch of Calvin's life, I will give an overview of Calvin's framework and key theological insights, before dealing more closely with the way Calvin conceived the relationship between God and humans. Like in Chapter I, the last part contains a systematic outline of Calvin's doctrine on the common priesthood.

To verify how Luther and Calvin understood the doctrine of common priesthood, the study focuses in the last parts of both chapters on the following elements of common priesthood: its fundament, mode of participation, its finality and exercise: functions, the relation between common priesthood and ministry and, finally, the element of mediation (ascending and descending dimensions).

Chapter III contains an evaluation of the doctrines of common priesthood in Luther and Calvin from a Roman Catholic perspective. The doctrines will be evaluated by, firstly, comparing the common priesthood in Luther and Calvin, and secondly, by identifying the points of connection and divergence between Reformation and Catholic doctrine. Thirdly, some general theological implications of the Reformed understanding of common priesthood will be discussed. Finally, to clarify the mutual relationship between common and ministerial priesthood, some key elements of recent Catholic doctrine (since the Second Vatican Council) will be presented, followed by a conclusion.

CHAPTER 1
COMMON PRIESTHOOD IN LUTHER

«This not only praises our works as good fruit on earth, but it also elevates them toward heaven and offers them to God as sacrifices acceptable to Him for His special honour and His highest service. How could a Christian life be extolled more? And how could a person be urged and exhorted more strongly to live a Christian life than by the prospect of bearing such fruit, of serving such a purpose, and of enjoying such honour with God?».[1]

«Christ's merit and sacrifice stands in contradiction to my sacrifice and work. Only one can be valid: either Christ's or my own».[2]

1. Relevant elements of luther's life and person

1.1 Historical context
The Reformation is an extremely complex phenomenon. There are many historical factors to be taken into account, such as the state of religion (spirituality), theology, philosophy and culture (humanism, renaissance), politics (the emergence of the nation-states), economy (taxation) and science (invention of the printing press), just to name a few. This section only deals with two issues, which are relevant for understanding Luther's ideas on the common priesthood: the division of society and Church in so-called "estates" and the poor spiritual state of the spiritual estate.[3]

1.1.1 Society divided into estates
According to the historian Johan Huizinga, the structure of medieval society was based upon distinct "orders" and "estates"—almost synonymous

---
1 LW 24:243.
2 LW 13:328.
3 General biography used for this section: J. HUIZINGA, *The Waning of the Middle Ages*, Doubleday, New York 1954, 56-67; C. TAYLOR, *A Secular Age*, The Belknap Press of Harvard University Press, Cambridge, Massachusetts, London 2007; LORTZ, *Geschichte der Kirche*, 68 ss; H. PIRENNE, *Histoire de l'Europe des invasions au XVIe siècle*, Nouvelle Société D'Éditions, Bruxelles 1939.

notions—which, in late medieval times, long after nobility and feudalism had ceased to be really essential factors in society, continued to impress the mind as dominant forms of life.[4] Late European medieval society was divided into three estates, the so-called "estates of the realm": i) nobility, ii) the spiritual estate (*geistliche Stand),* consisting of clergy and religious, and iii) the common people (peasants, serfs and later bourgeois). Everyone belonged to one of these estates, each one forming a little world of its own, with its own rules, norms and practices. In short, each estate had its own particular way of life. Although, free movement between the estates was possible—one could go from one to the other—[5] the overall system of estates was rather rigid; one's belonging to a particular estate determined one's life, work and identity, in principle, for once and for all.[6] There was a strong sense and awareness of the existence and necessity of, as well as the belonging to, different estates as building blocks for the society.

The role of the religious and the clergy was to pray and to administer the sacraments: to celebrate the Holy Mass, to hear Confession, to baptise, to preach the Gospel and to instruct the people. The clergy performed these tasks for and to the other two estates: the nobility and the common people. The nobility was subject to a sovereign lord, a King or Emperor, who was governing with God's mandate and authority over a territory. The nobles had sworn an oath of loyalty; they were given privileges and were bound to supply military support to their sovereign upon request. Moreover, they owned their territories and ruled over the peasants, who lived and worked on their fields and, in turn, were given shelter, food and protection.

This system of estates had a hierarchical structure, which was considered to be instituted by God.[7] According to Charles Taylor: «the famous medieval adage "the nobility fights for all, the clergy prays for all and the peasants work for all" encapsulates the medieval idea that society is organized in complementary functions, which are nevertheless of unequal

---

4 Cfr. HUIZINGA, *The Waning of the Middle Ages*, 57. According to Huizinga, the notion of "orders" was not fixed, but designated a great variety of social realities, functions, trades, matrimony and virginity and social groups.

5 Especially the spiritual estate, i.e., the clerics and religious, was open to both the nobility (bishops) and the common people (clergy and religious).

6 In the words of Huizinga, «the conception of society in the Middle Ages was statical, not dynamical», HUIZINGA, *The Waning of the Middle Ages*, 58.

7 Huizinga observes «that which, in medieval thought, constitutes unity (…) is the conviction that every one of these groupings represents a divine institution, an element of the organism of Creation emanating from the will of God, constituting an actual entity, and being, at bottom, as venerable as the angelic hierarchy», HUIZINGA, *The Waning of the Middle Ages*, 58.

dignity. (…) People tended to see these relationships in terms of a kind of exchange».[8]

1.1.2 Luther's ecclesial world[9]

In late medieval European society, there was formally one Church and one faith, embodied in the Roman Catholic Church. Practically all people (except Jews and Muslims) were baptised and, formally at least, belonged to the Church. Although Church and worldly governance, in theory, were not to be identified, in practice, however, it was not always easy to separate them. For example, there was the figure of the Prince-Bishop, who ruled his diocese as pastor and, at the same time, governed the city in temporal affairs. It was easier to distinguish the Church from the world in the case of monks and nuns who had "left" the world and temporal affairs to dedicate themselves fully to God. In any case, it is important to note that the people generally tended to identify the Church as such with the spiritual estate, as described above.

The Church, like society, was structured hierarchically as well. The hierarchy of the Church was understood in two senses: i) there was a hierarchy of "holiness" or "perfection" and ii) a hierarchy of "authority".[10] The hierarchical structure implied two mayor divisions between the believers within the Church.[11] Firstly, believers were divided into a spiritual and a secular sector of Christianity according to their vocation and position in the world. Secondly, a division was made between believers into clergy and laymen as to the "authority and spiritual powers" they possess.

These divisions between believers were also institutionalised in estates[12]; the Church recognised three of them: religious, clergy and laity.[13] All estates have in common the sacrament of Baptism. After

---

8 TAYLOR, *A Secular Age*, 45.
9 Expression borrowed from VOSS, *The priesthood of all believers*, 187.
10 It is clear that in practice "holiness" and "authority" do not necessarily coincide, although they obviously ought to go together. The term "authority" comprises the sacred power to act in the person and the name of Christ in the sacraments, public preaching and Church discipline.
11 Also Voss and Eastwood draw attention to these distinctions. Cfr. VOSS, *The priesthood of all believers*, 187-188; EASTWOOD, *An Examination of Doctrine till Present Day*, 12-13.
12 Cfr. J.L. ILLANES, *On the Theology of Work*, Scepter, Dublin and Chicago 1968, 29.
13 These distinctions can cause some confusion. For example, whereas the famous Decree of Gratian (1140) makes no distinction between hierarchy of "holiness" and "authority" and stipulates: «*Duo sunt genera Christianorum: (…) clerici et (…) laici*» (there are two types of Christians: the clergy and the laity) in: *Decretum Gratiani C.12, q.1, c.7*, the CIC of 1917 made a distinction between three hierarchical estates: clergy (c. 107), religious (c. 487) and laity (c. 682).

Baptism, there were two ways to differentiate between the baptised Christians. Firstly, by taking vows, a Christian man or woman changed estates, and became a religious, that is, part of the spiritual sector of Christianity and, secondly, Christian men (religious or lay) could become member of the clergy by being "separated" from the other believers in order to be "consecrated" and to be ordained to God in a special way, in view of the mission to sanctify the world (*consacratio mundi*). The clergy could be either "religious" or "secular".

First division: holiness
To the spiritual sector belonged the religious: men and women who had taken vows of obedience, poverty and chastity. It was regarded to be a specific way of following Christ more intimately. These monks and nuns followed a divine vocation, consisting of renouncing or "leaving" the world and putting themselves at a certain distance from it, in order to sanctify themselves and the world, by giving a testimony of the eschatological character of the final destiny of humans. Late medieval Christianity granted to those who followed the counsels of perfection a special position. By taking vows, they entered the spiritual estate and were regarded to be the *elite* members of Christianity.[14]

To the secular sector of Christianity belonged the laity, men and women, nobles and peasants, who had not taken any vows and were not following the counsels of perfection but were living ordinary lives in the world. They were part of the Church, but not so much identified with it. With respect to their holiness or perfection, they were regarded to be second-class. Holiness in the world was not just considered difficult, but unattainable.[15] To become holy, one should "leave" the world. People belonging to the secular estates should content themselves with "being saved".[16]

Second division: authority
The second major division within Christianity was between clergy and laity. The Pope, successor of the apostle Peter, being the visible substitute of Christ on earth, governed the Church, together with his bishops and ministerial priests. Christian men entered the priesthood by ordination,

---
14 Cfr. PIRENNE, *Histoire de l'Europe des invasions au XVIe siècle*, 306.
15 Cfr. ILLANES, *On the Theology of Work*, 28-29.
16 In *strictu sensu*, theologically speaking, there is no difference between "holiness" and "salvation". However, in the collective imaginary at that time "salvation" was equated with complying with the minimum moral standard of the negative commandments of the Decalogue: thou shall not kill, etc.

which gave them the spiritual "power" to represent Christ in person, in preaching the Gospel and administering the sacraments. They were endowed with the authority of Christ on earth to govern the Church. The clergy were the chosen custodians of divine authority and the officially appointed channels of divine grace through the sacraments that had the effect *ex opere operato*,[17] that is, just by performing the sacraments, divine grace was administered by the priest to the believer.[18] The clergy represented the Church visibly and had the task of preaching the Gospel and instructing the people. It divided the Church in the sense that there are persons who rule and others who are being ruled. These priests also changed estate by their ordination and entered the class of the clergy, which formed part of the spiritual sector of Christianity.

Consequences of the divisions
The overstressing of these divisions had led—in general, concerning the large majority—to a rather passive laity, who did not take much responsibility for the Christian cause, but naturally left everything to the spiritual estate. In fact, in late medieval consciousness there existed two equations. Firstly, people tended to identify the Church with the religious and the clergy (the hierarchy)[19] and secondly, holiness or perfection was considered reachable only for the religious—and to a much lesser extent for the secular clergy.[20] The others, the laity, were not aiming at perfection, but only at salvation.[21]

According to Taylor, «medieval society had reached an equilibrium in the tension—without taking it away—between the radical demands of holiness and ordinary human flourishing, people could "travel at different speeds", in various states or walks of life, in "higher" and "lower" vocations: religious, clergy or lay Christians, which were regarded to be complementary. The celibate, renunciative vocations were seen as higher, but this did

---

17 Cfr. EASTWOOD, *An Examination of Doctrine till Present Day*, 11-12.
18 This doctrine—which supposes the existence and a context of faith—expresses the reality that in the liturgy certain acts have God himself as subject, and not only the Church; Christ is acting through the ministerial priest (words and gestures) to render himself present in the Church, a "power" which a priest does not have by himself, but a prerogative given to him by God due to his special configuration with Christ (cfr. CCC no 1128).
19 Cfr. LORTZ, *Geschichte der Kirche*, 5.
20 In this respect, it is interesting to note that the first diocesan priest ever to be raised to the altars was Saint Jean-Marie Vianney, who was canonised in 1925. The remarkable fact is that he wanted to go at the end of his life to a monastery. Cfr. C.F. TROCHU, *le curé d'Ars, Jean-Marie-Baptise Vianney (1786-1859)*. Librairie Catholique Emmanuel Vitte, Lyon-Paris 1925, 400 ss.
21 Cfr. ILLANES, *On the Theology of Work*, 28-29.

not prevent them from balancing the other, lower modes of living the Christian vocations, in a functional whole».[22] It meant, however, accepting that «the vast majority of Christians were not going to live up fully to the demands of the Gospel in their daily lives in the midst of the world».[23]

1.1.3 The poor spiritual state of the spiritual estate
Although there were exceptions, which must be given credit, unfortunately, the mix of spiritual with worldly powers had led to many abuses by popes and bishops. Several popes did not behave according to the dignity and demands of their ministry, as successors of St. Peter and vicar of Jesus Christ on earth. They often seemed more interested in exercising worldly power to the benefit of the pontifical state and family interests, and governed as absolute monarchs, rather than promoting the Kingdom of God.[24]

Also, many Bishops were not so much pastoring the flock but thinking more of their own well-being. They possessed a rather poor knowledge of theology, did not celebrate Mass, nor paid any attention to the formation of future priests. They lived an easy life (accumulating offices) and often even an immoral one.[25]

The lower clergy did not enjoy much prestige either. Although they were rather poor materially, they did not compensate this with spiritual richness. On the contrary, they often lacked a divine vocation, interior life, culture or proper formation, and living in concubinage was common. The pastoral activity was limited to saying Mass, but without any instruction, preaching and apostolic zeal.[26]

Finally, the religious generally did not live up to high moral standards either, which they pretended to attain. In theory, they had left the world, but in practice many had become worldly, lacking piety and discipline, and even the necessary vocation, but they amassed wealth and privileges instead.[27]

In sum, the church in Luther's time seemed to emphasize external acts performed by priests in liturgy and sacraments, saying formulas of standard prayers, while leaving the common people ignorant about the mysteries of faith. Personal faith appeared not to count because grace was distributed by acts of spiritually poor and sinful men *ex opere operato*,

---

22 TAYLOR, *A Secular Age*, 45.
23 *Ibidem*, 61-62.
24 Cfr. LORTZ, *Geschichte der Kirche*, 28-29.
25 Cfr. *Ibidem*.
26 Cfr. *Ibidem*, 51-52.
27 Cfr. *Ibidem*, 53.

and the insistence on performing "good works" to reach righteousness before God: indulgences, penitence, worship of relics, processions, pilgrimages, etc. This was the setting in great parts of Europe when Luther entered the scene.

1.2 Luther's experience of salvation

Martin Luther[28] (1483-1546) was born in Eisleben, Saxony (Germany). His parents were small farmers, and his father later became a miner. He received his first formation at a primary school of the brothers of the Brethren of the Common Life, and later studied philosophy and theology at the University of Erfurt. In 1505, at the age of 23, he took his vows, entered the monastery of All Saints in Wittenberg as an Augustinian hermit, and became part of the spiritual estate of Christendom. Two years later, he was ordained priest, which made him part of the clergy. In 1522, he became a professor of sacred theology and Bible exegesis at the University of Wittenberg. Luther was known to be a hard worker and expert in languages and Scripture. As an Augustinian friar, he was especially influenced by the Church Father St. Augustine, but also by the apostle Paul, who played a vital role in the development of his theological insights. He translated the New Testament into German in 1522 to be followed by a translation of the Old Testament in 1534.

Luther was a theologian and teacher, but, above all, he was a fervent believer with a deeply religious nature. He had a special sensibility to the existence of sin. Luther's ideal and main concern were to please the Lord; his greatest desire—turning often into anxiety—was that God would look upon him favourably.[29] Luther had, therefore, a keen interest in the issue of his salvation. His primordial question was: how do I know for certain that I am saved? By taking his vows and becoming a monk, he had entered the spiritual estate and formed part of the *elite* of Christendom. He had tried everything and had followed every advice of his spiritual directors

---

28 General bibliography on Luther: C. METHUEN, *Luther's life*, 7-27 in: R. KOLB, I. DINGEL, L. BATKA (eds.), *The Oxford Handbook of Martin Luther's Theology*, Oxford University Press, Oxford 2014; LORTZ, *Geschichte der Kirche*, 78-129, E. ISERLOH, *Martin Luther und der Aufbruch der Reformation (1517-1525)*, in: H. JEDIN (ed.), *Handbuch der Kirchengeschichte, Bd. 4, Reformation, katholische Reform und Gegenrefomation*, Herder, Freiburg 1979; GARCÍA VILLOSLADA, *Martin Lutero* (2 Vol.).

29 LW 54:75, Table Talk n. 461, «Beware of melancholy, for it is forbidden by God because it is so destructive for the body. Our Lord has commanded to be cheerful. In this world sadness generally springs from money, honour, study, etc. My temptation is this, that I think that I don't have a gracious God. This is [because I am still caught up in] the law». Cfr. GARCÍA VILLOSLADA, *Martín Lutero, Vol. 1*, 143-144.

to please the Lord and to become holy.[30] Yet, he still experienced sin in his life. After all his efforts, mortification and penance, he regarded—and felt—himself to be a great sinner, that he could not be propitious to God at all, and that it was impossible for him to comply perfectly to God's law by himself.

Around 1515 his deeply felt longing for salvation was resolved. While studying the Letter of Saint Paul to the Romans in his room in the tower, Luther finally learned and experienced—the so-called *Türmerlebnis*— that salvation was not the consequence of any human works, but solely a consequence of faith in Jesus Christ.[31] Jesus Christ has saved us by his sacrifice on the cross, once and for all. For Luther, this experience was not just an experience of consolation, but he thought of it as a real conversion from his former erroneous "pelagian" concept of the Gospel trusting exclusively in one's own works to the "true" version of the Gospel, which is that God is merciful, if you only have faith in Christ.[32] Humans cannot rely on works, because they are sinful and therefore, «we cannot find any consolation in them».[33] For Luther, salvation is a pure gift from God, without any reciprocity,[34] and the gateway to it is personal faith in Jesus Christ.

Above all things, Fr. Martin yearned for certainty in his relationship with God. The kind of certainty he was longing for was not just moral certainty about whether one is walking on the right path and doing—or trying to do—God's will, but rather he was looking for what we could call "eschatological certainty": the certainty of his salvation and destiny after earthly life. In order to obtain this kind of certainty, Dr. Luther put the emphasis in his relationship with God decisively on God's role, to such an extent that his own role was minimised and reduced to nothing.[35] In this way, he safeguarded and secured the absolute primacy of God in relation to humans, who totally depend upon God, and at the same time, he

---

30 Cfr. METHUEN, *Luther's life*, 8, and GARCÍA VILLOSLADA, *Martín Lutero*, Vol. 1, 110.

31 Cfr. EASTWOOD, *An Examination of Doctrine till Present Day*, 10. Eastwood points out that this was no mere academic conclusion, but Luther's personal history.

32 Cfr. B. HAMM, *Martin Luther's Revolutionary Theology of Pure Gift without Reciprocation*, «Lutheran Quarterly», XXIX (2015), 147; Cfr. LW 48:12; LW 54:75.

33 Luther once remarked: «After Confession and the celebration of the Mass I was never able to find rest in my heart, for the conscience cannot have sure comfort on the basis of works», LW 5:157.

34 According to Hamm this is the essential characteristic of Luther's theology. HAMM, *Martin Luther's Revolutionary Theology of Pure Gift without Reciprocation*, 125-161.

35 LW 26:66, «(…), I attribute everything solely to God and nothing at all to men. (…). Still my doctrine is one that preaches and worships God alone, and it condemns the righteousness and wisdom of all men. Here I cannot go wrong, for both to God and to men I ascribe what properly and truly belongs to each».

established a firm basis for certain knowledge of his salvation. For only if God takes care of everything,[36] and humans have no role to play whatsoever, believers can be sure that everything in their relationship with God is well.[37]

1.3 Luther's objections to the Catholic Church

Luther's main objection to the Church *of his day* was of a spiritual nature— the prevalent general lack of faith and interior life. Instead of simply believing in Christ, Luther saw a Church that was much occupied with trying to reach salvation by its own means, i.e., without Christ. For Luther, it is not only not necessary for humans to contribute to Christ's sacrifice, but even more, to pretend to contribute to this sacrifice is blasphemous: an attempt to "buy" God's favour, which is tantamount to self-righteousness, and trusting merely in one's own works, without relying on Christ's salvific work. Luther was thus convinced that the church people of his time were self-righteous and did not rely on Christ, but solely on their own works and means. He regarded the participation in processions, pilgrimages, the adoration of relics, people leaving the world and doing penance, indulgences, and the celebrating of a lot of (private) Masses for money, as mere proprietary works.[38] The emphasis on the Church was very much laid on the exterior forms, practises and norms, while at the same time the essence of the interior faith was neglected, and even in many cases wholly absent. According to Luther, the common people were left totally ignorant about the essence of faith, that is, as understood by Luther.[39]

Luther held the Roman Catholic Church to be responsible for this state of affairs.[40] He considered the Roman clergy (Pope, bishops and

---

36 ALTHAUS, *The Theology of Martin Luther*, 107, «God who causes all things is also the only causal agent. For the agent who really works in all things is God, and not the personal and impersonal powers of the world which we think of as causes. (...) They are only tools which he uses in the service of his own autonomous, free and exclusive working; they are the masks under which he hides his activity». And LW 45:331, «Indeed, one could very well say that the course of the world, and especially the doing of his saints, are God's mask, under which he conceals himself and so marvellously exercises dominion and introduces disorder in the world».

37 LW 33:289, «But now, since God has taken my salvation out of my hands into his, making it depend on his choice and not mine, and has promised to save me, not by my own work or exertion but by his grace and mercy, I am assured and certain (...)».

38 Cfr. LW 13:327.

39 Cfr. LW 13:326.

40 Luther's intention was not so much to correct "lack of discipline" or "bad practices" of the Church of his days, which undoubtedly existed and will always in some form exist. At the heart of the matter lies a fundamental (dogmatic) opposite point of view of the

priests) to be obstacles to the salvation of the common believer. Firstly, he claimed that they neglected their most important task: preaching justification by faith alone, the essence of the Gospel—that God is merciful, and would save humans if they only would have faith in Christ's sacrifice and God's grace. According to Luther: «they [the Roman clergy] teach the people absolutely nothing concerning this priestly office of Christ[41] (...). All of us had been taught that we ourselves must render satisfaction for our sins (...)».[42]

Moreover, the Roman clergy had put themselves in between Jesus Christ and the believer, claiming exclusive rights and control over the distribution of sacramental grace, not demanding any faith whatsoever, but mere works as the sole requirement for salvation, of which the controversy about the selling of indulgences was the most conspicuous example. In Luther's vision, the Roman clergy and the religious had placed themselves above—and therefore outside—the community, since they belonged to a different estate and formed a special class.[43]

The Catholic Church had succumbed to the same temptations as Israel, by confusing the means of Revelation with Revelation itself, interpreting their election as an exclusive privilege and trying to control the means of salvation—the sacraments—by means, which God did not own.[44] Luther regarded the preaching of the pure Word of God as one of the marks of the real Church. Consequently, the Roman Church was not the real Church, because the Word was not preached properly.[45]

Luther argued that the wonderful reality of Baptism, through which the "old man" was regenerated into the "new man", was forgotten,[46] in favour of other realities, such as canon law, philosophy, religious life (people "leaving" the world), ministerial priesthood, which have no explicit basis in Scripture. Thus, according to Luther, «the spiritual estate has been established and ordered by men's laws and regulations in such a way and has become so deeply entrenched in the course of time, that one thinks it is founded on Scripture, even though it is more than twice as worldly as

---

relationship between God and humans. Luther's concern and the Catholic Church's "abuse" consisted in its alleged "own-works-righteousness" and the "preaching of self-righteousness", while denying Luther's version of the "true" Gospel.

41 Luther means with the priestly office of Christ, his sacrifice on the cross to redeem men from sin without any merit on their part.
42 LW 13:326 .
43 LW 13:329: «the pope has usurped the term "priest" for his clergy and in this way, they have separated themselves from the ordinary Christians (...)».
44 Cfr. EASTWOOD, *An Examination of Doctrine till Present Day*, ix.
45 Cfr. LW 39:155.
46 Cfr. LW 44:356.

the world itself while calling itself and pretending to be spiritual».[47]

In short, based on his analyses of the state of affairs, Luther proposed to solve these problems by proclaiming and preaching the "true Gospel" over and against the version of the Roman Catholic Church, which, according to him, preached a mere human version.[48] Luther wanted to go back to the original Gospel by purifying it from all human elements that had crept at some point in time into the Roman Catholic version of the Gospel. Thus, according to Luther, Catholics practised a form of disbelief, by refusing the true gospel of free grace, which is a blasphemy against Christ and an abomination of his promises.[49]

Luther's claims started the process, which eventually led to a schism in the Church, which continues until the present day. Today the Lutheran World Federation, a federation of Lutheran Churches, represents communities from the Lutheran tradition in 99 counties, of which the largest are in Germany, Ethiopia, Tanzania, Scandinavia and the USA, with over 75 million believers.[50]

---

47 LW 39:155. Luther has a point here. The "estates" in the Church are in part copied from Ancient Roman and Medieval society. The way we look at society partly reflects the way we see the Church, which is not only divine but also human. This reciprocal dynamic between society and the Church is present in all episodes of history. Our understanding of society can help to understand and explain the Church if we duly respect the fact that we are dealing with an analogy.
48 Luther held that the Holy Spirit had ceased to preach the real Gospel through the Roman Catholic Church and its ministers. Cfr. *Large Catechism*, Art. III, 43-45.
49 Cfr. LW 35:369.
50 According to www.lutheranworld.org (consulted May 2020).

2. Luther's relationship with God

As we have pointed out, Luther's *forma mentis* is shaped by his longing to ensure eschatological certainty by maximising God's role and minimising the human role in their mutual relationship. This principle configures his concept of faith. It provides a hermeneutical key to Luther's doctrine and spirituality and should continuously be taken into account while studying it.[1]

To grasp Luther's understanding of the priesthood and its excecise by all believers, it is worthwhile to have a closer look at his own religious experience and the way he conceived his relationship with God. The main theme of this section is the gap between God and humans; a gap which undoubtedly exists, but which Luther enlarged and in his experience is never really bridged. The following theological insights are discussed: God's glory versus human sin, the role of the law, God's saving action, the true knowledge of God, the experience of salvation in faith, spiritual identification and participation in free eschatological benefits, direct access to God, and God's mercy.

2.1 Widening the gap

2.1.1 God's glory versus human sin

God is God and humans are humans. God is the absolute sovereign Creator and Redeemer, and humans are his redeemed creatures. Between them, there exists an abyss. In Luther's experience, however, the contrast between God's holiness and humans' sinfulness is accentuated.[2] The existing abyss is made wider, for not only is God considered exclusively holy in himself, but also human nature and being are regarded as sinful

---

[1] Strohl mentions the work of Ulrich Asendorf (*Eschatologie bei Luther,* Vandenhoeck & Ruprecht, Gottingen 1967*)*, who «sought to demonstrate that all the important aspects of Luther's thought are explicit in their eschatological orientation. Whether it be soteriology, Christology, or ecclesiology, the overarching eschatological framework serves the compelling dynamic of the now and the not yet, which accounts for the paradoxical quality of Luther's teaching», J.E. STROHL, *Luther's eschatology*, 354, in: R. KOLB, I. DINGEL, L. BATKA (eds.), *The Oxford Handbook of Martin Luther's Theology*, 353-362.

[2] L. BATKA, *Luther's teaching on sin and evil*, 233, R. KOLB, I. DINGEL, L. BATKA (eds.), *The Oxford Handbook of Martin Luther's Theology*, 233-253, «Characterizing humans as essentially guilty and condemned, and God as Justifier and Saviour, is fundamental, though not new, for Luther: (…)».

"in themselves".³ Luther appears to equate "sinfulness" with "reality", i.e., the sphere of common experience.⁴ As Althaus puts it, «man and God in his majesty are enemies».⁵ Only in this way, Luther argued, can humans come to apprehend 'the deepness and seriousness of sin'. Humans are *incurvatus ad se*, always referring everything to themselves, thus automatically excluding God and the others. Fallen human nature is characterised by concupiscence—sinful in itself—which Luther understood as the invincible human tendency to pride; to affirm oneself before God, i.e., to rely on one's works for salvation and to claim to have one's own title before God, instead of relying on Christ's sacrifice and his mercy and grace alone.

2.1.2 The role of the law

Humans regard God at first, i.e., before the experience of faith, with uncertainty and therefore, distrust. According to Althaus, as long as man does not yet believe, he only has a superficial knowledge in his heart and reason of who God really is and what his intentions are with him.⁶ This knowledge includes the awareness that God is the giver of all good, that he is kind, gracious and willing to help a man who calls upon him in time of need, but it does not give certainty that God wants to help *me* personally, because experience shows another reality.⁷

Humans know, or think they know, that God is righteous and judges them with a strict application of the law, which he has imprinted in each

---

3 LW 32:224f: «Our weakness lies not in our works, but in our nature; our person, nature and entire being are corrupted through Adam's fall». Luther *formally* recognised that God's creation, including the first humans, is good. However, he *materially* situated sin at the heart of the fallen human being: fallen human nature is intrinsically and essentially corrupt. He, therefore, had some problems of harmonising the concepts of Adam's original, complete and natural holiness, his freedom and his falling into disgrace. Cfr. ALTHAUS, *The Theology of Martin Luther*, 158-159 and J.A. MÖHLER, *Symbolik*, 66-81.

4 Cfr. P. O'CALLAGHAN, *Luther and 'sola gratia': The Rapport between Grace. Human Freedom, Good Works and Moral Life*, «Scripta Theologica» 49 (2017), 201.

5 ALTHAUS, *The Theology of Martin Luther*, 21, «Since our corrupted nature is completely unable to grasp the Divinity, we are not able to bear the sight of God as he is, God has, therefore, chosen to take hold of our nature which is corrupted, and infected with satanic poison and to involve it in these external manifestations and sacraments so that we may be able to grasp him», WA 39 I:217.

6 *Ibidem*, 15, «God has given a general knowledge of himself to all men, which cannot be eradicated from the human heart». The question arises how this statement relates to Luther's position that due to original sin «our person, nature and entire being are corrupted».

7 *Ibidem*, 16; WA 19:296: «It [reason] believes that God has the power to help, but doubts that God wants to help—because in times of trouble it feels that the opposite is true».

human heart. However, at the same time, they experience that his demands clearly exceed their powers and are even contrary to their nature.[8] Luther based this assertion on the experience of every age and of his own heart, which after all is impossible to control by an act of will.[9] From this, Luther concludes that man continuously stands under God's wrath and is always liable to eternal condemnation.[10]

2.2 Bridging the gap

2.2.1 God's saving action

As we have seen in the prolegomena, Luther allowed only one possible path—a narrow bridge—for true knowledge of God: a personal encounter with Christ on the cross. Although Luther presented his theology of the cross as a bridge between God and humans, it actually manifests the existence of the infinite abyss between them. Humans are obliged—due to the frame of radical paradox—to reject their own reasonable experience in order to come to the true spiritual knowledge of God and humans in faith, which is always exactly contrary to the human reasonable knowledge of common experience.

Due to the fact that Luther situated sin in human nature itself, the problem is raised how sinful human beings could ever be capable of receiving divine Revelation if they automatically pervert everything into the opposite. In principle, humans are not *capax Dei*, because—due to original sin—they have practically lost God's image. Luther solved this problem by eliminating humans' role in favour of God's determining action. The triune God saves humans—each of the three Persons of the Trinity has his own task and jointly works for the same end: humans' salvation and holiness.[11] God, who has revealed part of himself in Jesus Christ, continues to reveal himself through the work of the Holy Spirit. Since humans cannot trust themselves or any other human being, they can only rely directly on God, who works all in all. Luther taught that God must miraculously renew and regenerate human reason before it can believe the Gospel.[12] Moreover, Luther held that «the *real* knowledge is taught *only* by the Holy Spirit»,[13] for «He Himself puts His word into the

---

8 Cfr. *Ibidem*, 151.
9 Cfr. *Ibidem*.
10 Cfr. WA 17 II, 203 and LW 14:58.
11 «For as the Father is called Creator, the Son Redeemer, so the Holy Spirit, from His work, must be called Sanctifier, or One that makes holy», *Large Catechism* (1929), Article III, 36.
12 Cfr. ALTHAUS, *The Theology of Martin Luther*, 69 and LW 34:144.
13 Cfr. WA 19:206f, italics added.

hearts and mouths of people so that they will accept it and preach it».[14] This true, specific and evangelical knowledge of God is opposed to the general, superficial and legalistic knowledge of God, which each man carries in his heart and reason. In order to come to the former, humans have to reject the latter.[15]

2.2.2 Personal encounter: despair and faith

The Holy Spirit stimulates humans' imagination and provokes a decisive spiritual encounter with Christ in the human mind. The natural surroundings of this encounter is the church, for the Holy Spirit «leads us into His holy congregation, and places us in the bosom of the church, whereby He preaches to us and brings us to Christ».[16] The preeminent focus is humans' encounter with Christ on the cross, for it is only in this event that they can truly know and learn who God really is.[17] Through preaching, i.e., anamnesis,[18] humans are placed spiritually right in front of Christ, who has suffered and died for us. They come to realise that Christ has suffered and has given his life not in general, but *for me personally*. In this spiritual encounter, humans now recognise the infinite goodness of God in Christ.

The Holy Spirit shows humans in this spiritual encounter the abyss between, on the one hand, the holiness and goodness of God in Christ and, on the other hand, the deep sinfulness of humans, their absolute incapacity and nothingness in relation to God.[19] Humans now come to

---

14 LW 13:325. See also LW 13:317.
15 ALTHAUS, *The Theology of Martin Luther*, 19, «There are two types of knowledge about God, legalistic (law) and evangelical (gospel). Reason is limited to the first and knows God's "left hand", evangelical knowledge knows God's "right hand". To really know God, one must hold to his "right hand". Only then do we know what God really thinks of us and what his intentions are towards us. «The God whom we learn to know through the law shows us his back (Exod. 33:18-20); it is through the gospel, through Christ, that "we learn to look straight into the face of God"». LW 22:153, 157.
16 *Large Catechism*, Article III, 37.
17 Luther recognised the importance of the Incarnation as well. "Inner" knowledge is given by the Holy Spirit and the incarnation. Knowledge of the Trinity includes knowledge of the incarnation of the Second Person, and it is this knowledge of the incarnation, which teaches us how God feels about us in his heart. Cfr. ALTHAUS, *The Theology of Martin Luther*, 16.
18 Luther taught that humans in the Church hear that «the work is done and accomplished; for Christ has acquired and gained the treasure for us by His suffering, death, resurrection, etc.». *Large Catechism* (1929), Article III, 38.
19 Luther put it as follows, mixing his own words with those of Christ when he said: «But Christ throws on the ground your clay vessel, and says: "Don't trust in the [fulfilment of the] law, but in Christ. You [man] are not good, but I [Christ] am good". This is the way to leap from my sin to Christ's justice, holding for certain that his justice is mine». Tischr. 1351 II, 64-65.

realise and acknowledge that they cannot fulfil God's law by themselves. The abyss constitutes the essence of the human being before God,[20] while the acknowledgement of this abyss is the formal cause of his salvation. Luther's concept of faith thus includes the explicit recognition of the believer's intrinsic corrupt nature and being.[21] The Holy Spirit produces in humans, not contrition for their sins,[22] filial trust or hope, but desperation.[23] This despair is a constitutive element in the process of provoking humans' genuine and authentic response of faith. Only from the awareness of despair, and even hate against God's law,[24] humans can believe and make an act of faith by considering that the true God as manifested in Christ is exactly the opposite of how God has always appeared *to me* until now as the wrathful God of the law, requiring from me impossible things.[25]

2.2.3 Identification and free benefits

Although humans' salvation is completely attributed to God,[26] who provokes the act of faith by means of the law and despair, the human part, so to speak, in the act of faith is his desperate acknowledgement that the

---

20 Cfr. N. SLENCZKA, *Luther's anthropology*, 215, in: R. KOLB, I. DINGEL, L. BATKA (eds.), *The Oxford Handbook of Martin Luther's Theology*, 212-232.
21 *Ibidem*, «This acknowledgement of Christ and of God who is acting in him as the true origin of all the good that human beings produce is both the acknowledgement that in the human being there is no good, and the acknowledgement of God as the '*summum bonum*'».
22 For Luther, humans can never trust on their own capacities and they lack the capacity to produce so-called "true contrition" for their sins. Instead, humans can only trust the promise of salvation. Indeed, if human fallen nature is considered intrinsically corrupt and God's demands to exceed human powers and contrary to human nature, true contrition becomes impossible. Any pretended "contrition" is in reality "pride": wounded self-love when confronted with one's own imperfection. "Contrition" in this framework becomes "acknowledging your nothingness", which is the same as "humiliation".
23 For reasons of pedagogy, «God makes himself look like a devil», WA 41, 675.
24 Cfr. ALTHAUS, *The Theology of Martin Luther*, 175.
25 The paradoxical mind, for whom dialectics is the essence of the process to acquire "true" knowledge, can simply exchange real or imagined opposites: contrition and pride, despair and faith, justice (law) and love, God and devil.
26 Luther taught that men's salvation is an exclusive action by the triune God: The "work" is accomplished by Jesus Christ, God the Father sends «the Word to go forth and be proclaimed, in which He gives the Holy Spirit to bring this treasure home and appropriate it to us», so that it can be «enjoyed». Cfr. *Large Catechism* (1929), Article III, 38 and LW 12:377, «But we teach and believe differently about grace, namely, that grace is the continuous and perpetual operation or action through which we are grasped and moved by the Spirit of God so that we do not disbelieve His promises and that we think and do whatever is favourable and pleasing to God. The Spirit is something living, not dead».

believer *in the temporal-earthly sphere* cannot do anything relevant towards God by himself. As a consequence of this acknowledgement, the believer is *spiritually identified with Christ in faith*; a spiritual identification that seems to be conceived in dialectical and exclusive opposition to an identification with Christ in the temporal-empirical sphere of common experiences.

Luther described the spiritual unity of the soul with Christ in different ways and wordings: as "heritage", "joyous exchange" (*fröhliche Wechsel, admirabile commercium*) and "marriage" between Christ and the believer. It seems that the centre of attention for Luther is not so much the identification and union with Christ, but the result thereof: the acquisition of the benefits of forgiveness of sins (righteousness), direct access to God (priesthood), certainty of salvation (freedom), holiness and eternal life.[27] All these analogous expressions have this in common: that they indicate that the believer has a title to obtain spiritual benefits from Christ. The Christian, being an adoptive child and heir in Christ, receives from God the same goods as Christ.[28] In the joyous exchange, humans give to Christ their reality of sin as experienced in the temporal-empirical sphere and obtain in faith Christ's righteousness and holiness.[29] The analogy of marriage serves to indicate that between Christ and the believer, there exists a community of (spiritual) goods.[30]

---

27 According to Kolb, «Luther used a metaphor [joyful exchange] in which the "union" of the two [Christ and the sinner] is defined by each person's retaining his or her distinct characteristics. This reinforces what Jüngel sees as a basic presupposition of *On Christian Liberty*: 'we are to be human, not God ... This is the summa'». KOLB, *Luther's hermeneutics of distinctions,* 181, in: R. KOLB, I. DINGEL, L. BATKA (eds.), *The Oxford Handbook of Martin Luther's Theology,* 168-184. Arnold points out that Luther rejected the mystical concept of a fusion of persons, but that «for him, this joyful exchange more implies a whole community and an exchange of goods between persons», M. ARNOLD, *Luther on Christ's person and work,* 286, in: R. KOLB, I. DINGEL, L. BATKA (eds.), *The Oxford Handbook of Martin Luther's Theology,* 274-293.

28 «Christians are children and heirs, born in a spiritual and heavenly manner, without any human activity, but through the unique activity of God working through the Gospel and Holy Baptism. Such children are the true children of a priest and inherit the same name from their father. Consequently, every baptised Christian is a priest already, not by appointment or ordination by the pope or any other man, but because Christ Himself has begotten him as a priest and has given birth to him in Baptism»: LW 13:329.

29 Fr. Martin expressed his almost mystical and poetical experience in a moving letter to console a fellow monk (Spenlein) as follows: «Lord Jesus, you are my righteousness, just as I am your sin. You have taken up what is mine and have given to me what is yours. You have taken up yourself what you were not and have given me what I was not», LW 48:12.

30 «For since Christ is the Groom and we are the bride, the bride has everything that the Groom has, even His own body. When He gives Himself to the bride, He gives Himself

The believer receives the benefits as a free gift. Although formally, believers do nothing to merit these gifts, it is precisely in the acknowledgement that they *in the temporal-earthly sphere* cannot do anything relevant towards God that they become spiritually one with Christ and "merit" and "receive" the benefits, such as a peaceful conscience, *in faith*.[31] These spiritual gifts do not alter the human condition and they do not render believers capable of doing any supernatural acts in the world.[32] The spiritual-supernatural sphere and the temporal-empirical sphere remain separated and believers continuously confess themselves incapable and unworthy. At the same time, they perform acts of thanksgiving for the spiritual benefits received, i.e., the psychological certainty that God will fulfil his promise to save believers by being merciful.

2.3 Leaping the gap

The believer's desperate act of faith, while considering Christ on the cross and confessing his incapability, produces a simultaneous "second" encounter. The believer "leaps" the gap, or to put it differently, transcends space and time, which separates him from God, and encounters God the Father immediately and directly, face-to-face. Due to this spiritual identification with Christ and the consequent benefits obtained, he receives a free passage and finds himself in the direct presence of God the Father, before his throne.[33]

---

entirely as what He is; and the Bride, in turn, gives Himself to Him», LW 30:53-54; Cfr. VOSS, *The priesthood of all believers*, 200 and EASTWOOD, *An Examination of Doctrine till Present Day*, 9.

31 LW 36:57, «For this testament of Christ is the only remedy against sins, past, present and future, if you but cling to it with unwavering faith and believe that what the words of the testament declare is freely granted to you. But if you do not believe this, you will never, anywhere, by any works or efforts of your own, be able to find peace of conscience. For faith alone means peace of conscience, while disbelief means only distress of conscience».

32 According to a Catholic understanding, the concepts of the adjectives "spiritual" and "supernatural" are not identical (e.g. the human intellect is both a natural and spiritual capacity). For Luther, however, the spiritual and the supernatural does coincide, and for him, the spiritual goes against the natural. The human intellect nor his will can reach the spiritual and supernatural or, said in another way, humans cannot participate in the spiritual and supernatural in the temporal earthly sphere.

33 One of the benefits granted to the believer, and which is closely linked with the priesthood, is the benefit of "direct and immediate access" to God the Father in Christ through the Holy Spirit. All believers have the capacity and duty to present themselves freely before the Lord to pray and intercede for others, «for to stand before God's face is the prerogative of none except priests», M. LUTHER, *Reformation Writings of Martin Luther*, Bertram Lee Woolf (ed. and tr.), Lutterworth Press, London 1952, I.366.

In this encounter, while standing next to the crucified Christ before God the Father, the believer experiences that God the Father has another face. Apart from the mask of a judge, who requires that his law should be fulfilled completely without any imperfection, God now shows himself to the believer in his most inner being, which is not "justice", but "mercy" and "love". The believer is still completely sinful but experiences a wonderful thing—that God the Father, due to the work and merit of his Son, forgives him his sins. The believer, who is in absolute despair due to his sinful condition, but full of faith[34] and trusting confidence in Christ's saving work, experiences that God does not exercises his rights to demand full compliance with the law and to hold the believer responsible for his actions, but forgives by not attributing sins to him, due to Christ's sacrifice[35] and continuous intercession. Instead, the Father covers sinful human nature with "the blanket of love" and tells the believer directly that he can trust the promises fulfilled in Christ. In this personal experience, the believers' despair turns into certainty[36]—about his salvation, holiness, eternal destiny and his capacity to be propitious to God in whatever he does.[37]

Luther regarded the whole experience of his redemption, transcending time, in and by faith, as a complete new divine creation of his mind, being and person.[38] According to Althaus, «the believers' experience of reason

---

[34] Catholics would introduce here the concept of hope. However, hope implies risks and uncertainty. For this reason, in Luther's experience and framework, the concept of hope is dissolved into his concept of faith.

[35] LW 13:320: «Christ has won for us our salvation by His sacrifice on the Cross, by which he willingly and without price mediated between God's wrath and our sin».

[36] Thus, it seems that for Luther, even *in faith* believers are not saved in the temporal earthly sphere, because they remain sinful. However, they can be certain of the promise of salvation. God will always render believers just, as long as humans have faith (*Heilsgewissheit*). After all, God is not only merciful but omnipotent as well and keeper of his promises; the only obstacle for God's justice to be realised, is lack of faith. For Luther, the biggest sin, therefore, is incredulity. Cfr. LW 31:350.

[37] Luther stated, «He [Christ] brings our prayers to God and assures us that such prayers are pleasing to God and will be heard for His sake, just as He promised (John 15:16): "Whatever you shall ask the Father in My name, that He will give you"», LW 13:320-321.

[38] According to Schwanke, «Luther does not allow himself to be distanced from God's creative work by any isolated, past original history, by any "beginning of things", but instead sees himself placed in the most radical fashion in the creative event of primordial history of the present. Luther's personal and present environment is the effective sphere of divine creativity. (…). In an interlacing of times, past, present, and future come together in a single moment, pervading time, Gods living creative Word is without end and remains ever "effective" to this very day, is *verbum efficax*». J. SCHWANKE, *Luther's theology of creation*, 203, in: R. KOLB, I. DINGEL, L. BATKA (eds.), *The Oxford Handbook of Martin Luther's Theology*, 201-211.

and reality is in a constant struggle with his faith, in which God gives him another experience and another insight.[39] The more the latter increases, the former decreases, and his remaining sin becomes less and less a burden and trail to him.[40] This tension will only be fully resolved eschatologically when believing becomes seeing in God's new heaven and new earth».[41]

---

39 ALTHAUS, *The Theology of Martin Luther*, 63.
40 *Ibidem.*
41 *Ibidem.*

3. Luther's theological framework

Luther's theological framework is based on the feature that each believer has direct and immediate eschatological access to God the Father in Christ and through the Holy Spirit. In order to minimise the human part and role in their relationship with God, Luther deemed it necessary—rather paradoxically—to grant every believer "direct and immediate access" to God, which feature is closely connected with the common priesthood.[1] After all, only in this way no believer depends on any other corrupt human being and any false human realities, but only and directly on God. All believers are priests so that they may learn and hear directly and immediately, anytime and anywhere from the triune God the Word that they are saved, and that God has the best intentions for them.[2]

Luther seemed to have paid a high price for this kind of certainty. By framing the paradigmatic experience of his salvation as a direct and immediate eschatological access to God the Father in Christ by the Holy Spirit, he also reframed the whole relationship between God and humans. In Luther, the centre of gravity in the relationship with God changed and shifted to the believer's eschatological situation of direct access to God, which becomes the paradigmatic "situation" of all believing Christians and the exercise of their priesthood, here and now, while they are still travelling in the temporal-earthly sphere.

3.1 Main features

This manoeuvre implies that in Luther, the relationship between God and humans is characterised by, firstly, a dialectical and exclusive antagonism between God and humans, and as a logical consequence thereof, he introduced a separation between the spheres of faith and temporal-earthly reality, laying the basis for dualism in his theology. Secondly, the believer's experience of salvation and faith in Christ is a personal one, but

---

1 «Every priest (Heb. 5, 1) is appointed in order that he might pray for the people and preach. Thus every Christian in his own may pray in Christ and have access to God (Rom 5, 2) (…). Thus every Christian is himself taught and instructed by God (Isa. 54 (:13): "And I will grant that all your children shall be taught by God". (…) Hence, it comes that Christ says in John 6 (:45): 'It is written in the prophets, "And they shall all be taught by God"», LW 36:138-139; Cfr. voss, *The priesthood of all believers*, 205.
2 ALTHAUS, *The Theology of Martin Luther*, 16, «"Inner" knowledge about how God the Father really feels about us is given by the Holy Spirit and the Incarnation. Knowledge of the Trinity includes knowledge of the incarnation of the Second Person, and it is this knowledge of the incarnation, which teaches us how God feels about us in his heart».

merely subjective.³ Thirdly, a merely passive role for humans, who only receive eschatological benefits, but fundamentally lack the capacity and freedom to give anything back to God. Finally, in this framework, a communion between God and humans *in statu viae*, i.e., as pilgrims in the temporal-earthly sphere seems hardly possible.

3.1.1 Dialectical, exclusive and dualistic

Firstly, essential to Luther's way of proceeding is by establishing a fundamental opposition between God and humans, which, during human earthly existence, is never overcome. This opposition is, therefore, not only dialectical but also exclusive. This is expressed in the famous formula, which is the answer to the question of men's salvation: *per sola fide, sola gratia, sola scriptura, solo Christo et solo Deo*. These affirmations are dialectically opposed to humans and their realities, such as human works, human reason (philosophy), magisterium and tradition, roman priesthood (pope, bishops and clergy) and religious life. The reductionism follows from and is expressed in the word *solus*.

As we have seen in the prolegomena, paradox and dialectics play an essential role in Luther's doctrinal framework, which not only contains a radical opposition between God and humans, but as logical consequence thereof, also imply a separation between the sphere of "faith" on the one hand and the sphere of "temporal-earthly experience" on the other. The latter has to be denied to make room for faith. Thus, Luther created two kinds of experiences, which are *per definition* in conflict with and are radically opposed to each other: the reasonable experience of my common reality, which is always "false", and the experience of my faith that gives me the "true spiritual and supernatural reality".

3.1.2 Subjective act of faith

These two separate spheres, the "true spiritual reality" on the one hand, and on the other the "false apparent reality of common experience", always seem to run completely parallel to—without ever touching—each other. The two spheres are inverted exclusively in the believers' mind by a subjective act of faith, since *for the believer*, and only for him, "spiritual things", like salvation and holiness, become "true spiritual reality" and "false apparent reality", like sin, becomes the opposite in the sphere of "true spiritual and supernatural reality": God's glory.⁴ Since the emphasis

---

3 Cfr. *Ibidem*, 115, «Man can never reach the objective view but must always—being a creature and not the Creator—remain in his subjective views».

4 *Ibidem*, 118-119, For Luther, «God always creates *ex nihilo* and out of its opposite. God creates life out of death, righteousness out of sin, exaltation out of humiliation. Confess-

on the relation between God and the believer is laid upon the act of faith by the believing subject, the phenomena of "hope" and "love" seem to dissolve into the concept of "faith".

3.1.3 Passivity towards God
In Luther's experience and framework, humans *per definition* cannot give anything to God, because allowing this would increase the human role in their mutual relationship, and consequently, decrease the believers' certainty of salvation. The issue here is not the evident fact that humans have received everything as a free gift of grace from God by creation and redemption, but rather to which extent humans, in their capacity as redeemed creatures and children of God are capable of giving freely, with God's aid, back to God what they have received from him, and in this way could cooperate with Christ in the temporal-earthly sphere of common experience. For Luther, it is far too risky to give humans any role—even a small one—in the temporal-earthly sphere towards God.[5] He deemed it safer to move around exclusively in the sphere of faith, denying any human supernatural role in, and thus "withdrawing" from, the sphere of temporal existence.[6]

3.1.4 Impossibility of communion in the temporal-earthly sphere
Finally, the preceding discussion implies—and that was the price Luther paid for his certainty—that communion between God and humans in this temporal-empirical sphere seems hardly possible. Even more, it appears that in Luther's framework, the human recognition that communion between Christ and the believer *in the temporal-earthly sphere* is not

---

ing faith in the Creator thus means confessing one's own inability and that one expects everything from God alone». Cfr. *Ibidem,* 142, «Making sin great is inseparably connected with exalting and praising grace».

5 LW 26:66: «Furthermore, it is much safer to ascribe too much to God than to men».

6 This attitude is also reflected in Luther's writing against Erasmus, *De servo arbitrio* (1525), after having argued against human free will, at the end of his writing, Luther stated the following: «For my own part, I frankly confess that even if it were possible, I should not wish to have free choice given to me, or to have anything left in my own hands by which I might strive toward salvation. For, on the one hand, I should be unable to stand firm and keep hold of it amid so many adversities and perils and so many assaults of demons, seeing that even one demon is mightier than all men, and that no man at all could be saved; and on the other hand, even if there were no perils or adversities or demons, I should nevertheless have to labour *under perpetual uncertainty* and to fight as one beating the air (1 Cor. 9:26), since even if I lived and worked to eternity, my conscience would never be *assured and certain* how much it ought to do to satisfy God», LW 33:288-289, italics added.

possible constitutes a prerequisite for the believer's salvation *in faith*, or better, the believer's *certainty* of salvation in faith.

3.2 Back in the world

In the meantime, while standing in faith before God's throne, believers find themselves also in the world, where they are supposed to be holy and acceptable to God in everything that they do. The situation of "direct and immediate access" represents the eschatological situation of the believer standing before God the Father face-to-face, which is not only a *right* of the believer but also entails an *obligation* to appear before God's throne. Luther's manoeuvre to grant each believer direct and immediate eschatological access to God the Father by faith in Christ and through the Holy Spirit is theologically questionable. What Luther deemed impossible for humans in the temporal-earthly sphere[7] becomes possible *only* in an act of faith, which is diametrically opposed to human sinful reality and experience in the temporal-earthly sphere. Luther is so eager to hear God's positive and definitive verdict now that he anticipated particular judgement, which is perhaps possible to a certain extent in prayer and examination of conscience, but not fully in the temporal-earthly sphere, for we are not yet standing in actual sense before God's throne, not even in a faithful examination of conscience.[8] In any case, Luther saw himself forced by reality to harmonise his spiritual experience of anticipated eschatological redemption in faith with that of the temporal-earthly sphere in which believers are still travelling. To maintain his theological position that all Christians have the right and obligation of "direct and immediate access", Luther developed various doctrines, both on individual and community levels, which are relevant for his understanding and exercise of the common priesthood.

3.2.1 On the individual level

Without the pretension of being exhaustive, I will discuss the following doctrines of Luther to harmonise his experience of salvation in faith with the experience in the temporal sphere on the individual level: salvation is identical to holiness, *simul iustus et peccator*, the promised benefits,

---

7 ALTHAUS, *The Theology of Martin Luther*, 21 «The corrupted nature of sinful man cannot achieve knowledge of God in himself, in his majesty, as he is in heaven. Sinful man is not capable of dealing with this divinity». Cfr. LW 14,1.

8 Not even Roman Catholic priests claim to have this kind of direct access. Luther seems to have mixed up eschatology with the present life and state of believers *in statu viae*. The current relationship between God and humans is characterised by the elements of space and time. Humans do have access to God, but this access is not yet direct and definitive in the sense Luther proposed.

regeneration as a continuing event, redemption as a recreation *ex nihilo,* and practical dualism.

i) Salvation is identical to holiness

Besides certainty about one's salvation, spiritual identification and direct access also imply instant holiness, for salvation and sanctification are identical realities; once the believer is saved, he is also holy: after having received the treasure, there is nothing more to receive or to do other than to enjoy it.[9] If the believer in faith understands that everything is done, and God is well pleased with him, in the temporal sphere, there is nothing left to be done. The requirement for holiness of the believer is the same as for his salvation; his recognition that he is not able to do anything relevant towards God *in the temporal-earthly sphere,* but at the same time trusting that whatever he does is propitious to God the Father *in the sphere of faith,*[10] because Christ has done it all.[11] Humans seem, therefore, to be holy only in the spiritual sphere of faith, and not in the temporal-empirical sphere. Christ's holiness is imputed to them in the temporal sphere, just as his righteousness.

ii) Simultaneously just and sinner

Luther taught the doctrine of *simul iustus et peccator*: the believer is *completely* justified and holy, and at the same time *completely* sinful. This doctrine can only be properly understood in his framework in which temporal-earthly reality and faith are considered as two separate and opposite spheres. That the believer is completely justified and holy in faith is due to the anticipated eschatological character of the received spiritual benefits. There is no room here for gradation, but standing before God's throne, it is all-or-nothing. The believer receives everything in faith, however, at the same time, i.e., in the temporal-empirical sphere, the believer is completely sinful by nature. This sinfulness is, moreover, a

---

9 «That this treasure, therefore, might not lie buried, *but be appropriated and enjoyed,* God has caused the Word to go forth and be proclaimed, in which He gives the Holy Spirit to bring this treasure home and appropriate it to us (heimzubringen und zuzueigenen)», Luther's *Large Catechism* (1929), Article III, 38, italics added.

10 Believers acquire the benefit of (certainty of) being able to please the Lord and to be propitious to him. Whether this is really the case is a question which is irrelevant in Luther's framing. For him, putting this question—which had haunted him in his earlier life as a Catholic monk before his "conversion"—would be tantamount to "lack of faith". What matters is the certainty.

11 According to Luther, «sanctifying [by the Holy Spirit], is nothing else than bringing us *to Christ to receive this good* [the treasure of salvation] *to which we could not attain of ourselves*», *Large Catechism* (1929), Article III, 39, italics added.

necessary condition for the believer's justification, since the act of confessing one's complete inability in the temporal-earthly sphere makes the believer completely justified in faith.

iii) Promised benefits

To obtain absolute certainty about his eschatological destiny, Luther believed firmly that God had already conferred upon him these eschatological benefits, here and now. In this kind of faith, the eschatological benefits are anticipated and become already present in faith, but not in the temporal sphere of common experience. The fact that believers are travellers *in statu viae*, obliged Luther to "reintroduce" the concept of promise[12] and to make a distinction in benefits "received now" and the promised benefits to be received "in the future". In the sphere of faith, the believer is already completely justified and holy, but in the sphere of temporal-earthly experience, the believer should hold on firmly to the promise.[13] The benefits the justified believer receives now can be summed up by certainty of one's (future) salvation, a peaceful conscience, freedom,[14] forgiveness of sins and consolation. Luther regarded as benefits to be received in the future: true holiness and perfection, the resurrection of the flesh and eternal life.[15]

iv) Regeneration as a continuing event

To keep up and recover the element of time in the temporal-earthly sphere, Luther conceived of salvation and sanctification as a "continuous event" or "process of regeneration". The Holy Spirit[16] continuously congregates humans into the Church to hear the Gospel, i.e., to bring them spiritually

---

12 LW 36:42: «For anyone can easily see that these two, promise and faith, must necessarily go together. For without the promise there is nothing to be believed; while without faith the promise is useless, since it is established and fulfilled through faith».

13 Cfr. F. BRAVO, *El sacerdocio común de los creyentes en la teología de Lutero*, Editorial ESET, Vitoria 1963, 306. Bravo remarks that since faith guarantees certainty of salvation, justice is considered a present reality and at the same time a future reality.

14 Salvation for Luther meant, above all, being saved from judgement and being freed from worrying. Thus, the attention shifts from the liberation from sin to the liberation from the anxiety over sin, also called "the existential liberation from sin". Cfr. KOLB, *Luther's hermeneutics of distinctions*, 180. Since the believer is completely justified by God, he is totally "free" to give everything to his neighbour, for he does not have to take care of his own salvation, which was won for him by Christ. So, Luther also regarded Christian freedom in this sense a benefit of faith.

15 Cfr. *Large Catechism*, Article III, 55-58.

16 Cfr. *Large Catechism*. The Holy Spirit continuously "appropriates the treasure to us" and "brings us to Christ to receive this good" and "illumines and enkindles our hearts so that we understand it, accept it, cling to it, and persevere in it".

before Christ's cross, provoking despair, humility and faith. As result, they are spiritually identified with Christ, which opens the door of heaven, so that they leap the abyss and stand before God the Father, where Christ continuously prays[17] on their behalf. On these grounds, believers can continuously experience God's mercy and love. In this sense, Luther allowed for a gradation in their process of sanctification; believers increasingly come to recognise their inability in the temporal-empirical sphere towards God, which means more certainty of salvation and "greater holiness".[18]

v) Redemption as a new creation ex nihilo
As already remarked a few times, another way for Luther to harmonise his experience of spiritual identification with Christ in faith with the impossibility of communion with Christ in the temporal-empirical sphere is his view that God only redeems and sanctifies human nature by a new creation, i.e., a *creatio ex nihilo*.[19] Fallen human nature is corrupt to such an extent that God can only "redeem" and "sanctify" it by a new act of creation out of nothing.[20] This act of new creation is God's own Word, which the believer hears directly from the triune God while standing before God's throne.[21] For Luther—so it seems—St. Paul's image of "the old man" in chapter 6 of his Epistle to the Romans represents man as he

---

17 The benefits of Christ's sacrifice are conferred upon humans by Jesus Christ's prayer. Luther considered: «the power and merit of His sacrifice, i.e., forgiveness of sins, righteousness and eternal life, are won for us and communicated to us by Jesus his priestly prayer for us in Chapter 17 of the Gospel of St. John. Prayer like that is valid forever and works its power in all Christendom, which He continues to pray as our Mediator and Advocate before God», LW 13:320.

18 Silcock puts it as follows: «Christians progress by continually going back to their baptism and re-appropriating its promise every day anew (...). Therefore, progress in the Christian life remains hidden (...). It is not marked by an increasing absence of sin but rather by a deeper awareness of sin and the sufficiency of God's grace». SILCOCK, *Luther on the Holy Spirit and his use of God's Word*, 304-305, in: R. KOLB, I. DINGEL, L. BATKA (eds.), *The Oxford Handbook of Martin Luther's Theology*, 294-309.

19 As we have seen, Luther regarded all God's actions as creations *ex nihilo*. Cfr. ALTHAUS, *The Theology of Martin Luther*, 118-119; see also SCHWANKE, *Luther's theology of creation*, 210.

20 God's attributes are by their very nature creative. In the spiritual identification God «showers us with his own being», giving us what he is and sharing his attributes with men. ALTHAUS, *The Theology of Martin Luther*, 117.

21 According to Kolb, «Luther transformed the core definition of what it means to be Christian into a relationship based on God's approach to sinful human beings, in his Word. It is his creative and re-creative instrument, whereby he brought the universe into being (Gen. 1) and through which he changes the identity of sinners, making them his children by giving them trust in Christ and his atoning work in dying and rising». KOLB, *Luther's hermeneutics of distinctions*, 169.

is in the temporal-earthly sphere. This man always remains the same—and must remain the same—so that God can continuously create "a new spiritual man" *ex nihilo* over and over again.²² This way of framing seems to confirm the impression that in Luther's perception there is a dualism: the "old" and the "new" man is not the same man, but two different men.

By framing redemption and sanctification as a divine creation *ex nihilo*, Luther leapt back over the abyss, from the sphere of faith to the temporal-empirical sphere, exchanging his sins for Christ's holiness. What Luther heard from the Father in Christ standing before God's throne, he regarded "true spiritual reality" (holiness), which is exactly the opposite of the "false apparent human reality" as experienced in the temporal-earthly sphere (sin). Luther could, therefore, maintain that he believed that God's Word really alters reality, thus that if God *considers* a man just, that man *is* just.²³ There is no need to say that this "true spiritual reality" necessarily is merely interior and invisible, apart from Luther's own faithful eye.²⁴

Furthermore, by equating redemption and creation, Luther seemed to appropriate and grant himself the divine quality and prerogative of creation and was able to affirm that believers really share in God's power of creation and cooperate in God's own work.²⁵ It is striking that in Luther's view, he regarded himself unworthy to redeem with Christ, but that this humility did not prevent him from recognising that he could co-create with God.

Due to this framing, Luther also appears to deny the continuation of our current body *in statu viae* and the human body in its final glorious

---

22 ALTHAUS, *The Theology of Martin Luther*, 106, «God's constant preservation of creation at every point of space and time is an ongoing act of new creation». LW 22:27.

23 Cfr. MATTES, *Luther on justification as forensic and effective*, 265, in: R. KOLB, I. DINGEL, L. BATKA (eds.), *The Oxford Handbook of Martin Luther's Theology*, 264-273.

24 In this doctrine—together with the method of radical paradox—it becomes clear that the two spheres of faith and temporal-earthly experience run merely parallel and are inverted exclusively in the believers' mind by a subjective and paradoxical act of faith; since *for the believer*, salvation and holiness become "true spiritual reality", whereas the false apparent reality of sin becomes its exact opposite in the sphere of "true spiritual reality": God's glory.

25 Schwanke puts it as follows: «For Luther, the government and rule of human beings is grounded in the fact that God does not keep the power of creation for Himself (…). As a God who shares Himself with his creatures without reservation, God gives human beings a share in the divine attributes (…). With this gift of God's participation and the resulting participation of the human being, a marvellous cooperation of divine and human energies takes place in the strictest sense: God gives Himself into human hands, into human mouths, gives human beings divine creative attributes, and therewith a share in God's own work». SCHWANKE, *Luther's theology of creation*, 209.

state. According to him, God does not sanctify our body now, but he will sanctify us fully by creating 'our body' totally anew after death.[26] Humans return to nothingness and from there God will create them anew and unite the new humans to himself.[27] Healing of the human existing body is, therefore, excluded, but its "sanctification" and "glorification" will be realised by a proper divine act of creation, *ex nihilo*.[28]

vi) Practical dualism: God or man
The fact that communion between God and believers in the temporal-empirical sphere is problematic also becomes manifest in the practical dualism which characterises Luther's doctrine. For Luther, it is always *either* God who acts, *or* humans, but never together. God acts in the world through humans, but without their cooperation, *or* humans act necessarily on their own without God, and thus, sinful, self-righteous, blasphemous and arrogant.

God's actions and those of humans appear to run completely parallel each other. In the true spiritual reality, the believers' holiness and good works are attributed fully to God. They are completely holy if they believe that God acts through them and that they themselves, in the apparent false reality, do not and can not participate in these good works ('Sola Dei Gloria'). From the latter perspective, believers' actions are completely sinful since their human nature is intrinsically sinful, and believers glorify God only in the act of confessing that they, in the temporal-empirical sphere, can do nothing at all towards God.[29]

---

26 LW 13:323-324, «He [Christ] must create an entirely new nature and being in us, so that we may also rise from the dead, in body and soul, and live with Him in eternal glory, in purity and perfection. This is the reason why He became our High Priest».
27 «Where does a man who hopes in God end up except in his own nothingness? ... Since he comes from God and his own non-being, it is to God that he returns when he returns to nothingness», WA 5, 168
28 *Large Catechism*, Article III, 57, «Meanwhile, however, while sanctification has begun and is growing daily, we expect that our flesh will be destroyed and buried with all its uncleanness, and will come forth gloriously, and arise to entire and perfect holiness in a new eternal life».
29 This practical dualism becomes manifest in Luther's following statement: «The first thing I ask is that people should not make use of my name, and should not call themselves Lutherans but Christians. What is Luther? The teaching is not mine. Nor was I crucified for anyone (...). How did I, poor stinking bag of maggots that I am, come to the point where people call the children of Christ by my evil name?», WA 8:68, cited in P. O'CALLAGHAN, *God and Mediation, Retrospective Appraisal of Luther the Reformer*, Fortress Press, Minneapolis 2017, 4.

Due to the frame and method of radical paradox, Luther spoke always about God and humans in categorical terms and universal statements.[30] This explains that in Luther's view, everyone who did not agree with his true version of the Gospel was automatically his adversary. Not only the Roman Catholic Church, which in a way understandably was his natural adversary, but he also considered his congenial former allies as *Schwärmer* — like Andreas Bodenstein von Karlstadt and Thomas Müntzer — and even antichrists.[31] For in Luther's view, God was enlightening him and working through him, though without his cooperation.[32] He could not do otherwise than preaching the true Gospel and to wage battle against anyone who did not agree, for the one who opposed it is necessarily on the other side.[33] This line of thought manifests an underlying principle; for Luther, it is always God who acts *or* humans, but never together.

---

30 Cfr. GARCÍA VILLOSLADA, *Martín Lutero, Vol. 1*, 358 and for example LW 39:278: «All those who work towards this end and risk body, property, and honour that the bishoprics may be destroyed and the episcopal government rooted out are God's dear children and true Christians. They keep God's commandment and fight against the devil's order. (…). On the other hand, all those who obey the government of the bishops and subject themselves to it in willing obedience are the devil's own servants and fight against God's order and law».

31 Cfr. GARCÍA VILLOSLADA, *Martín Lutero, Vol. 2*, 179-180 citing (against the heavenly prophets in the matter of images and sacraments, 1525): «Doctor Andreas Karlstadt has deserted us, and on top of that has become our worst enemy» and WA 15:220: «Müntzer, who is the personification of Satan. His voice is that of the devil» (my translation).

32 Cfr. LW 39:274: «I am certain that Christ Himself, who is the master of my teaching, gives me this title and regards me as one [minister and evangelist]. Moreover, he will be my witness on the Last Day that it is not my pure Gospel but his». Cfr. GARCÍA VILLOSLADA, *Martín Lutero, Vol. 2*, 131; LW 45:347: «But God has opened my mouth and bidden me to speak, and he supports me mightily». Cfr. GARCÍA VILLOSLADA, *Martín Lutero, Vol. 2*, 14; LW 26:66, «Whether it is St. Cyprian, Ambrose, or Augustine, or John, yes, or even an angel from heaven that teaches otherwise—I know this for certain, that what I teach is not from men but from God». Cfr. GARCÍA VILLOSLADA, *Martín Lutero, Vol. 2*, 85; LW 48:389-390, Letter n. 117 to Elector Frederick, March 5, 1522: «(…) I am convinced by more than human means of reckoning that I too have good intentions. (…). Your Electoral Grace knows (or, if you do not, I now inform you of the fact) that I have received the gospel not from men but from heaven only, through our Lord Jesus Christ, so that I might well be able to boast and call myself a minister and evangelist, as I shall do in the future».

33 Cfr. STROHL, *Luther's eschatology*, 356, «This consignment of his enemies to the Devil was characteristic of Luther. The list included not only Rome but spiritualists, Anabaptists, Zwinglians, Turks and Jews. Anyone who, in Luther's view threatened the truth of the gospel, refused to be corrected, and infected others with their false teaching was unconditionally condemned».

3.2.2 Community level

The paradigm of the authentic personal religious experience of direct access in faith as proposed by Luther also forms the basis of his ecclesiology.[34] Due to the spiritual identification with Christ, the individual believer in the congregation obtains all the (eschatological) benefits of Christ. The believer comes to share in *all* possessions of Christ, as Christ shares in *all* the possessions of the Church, i.e., by *all* Christians. All privileges, rights and obligations, which were given to the disciples, are bestowed upon all believers.[35] These benefits not only include salvation and instant holiness, but also the privilege of priesthood, understood by Luther as the believer's right and obligation of direct access to the Father, where he learns God's positive verdict for him and acquires certainty of eschatological salvation.[36] The eschatological confusion of Luther's personal experience of faith and experiences in the temporal-earthly sphere affects his concept of community as well. Luther's doctrine on the church reflects this eschatological confusion, as becomes manifest in his teachings on i) radical equality, ii) the absence of human mediation, iii) the nature of the church, iv) his doctrine of neighbour and v) the universal call to holiness.

i) Radical equality

All Christians are, in faith, radically equal while standing before God's throne. There are no fundamental differences or classes in Christendom. In principle, each Christian belongs to God's Church in the same way.[37] Luther, therefore, denied the divisions within Christendom among clerics, religious and laity. All Christians belong to the spiritual estate, for all Christians are spiritual.[38]

---

34 From Luther's point of view, he did not "leave" the Church or "started" another one. In his own words: «I believe that here below and throughout the world, there is only one Christian Church, the Church Universal, and that this Church is identical with the universal fellowship of the saints, i.e., the devout believers everywhere on earth», in: *Reformation Writings*, I.87-88.
35 Cfr. voss, *The priesthood of all believers*, 200.
36 Due to the personal character of this knowledge and experience, the centre of gravity and attention within the congregation shifts from the community to the individual; the community serves to provoke in the individual believer the knowledge of the certainty of salvation.
37 LW 13:330-331: «We all have one Baptism in common, one Gospel, one kind of grace, one kind of inheritance of the kingdom of heaven, one Holy Spirit, one God the Father, and one Lord Jesus Christ (Eph. 4:4-6). We are all one in Him, as He says in John 17:22 and as St. Paul says in Galatians 3:28 "You are all one in Christ Jesus"».
38 Cfr. LW 44: 127-128. Cfr. voss, *The priesthood of all believers*, 188-189.

By stating that all Christians are spiritually equal, Luther intended to "elevate" the laity in the Church—who coincided with the two other secular estates (nobility[39] and peasants[40])—to a "higher" level, represented by the spiritual estate (religious and clergy). The estates were merged into each other.[41] The effect of this operation was a levelling out of the estates; the elements of hierarchy—in terms of both holiness and authority—disappeared, as well as any distinction between the religious and secular sphere.

All believers have a common dignity and only differ as to the function, which they exercise.[42] Luther has always recognised the existence of ministries and the need for a (visible) structure of the community, even more so after the experience with the Anabaptists and the peasant wars. The New Testament, especially the letters of St. Paul, clearly speaks of different ministries, spiritual gifts, forms of service to be used to build up the Body of Christ, which is the Church (cfr. Ephes. 4, 11-12 and 1 Cor. 12). For Luther, each ministry is a calling, a gift and a service as any other service (1 Cor. 12, 5), as he affirmed: «A shoemaker, a smith, a farmer, each has his manual occupation and work; and yet, at the same time, all are eligible to act as priests and bishops. Every one of them in his occupation or handicraft ought to be useful to his fellows and serve them in such a way that the various trades are all directed to the best advantage of the community, and promote the well-being of body and soul, just as the organs of the body serve each other».[43]

---

[39] Therefore, Luther wrote in 1520 "To the Christian Nobility of the German Nation" explaining them that all Christians are spiritual and priests. Cfr. LW 44:127-128.

[40] The peasants were also informed of Luther's views on equality, which contributed to the start of the Peasants' War (1524-1525).

[41] Taylor sees the Reformation as an expression of a profound dissatisfaction with the hierarchical equilibrium between lay life and the renunciative vocations. The Reformation intended to close the gap by elevating lay Christians and to make over the Church to uniformly higher standards. All Christians alike were to be *totally* dedicated. From the beginning, the reformers refused to accept special vocations and counsels of perfection and any essential distinction between ministerial and common priesthoods. Cfr. TAYLOR, *A Secular Age*, 61-77.

[42] Cfr. VOSS, *The priesthood of all believers*, 189: «There is only one priesthood, but within that priesthood there are a variety of ministries».

[43] *Reformation Writings*, I.116. Bravo affirms that for Luther—although work should be done out of love for neighbour—the duty to work originates from his condition of being a sinner. According to Bravo, Luther's originality is not just his vision on the sanctification of one's professional work, but foremost in having annulated the dualism between active and contemplative life. Cfr. BRAVO, *El sacerdocio común en Lutero*, 348-350. According to Illanes, Luther and Calvin have never discovered the intrinsic sanctifying value of professional work. Cfr. J.L. ILLANES, *La santificación del trabajo*, Palabra, Madrid 2001, 60-61.

Although in faith all believers become equal before God, and heaven and earth seem to merge in the believer's mind, our experiences in the temporal-empirical sphere present us with an opposite view. Humans are, or it seems, not equal and heaven and earth are, or it seems, opposed to each other. Luther thought it necessary to introduce a variety of realms—taking the form of three estates of church, household and state, which are instituted by God—in which every human being is called by God to serve him equally.

ii) The absence of human mediation
Standing face-to-face before God, the believer only receives the treasure from the triune God "to enjoy it". This implies that the believer does not obtain the benefit of grace through other believers, nor that he himself brings the fruits of grace to others. Only Christ can give the benefits to each believer personally. Humans are worthy only as recipients of grace in *the sphere of faith* and not as distributors of grace *in the sphere of temporal-earthly experience*, for humans in the latter sphere necessarily would abuse the grace entrusted to them, as was the case of the Roman Catholic Church.[44] Justified believers become signs of spiritual salvation for others, but not real *other Christs* themselves.

iii) The nature of the church
Luther presented the church as a congregation of saints with Christ as its head and called together by the Holy Spirit in one faith, one mind, and understanding of the essence of the Gospel.[45] There is only one eternal holy Christian church, and it is found wherever the Gospel is preached in its truth and purity, and the sacraments are administered according to the Gospel.[46] The congregation of believers in Luther's framework appears to be characterised by non-communion with God in the temporal-earthly sphere. All believers jointly profess in faith that Christ has done everything for them and that they themselves in the temporal-empirical sphere cannot do anything relevant towards God, other than trusting in salvation realised by him. The liturgy is limited to preaching the Word to provoke acts of faith and the worship of God by praising and thanksgiving for the

---

44 Cfr. *Large Catechism*, Article 3, 43-45. It seems that Luther did not attribute the "abuse of ceasing to preach the real Gospel" to the Roman Catholic Church or its ministers, but to the Holy Spirit, since «He was not there to reveal it and cause it to be preached». Again, it becomes clear that for Luther, it is much safer that no Christian ("Catholic" or "Protestant") distributes divine grace to anyone (*Solus Christus*).
45 Cfr. *Large Catechism*, Article III, 51.
46 Cfr. *Augsburg Confession*, art. VII.

eschatological benefits received. The assembly has additional value, because «it is more precious, more appropriate, mightier, and also more acceptable when it [the spiritual offering of oneself] takes place with the multitude and in the assembly, when men encourage, move, and inflame one another to press close to God, and thereby attain without any doubt what they desire».[47] The scriptural basis of Christ's presence in these assemblies is given in Matt. 18:20, 19, «for Christ has so promised: where two are gathered in his name, there he is in the midst of them; and where two agree on earth about anything they ask, everything that they ask shall be done. How much more shall they obtain what they ask when a whole city comes together and praise God and to pray with one accord!».[48]

iv) Doctrine of neighbour
To keep the two spheres of faith (grace) and temporal-earthly reality (sin) separated, Luther developed his doctrine of neighbour in which he distinguished between two kinds of relationship: firstly, the vertical relationship of the believer with God and, secondly, the horizontal relationship of believers with their neighbours. The vertical relationship is one of faith, i.e., established and governed by faith and justification, in which the believer only receives from God and cannot give anything back to him. The horizontal relationship is governed by love, where believers are engaged in works of love and sacrifice (serving and offering), which are never directed to God, but only to humans, which would be pleasing to the Lord.[49] Now that believers have certain knowledge of their salvation and holiness in faith, they are in the temporal-earthly sphere totally free of concerns towards God[50], since they do not have to take care of their salvation anymore, which was won for them by Christ. This freedom would enable believers to give to their neighbour in the temporal-earthly

---

47 LW 35:98-99.
48 *Ibidem.*
49 «If man would offer his works to God, he would commit a double offence, for he is offering them to God who does not need them, and he is taking them from his neighbour where they truly belong. Since God does not require man's works, they must be offered in service to man's neighbour», EASTWOOD, *An Examination of Doctrine till Present Day*, 59; «Even if the Christian life, *coram mundo*, is characterised by action, its fundamental orientation *coram Deo*, is marked by passivity, for this is consistent with justification by faith and the reception of the Spirit», SILCOCK, *Luther on the Holy Spirit and his use of God's Word*, 305; and also Cfr. P. HACKER, *Das Ich im Glauben bei Martin Luther*, Styria, Graz 1966, 166-174.
50 The meaning of freedom here shifts from the freedom from sin and the capability to choose the good, towards the freedom of not having to worry about God's possible detrimental intentions with the believer.

sphere what they have received from Christ in faith.[51] Believers should imitate Christ in the temporal-earthly sphere, but apparently without him.

v) The insight of universal call to holiness
By anticipating eschatological realities, Luther gave a preview of the greatness of what is yet to come. For Luther, 'immediate and direct access' means not only a right of the believer but also an obligation to stand before God the Father in Christ, face-to-face, here and now. It follows that all Christians must be perfectly holy and are called—wherever they are, in whatever they do and at each moment in life—to the highest forms of contemplation, i.e., holiness in the world, while standing before God (*coram Deo*). Each Christian possesses the same authority and responsibility, to be exercised in the midst of the world in all daily activities.[52] As we have seen, all believers have a common dignity (Baptism) and only differ as to their function, which they exercise in the world, whether in the church, one's household or the state. For Luther, each ministry is a divine calling, a gift and a service, as any other service.[53] This means that there are no fundamental differences as to the persons who exercise the different ministries, nor as to the content of these ministries. Whether one is a shoemaker, a pastor or a civil servant, all honour God equally through their work. This is the greatness of the Christian life. This insight is closely related to the notion of common priesthood, as we will see in the next section.

---

51 LW 30:67, «Since we are still living here, we should do for our neighbour as God has done us and give ourselves to Him as God has given Himself to us. Thus it is faith that saves us. But it is love that prompts us to give ourselves to our neighbour, now that we have enough. That is faith receives from God, love gives to the neighbour».
52 Luther's intention was not to de-clericalize the Church, but to clericalize the laity. According to Voss, «Luther has been accused of turning the whole world into a monastery. There is a certain truth in this accusation; Luther himself would agree with the charge. The central text in this regard was Rom. 12:1, implying that all of life—at home or marketplace—was spiritual, an opportunity for priestly service», voss, *The priesthood of all believers*, 212. One of the accusers was Voltaire, who wrote about Calvin, Luther and Zwingli: «If they condemned celibacy in the priests, and opened the gates of the convents, it was only to turn all society into a convent. Shows and entertainments were expressly forbidden by their religion; and for more than two hundred years there was not a single musical instrument allowed in the city of Geneva», VOLTAIRE, *The works of Voltaire: vol. xxvii, Ancient and Modern History, vol. iv, Charles V., 1512—Philip II.*, 1584, E.R. Dumont, Paris 1901, 84.
53 Cfr. SCHWANKE, *Luther's theology of creation*, 209.

3.3 Preliminary conclusion

Luther introduced a dialectical opposition between God and humans and a separation between the spheres of faith and temporal-empirical experiences. Humans can reach God only in faith. For Luther, it appears that it is not Christ at the cross that forms the bridge between humans and God the Father, but rather the believers' recognition of—in a spiritual encounter—the event of Christ's cross (like a bridge), that the believer himself in the temporal sphere cannot use and does not have to use. In Fr. Martin's spiritual experience, he does not take the bridge, but rather, he appears to frame his identification with Christ in faith as a spiritual exchange. In this way, he avoided communion with Christ in the temporal-empirical sphere, but at the same time, ensured the acquisition of the benefits of full communion in a spiritual way. The spiritual benefits —for now, a peaceful conscience and certainty about one's eschatological destiny—do not have any effect on the human condition, which always remains corrupted. Instead of crossing the bridge—and to be really— sacramentally identified[54] with Christ on the cross, Luther leapt the abyss, which separated him from God the Father in an act of desperate faith, in which he obtained direct and immediate access. Only in this encounter Luther felt saved, not from sin, but from his worries about his eternal destiny. Since there appears to be no communion with Christ in the temporal-earthly sphere, believers also do not participate in Christ's life either. When Luther spoke of believers' participation in or with Christ, he referred to "spiritual participation in the eschatological benefits" of Christ, and not a participation in Christ's real life.

This way of framing leads to an inner contradiction and tension in Luther's theology and spirituality. On the one hand, believers are supposed to imitate Christ and serve their neighbours in the sphere of space and time, but doing all that without Christ, because in that same sphere believers have to acknowledge that they cannot be united with Christ.[55]

---

54 In the sacramental economy (cfr. CCC nos 1076–1109), the modality of presence of Christ is characterised not by an "immediate" or "direct" contact with Christ, like the historical experience of the Apostles who could touch Christ, but by an "mediate" contact by his ecclesial Body, which means concrete persons and in an eminent way the Eucharist. The sacraments ensure that believers can be in real communion with God, while at the same time remain humans, safeguarding the metaphysical difference between God, the Creator, and humans, his creatures. God leaps the gap—and enters his creation anew—so that humans may cross it.

55 Christ's cross in the temporal-earthly sphere here and now is reduced to an "*exemplum*" to follow, but not a "*sacramentum*", which pertains only to the sphere of faith. After all, the consequence of this kind of faith is that believers realise and hold for certain that «(...) Christ has acquired and gained *the treasure for us* (...)». The negative

Believers can only be united to Christ spiritually in the sphere of faith, which is diametrically opposed to the human experience in the temporal-empirical sphere. In this sphere, believers cannot give themselves together with Christ to their neighbours, but the focus shifts to giving consolation, preaching salvation in faith, and serving their neighbours. In this indirect way, believers please God in faith, while in the temporal-empirical sphere, the horizontal relations among believers are secularised.[56] The core of "altruism" shifts from the act of complete self-giving (love) to the act of complete self-denial. Luther taught that good works are supposed to be done with a complete lack of any personal interest.

This inner contradiction—that believers are supposed to carry Christ's cross, but without him—is the more remarkable, since that was exactly what Luther had reproached the Roman Catholic Church; that catholics performed self-righteous works of their own and on their own, that is, without Christ. Luther himself drew his courage and certainty from his belief, not that God *cooperated* with him, but that God did *everything* through him,[57] pretending that in this way he was not tempted by pride. In order to prevent this temptation, Luther reasoned, the good works of the believer are to be attributed fully to God in the sense that it is God who directly performs good works through the believer to other humans, without any human cooperation, but merely as an involuntary instrument.[58] What remains is the human part, which is always totally corrupt (*simul iustus et peccator*).

In this framework, only God can give honour to God. Humans cannot give anything to God in the temporal-earthly sphere, for they are unworthy. Believers only receive grace from God, but it is striking that the grace received does not make them worthy or capable to act in any

---

side of justification—i.e., believers as a sinner—obliges them to struggle against sin through mortification and penitence. These acts of mortification and penitence are not meritorious in the sense that it does not render believers just before God. According to Bravo the positive side of justification brings along the duty to preach the Gospel, whereas the negative side (*peccatum manens*) the duty to struggle through mortification and penance. BRAVO, *El sacerdocio común en Lutero*, 338.

56 Due to this framework with the coordinates of intrinsic sinful human nature without the possibility of communion with Christ in the temporal-earthly sphere, morality necessarily becomes exterior. Only external (human) law and authority can force the sinful human being to comply with any moral standard.

57 LW 34:111: «But having been justified by grace (…) we then do works, yes, Christ Himself does all in us».

58 So, it is true—as Luther asserted—that humans on their own can do absolutely nothing towards God. However, humans are not completely on their own, and in and with Christ, they can work for God and perform miracles in the temporal-empirical sphere.

relevant way towards God in the temporal-earhly sphere. Humans can, therefore, only honour and praise God *in faith* by an act of radical self-denial, i.e., the acknowledgement that humans *in the earthly sphere* cannot honour God due to their sinful condition and the recognition that everything is due to God's goodness: God the Son's sacrifice, the Father's mercy, and the Holy Spirit's consolation. Only in this way can believers hold for certain their ability to exalt and praise God's grace. However, it appears that even this self-denial is not really a human work, for Luther attributed the act of human self-denial to the triune God, who provokes in humans this act of faith. In fact, in the temporal-empirical sphere, humans can do absolutely nothing relevant towards God, not even sinning, since Luther appears to equate "reality" with "sinfulness". In Luther's spiritual theory, therefore, humans are supposed to deny "reality" by "an act of faith", but in practice, they cannot deny "reality" for they are completely sinful.[59]

---

[59] Moreover, if there is no human merit in relation to God, there can also not be any personal act of sin towards God, other than by imputation.

4. The common priesthood in Luther

Luther's doctrine on the common priesthood plays an essential role within his theological framework.[1] As we have seen in the preceding section, the priesthood of all believers is closely related and interconnected with the right and duty of spiritual, direct and immediate access to stand before God the Father, face-to-face, here and now. Only in this way can believers obtain eschatological certainty for the future, while in the present—that they are propitious to God in all that they do. This theological position is the axis around which Luther's whole doctrine and spirituality rotate.

This section contains a systematic outline of Luther's vision of the priesthood of all believers. Since Luther himself has not dealt with this doctrine in a systematic way, his views will be construed from passages taken from all over his writings.[2] To identify and grasp properly the role, concept and scope of the common priesthood in Luther, I will focus on the elements of the fundament of priesthood, the mode of participation by the believer, its finality, exercise and functions, the relation between common priesthood and ministries and the aspects of mediation.

4.1 Fundament of the priesthood

According to Luther, Jesus Christ is the true and only High Priest. In his commentary on Psalm 110, verse 4 ("The Lord has sworn and will not change his mind. You are priest forever after the order of Melchisedek"), Luther applied to Christ the eschatological figure of the priest-king Melchizedek.[3] The offices of King and Priest, which in the Old Testament were still separated, are united in Christ, who is everlasting King and Priest.[4] The nature of his Kingdom and Priesthood is spiritual, and neither

---

1 The direct need for Luther to legitimise this theological position was given in the Leipzig Dispute of 1519 with the Catholic theologian J. Eck. He challenged Luther to recognise the authority of the Pope and the Council of Constance (1415) who had condemned the teachings of Jan Hus. Luther sought to defend his position that an individual Christian, like Hus—and Luther himself—could possess the truth, even over and against the Pope and the Council, provided that the Holy Spirit illumines him.
2 Voss notes that secondary sources find evidence of the doctrine in over fifty of Luther's writings, of which Luther discusses the doctrine at length in some fifteen works. Cfr. VOSS, *The priesthood of all believers*, 186-187.
3 Voss points out that Luther's understanding of Christ's unique priesthood grew from his exegesis of Psalm 110 and its treatment in the Letter to the Hebrews, VOSS, *The priesthood of all believers*, 195.
4 Cfr. LW 13:304.

temporal nor of this world.⁵ Luther held that «nothing in Scripture is more comforting than what is said about the priestly office of our dear Christ and that this verse together with the Letter to the Hebrews (on this point) deserves to be written with golden ink».⁶ He regarded this verse as essential. «It is a treasure, the source of all Christian doctrine, understanding, wisdom and comfort. There is no single passage in Scripture, which expresses this so richly or completely. (…). It reveals all that our faith affirms and teaches».⁷

The reason for this comfort is that Christ has won for us our salvation by his sacrifice on the cross, by which he «willingly and without price mediated between God's wrath and our sin».⁸ By this sacrifice, Christ saved us and made us righteous and acceptable to the Father.⁹ Christ became our High Priest, «so that men also may arise from the dead, in body and soul, and live with Him in eternal glory, in purity and perfection».¹⁰ And to make that possible, «Christ must create an entirely new nature and being in us».¹¹

Only Christ could bring salvation, for he alone was without sin and could please God.¹² Luther claims that «everything Christ does is precious. God is thoroughly pleased in every way because Christ is totally without sin and guilt (Heb. 7: 26)».¹³ Christ is, therefore, the only mediator between God and humans capable of representing humans before God and to speak in their best interests. Luther affirms, «Being heard by God was His due; for He was the only one able to present Himself directly to God, without any intermediary and in His own right and power, to make intercessory prayer».¹⁴

Although Christ has performed and completed his once-and-for-all sacrifice on the cross on earth, he continues to exercise his office as mediator and advocate before God in heaven, as St. Paul tells the

---

5   LW 30:63, «The same is true with regard to the fact that we are all kings. "Priests" and "kings" are all spiritual names just as "Christians", "saints", and "Church" are».
6   LW 13:306.
7   LW 13:323.
8   LW 13:320.
9   Cfr. LW 24:246.
10 LW 13:323-324.
11 *Ibidem*. Luther understood God's action always as a continuous creation *ex nihilo*.
12 In Luther's framework, Christ's priesthood is exclusive. Humans cannot—as a matter of principle—participate in this priesthood in the temporal-earthly sphere for their human nature is intrinsically sinful. Luther thus opposed Christ's priesthood to any form of human priesthood in the temporal-empirical sphere.
13 LW 13:319.
14 LW 13:320.

Romans.[15] In this regard, Luther referred explicitly to Christ's «marvellously beautiful» priestly prayer in chapter 17 of the Gospel of St. John. The sacrifice «which he completed once and for all the world's sins is sufficient until the Last Day, but because we are still sinful, *Christ has to continue his intercession for us with the Father*».[16] Christ exercises his office as mediator by praying to the Father that he may regard us just, despite our sins. For Luther, «the power and merit of his sacrifice, i.e., forgiveness of sins, righteousness and eternal life, *are won for us and communicated* to us *by Jesus in his priestly prayer* for us in Chapter 17 of the Gospel of St. John. *Prayer like that is valid forever and works its power in all Christendom*, which *He continues to pray* as our Mediator and Advocate before God».[17]

Does this mean that—according to Luther—Christ's sacrifice has ended? Although it seems like it because Luther strongly stressed the past tense of Christ's salvific act, that is, Christ's sacrifice *has been* performed and completed, yet, elsewhere Luther affirmed that Christ, after his earthly sacrifice on the cross continues, in heaven, to offer himself for us to God.[18] Christ's intercession for humans before the Father is, therefore, twofold: by his prayer and the offering of himself.

4.2 The believers' participation in Christ's priesthood

Christ not only continuously intercedes for us in heaven—he also makes us participants in his intercession before God the Father. Luther observed:

> «Nor does He merely pray for us. He also *bestows upon us the power and the freedom to pray to God directly*. He brings our prayers to God and assures us that such prayers are pleasing to God and will be heard for His sake, just as He promised (John 15, 16): "Whatever you shall ask the Father in My name, that He will give you"».[19]

All believers have the capacity, due to their Baptism and their faith, to present themselves freely before the Lord to pray and intercede for others,

---

15 Rom. 8:34, «Who will condemn? It is Christ (Jesus) who died, rather, was raised, who also is at the right hand of God, who indeed intercedes for us».
16 LW 13:320, Italics added.
17 *Ibidem*, Italics added.
18 In his *The Treatise on the New Testament, That Is, the Holy Mass* (1520), Luther wrote extensively on the relationship between the Mass and sacrifice, affirming several times that Christ—besides interceding for us—also offers Himself for us in heaven. Cfr. LW 35:98-103.
19 *Ibidem*, 320-321, Italics added.

«for to stand before God's face is the prerogative of none except priests».[20]

Also, the Gospel testifies that Christians are priests.[21] Luther saw the royal priesthood mentioned by St. Peter (1 Pet. 2:9: "But you are a chosen race, a royal priesthood, a holy nation") in relation to the Melchisedekian priesthood of Christ. Furthermore, Luther connected the verse in John 15:4[22] with Christ's priestly prayer in chapter 17: «Christ says: 'If you remain in me, I will consecrate you to be holy priests—priests of my Father».[23]

Luther extended the priesthood to all Christians, in an equal manner, and in a spiritual way:

To all…

> «For it is certainly clear and manifest enough that the apostle [St. Peter] is addressing *the whole multitude, all Christians*, when he says: "You are a chosen race … a holy nation." Up to this point, of course, he has spoken about no one except those who are built on the Stone and believe. Therefore, it must follow that he who does not believe is no priest».[24]

Equally…

> «Peter speaks of the inward spiritual priesthood which all Christians possess and not the consecrated priesthood. (…) There are not two kinds of priesthood, a spiritual one and a churchly one, which he [Luther's opponent] calls "ecclesiastical"».[25]
>
> «It should be understood that the name "priest" ought to be the common possession of believers just as much as the name "Christians" or "child of God". We all have one Baptism in common, one Gospel, one kind of grace, one kind of inheritance of the kingdom of heaven, one Holy Spirit, one God the Father, and one Lord Jesus Christ (Eph. 4:4-6). We are all one in Him, as He says in John 17:22 and as St. Paul says in Galatians 3:28: "You are all one in Christ Jesus».[26]
>
> «But we are all priests before God if we are Christians. (…). It would

---

20 *Reformation Writings*, I.366.
21 Luther interpreted the priesthood and admitted its existence and explanation only based on Scripture. Cfr. LW 30:62 and LW 13:318.
22 John 15:4, «Remain in me, as I remain in you. Just as a branch cannot bear fruit on its own unless it remains on the vine, so neither can you unless you remain in me».
23 LW 24:242-243.
24 LW 30:62, Italics added.
25 LW 39:151-152.
26 LW 13:330-331.

please me very much if this word "priest" were used as commonly as the term "Christians" is applied to us».[27]

And spiritually...[28]

> «This is the *spiritual* priesthood, held in common by all Christians, through which we are all priests with Christ. That is, we are all children of Christ, the High Priest; we need no priest or mediator other than Christ. (...) Thus every Christian on his own may pray in Christ and have access to God (...)».[29]
>
> «The same is true with regard to the fact that we are all kings. "Priests" and "kings" are *all spiritual names* just as "Christians", "saints", and "church" are».[30]

Christians share in Christ's priesthood, because Christ bestows it (the power and the freedom to pray to God directly) upon them , and St. Peter testifies to it. But the question arises: what should humans do on their part to become participants in Christ's priesthood? There is not one clear answer, but it seems that it has to do with Baptism, faith, inheriting, joyous exchange, being Christian and abiding in God's love.

Through Baptism, Christians become members of the family of God—they are children of God the Father, and siblings of Jesus Christ—which has a priestly character.[31] Luther explained:

> «Christians are children and heirs, born in a spiritual and heavenly manner, without any human activity, but through the unique activity of God working through the Gospel and Holy Baptism. Such children are the true children of a priest and inherit the same name from their father. Consequently, *every baptised Christian is a priest already*, not by appointment or ordination by the pope or any other man, but because *Christ Himself has begotten him as a priest and has given birth to him in Baptism*».[32]

---

27 LW 30:63-64.

28 Since Luther conceived the spiritual sphere in a dialectical opposition with the temporal-earthly sphere (vid. section 3 above), the believer becomes a spiritual priest by explicitly rejecting that he can be one in the latter sphere. Here only Christ was our one-and-true High Priest, who has performed the once-and-for-all sacrifice on the cross. The spiritual nature of the priest's sacrifices will be discussed in section 4.4.3.

29 LW 36:138-139, Italics added.

30 LW 30:63, Italics added.

31 LW 41:154.

32 LW 13:329, Italics added. Cfr. voss, *The priesthood of all believers*, 197.

Luther regarded Baptism as the maxim of the new regeneration and justification in Christ, but also faith is a constitutive element of Luther's priesthood since the baptised *believer* is a priest. According to Luther, «we are all spiritual and priests, to the extent that *we believe* in Christ».[33] For Luther, faith is a key concept and Baptism is an expression of faith. If faith is lacking, Baptism and priesthood become meaningless. Voss observes that not simply Baptism makes a Christian a priest, but rather Baptism plus the Word and the response in faith.[34]

Furthermore, Luther taught that Christians share in the priesthood of Christ due to the "joyous exchange" between Christ and Christians: All Christians share in *all* possessions of Christ, as Christ shares in *all* the possessions of the Church, including the priesthood and its functions.

Finally, commenting on John 15:9 ("abide in my love") Luther asserted: «Only if we abide in Him, we will be priests. If not, our works will become self-devised priestcraft, but will not be the true service of God».[35]

4.3 Finality of priesthood

The finality of Lutheran priesthood is to give honour to God and to serve him.[36] If believers honour and serve God, they are regarded to be God's servants, and all their works become pleasing to God. For Luther, this is the true honour of Christian life, as he affirmed: «Christians are honoured by God because He regards them His servants».[37]

Lutheran priesthood means that a Christian should offer holy and acceptable sacrifices to God unceasingly, for «Christ says: "If you remain in me, I will consecrate you to be holy priests—priests of my Father. Whatever you do, will not only be proper and acceptable but also the precious service of God"».[38]

---

33 LW 39:159, Cfr. LW 30:62, Italics added.
34 voss, *The priesthood of all believers*, 193. Similarly, Roman Catholic priests—although baptised—are not priests, if they lack faith. In Luther's framework, this makes perfect sense since priesthood is regarded as a mere spiritual phenomenon.
35 LW 24:244.
36 Again, it should be noted that believers seem to honour God spiritually by denying that they can do so in the temporal-earthly sphere.
37 LW 24:243.
38 LW 24:242-243. Voss remarks that for Luther, precious service to God is, firstly, priestly temple service, a service that was previously reserved to the clergy, but could now be rendered by all believers, and secondly, Luther extends the scope of the precious service to God by applying it to all the works of a Christian. All activities of a believer can and should be a precious service to the Lord, everyone can praise the Lord by rendering his own *Beruf* (profession, vocation) a service to his fellowmen and the community (LW 36:78 and 44:130). voss, *The priesthood of all believers*, 201.

And,

> «This not only praises our works as good fruit on earth, but it also elevates them toward heaven and offers them to God as sacrifices acceptable to Him *for His special honour and His highest service. How could a Christian life be extolled more?* And how could a person be urged and exhorted more strongly to live a Christian life than by the prospect of bearing such fruit, of serving such a purpose, and of enjoying such honour with God?».[39]

The common priesthood is also closely linked to the process of justification of others: «Therefore a priest is ordained for the sake of sinners *in order to reconcile them and to plead as the sinners' advocate*. If people were holy and without sin, there would be no need of a priest to sacrifice and pray for them. But if we accept the Lord Christ as Priest, it follows that we must believe and confess that we are sinners».[40]

4.4 The exercise of the priesthood: functions

Although the whole life of a Christian has a priestly character, Luther recognised at the beginning, the three specific priestly functions of sacrificing, praying and preaching, to which he later added four.[41] The following text gives us an important indication and sheds light upon Luther's vision on and understanding of the common priesthood.

> «Now Christ is the High and Chief Priest anointed by God Himself. He also *sacrificed* His own body for us, which is the highest function of the priestly office. Then He *prayed* for us on the cross. In the third place, He also *proclaimed the Gospel and taught* all men to know God and Himself. These three offices He also gave to all of us. Consequently, since He is the Priest and we are His brothers, all Christians have the authority, the command, and the obligation **to preach**, to come before God, **to pray** for one another, and **to offer themselves** as a sacrifice to God».[42]

In this text, Luther described the priestly functions of Christ and the priestly functions of the believers, but inverting the order. The first and most important priestly act—the one that is *truly* priestly—is Christ's

---

39 LW 24:243, Italics added.
40 LW 13:321, Italics added.
41 For an overview of the development of Luther's doctrine on priestly functions see voss, *The priesthood of all believers*, 202-207.
42 LW 30:53-54. Italics and bold added.

(one-and-only) bodily sacrifice, followed by his prayer for us to the Father, and in the third place, Christ's preaching and teaching to all men. The Christian believer participates firstly in the priestly function to preach, then to pray and intercede for others, and on the third and last place, the believer can and should offer himself up as a sacrifice to God.[43]

I will follow this order of the three priestly functions as established by Luther, and then briefly discuss the other four: Baptism, holy communion, the power of the keys (Confession), and judging doctrine.

4.4.1 Preaching and teaching

Since faith has priority, the main function of the common priesthood is bringing people to God for reconciliation and uniting them with him. Therefore, «a priest must be God's messenger and must have a command from God to proclaim His Word».[44] In the act of preaching, it is God who acts through the believer, both in the one who preaches as in the one who listens: «He Himself puts His word into the hearts and mouths of people so that they will accept it and preach it».[45]

The most important way for a priest to achieve reconciliation of humans with God is by teaching and preaching the Word of God (and not his own), i.e., the great things that God has done for humans so that they will do his will, and obey the ten commandments. However, due to the corrupt and sinful human nature, humans are not able to live up to the demands of the Decalogue[46]. Preaching should be aimed at informing the people how they can get rid of sin and God's wrath and obtain grace and righteousness. This is obtained by repentance of sins and faith in the promise of Christ that he has reconciled all humans by His sacrifice[47]. Its

---

43 Eastwood discussed Luther's doctrine on common priesthood by the seven outward marks of the Church, which are i) the preaching of the Word, ii) the sacrament of Baptism, iii) the Lord's Supper, iv) the Keys of Christian Discipline and Forgiveness, v) a called and consecrated Christian Ministry, vi) public worship, with prayer, praise and thanksgiving and vii) the holy Cross; i.e., suffering in many forms through with the Church must inevitably pass. Eastwood does not enter into the question of priority, but he followed the order which Luther had established, Cfr. EASTWOOD, *An Examination of Doctrine till Present Day*, 1.

44 LW 30:64.

45 LW 13:325. See also cfr. LW 13:317.

46 This is why—for didactical purposes—Luther's *Große Katechismus* (1529) first deals with the Ten commandments of God and then with the content of faith (Credo). Following this structure, the believer can only reach salvation, if he first experiences and recognises his total incapacity to fulfil the Law of God in the temporal-earthly sphere, followed by the experience and recognition of the necessity of faith and forgiveness in Christ in the spiritual sphere.

47 Cfr. LW 13:316-317.

function is «to proclaim the wonderful deed God has performed for you to bring you out of the dark into the light. You should also teach other people how they, too, come into such a light».[48]

Preaching should not only focus on faith but also pay attention to works. Priority is on faith, for «if one does not preach on faith, nothing but hypocritical works result. But if one confines one's preaching to faith, no works ensue. In brief, the outcome is either works without faith or faith without works. Therefore, the sermon must address itself to those who accept and apprehend both faith and works; the others, who do not want to follow, remain behind».[49]

Good preaching must lead to faith in God, which enables us to love our neighbour.

> «This is a proper way to preach: first to emphasize the faith, what it does and what its power and nature are, namely, that it gives us enough of everything necessary for piety and salvation, that one can do nothing except through faith, and that through it we have everything God has. Now, if God has dealt this way with us, has given us everything that is His, and has become our own, so that we have all blessings and enough of everything through faith, what are we to do now? Since we are still living here, we should do for our neighbour as God has done for us and give ourselves to Him as God has given Himself to us. Thus it is faith that saves us. But it is love that prompts us to give ourselves to our neighbour, now that we have enough. That is, faith receives from God, love gives to the neighbour (...)».[50]

4.4.2 Prayer

All believers have the capacity, due to their Baptism, to present themselves freely before the Lord to pray and intercede for others. Christians can and should intercede in Christ for each other, for, as we have already seen, a priest was «ordained for the sake of sinners in order to reconcile them and to plead as the sinners' advocate».[51] This means that the believer asks in and through Christ to God the Father that he may regard the others as righteous as well, i.e., to give the others faith that they may recognise Christ as the only mediator and that they stop regarding themselves "pelagians".

The reason that God the Father is pleased with these prayers and will attend to them is solely because of Christ, since «He brings our prayers to

---
48 LW 30:64.
49 LW 24:249.
50 LW 30:67.
51 LW 13:321.

God and assures us that such prayers are pleasing to God and will be heard for His sake, just as he has promised (John 15, 16)».[52]

For Luther, prayers are foremost acts of thanksgiving for the marvellous deeds of Christ, and acts of praise of God. However, he regarded public worship, with prayer, praise and thanksgiving mainly as a sacrifice,[53] because in these acts humans "acknowledge God's greatness and one's own nothingness".[54] The sense and meaning of a sacrifice of thanksgiving, prayer and praise is the recognition that God is everything, that he has given everything to the believer, who has received it by faith, and that the believer "gives" everything back to God and let God operate his salvation in the believer.[55]

4.4.3 Sacrifice

In his *The Treatise on the New Testament, That Is, the Holy Mass* (1520), Luther elaborated his views on the sacrificial character of the Mass and how the offerings of Christians become acceptable before God. Although it is a rather confusing text, Luther tried to harmonise contradictory theological positions,[56] which inevitably led to a change of concepts. It is worthwhile to scrutinise in detail certain passages from this treatise to shed light upon Luther's understanding of the relationship between the sacrifice of Christ and those of the believers.

---

52 LW 13:320. And also LW 35:99, «For this is why He [Christ] is also a priest (...) because He intercedes for us in heaven. He receives our prayer and sacrifice, and through Himself, as a godly priest, makes them pleasing to God».
53 The entire section in Eastwood on Prayer, Worship and Thanksgiving deals with these acts in terms of sacrifice, Cfr. EASTWOOD, *An Examination of Doctrine till Present Day*, 46-53.
54 LW 10:233 (Italics added): «God is rightly worshipped when we completely disparage ourselves and ascribe all praise and glory and whatever is in us to Him. For when we attribute to God what belongs to Him and keep for ourselves what is ours, then we keep nothing, and that very nothing is ours, but everything is God's, from whom we receive it. *Therefore, such a confession out of a true heart is itself the sacrifice of praise, namely, to confess that everything, whatever we are, is owed to God, and that there is absolutely nothing left for ourselves.* And this we must confess to Him not only in our heart but also in our deed, so that the works themselves bear witness that we are and appear nothing in ourselves. And on this basis it comes about that anyone, no matter how saintly, must necessarily think and confess in the presence of God concerning himself that he is totally evil and altogether nothing».
55 Cfr. EASTWOOD, *An Examination of Doctrine till Present Day*, 46-53.
56 Luther, at the same time, i) affirmed and denied the sacrificial element of the Mass, ii) affirmed that believers only receive from God, but also give to God and iii) stated that believers, and especially ministerial priests, do not offer Christ in the Mass, but then endeavoured to show that all believers in some way do offer Christ, both in the Mass and anywhere else.

i) Christ's sacrifice and the believers' sacrifices

As a first step, Luther endeavoured to ensure that believers realise that they do not "sacrifice" anything, admonishing against the peril «that we do not presume to give to God something in the sacrament [of the Mass], when it is he who in it gives us all things».[57] Undoubtedly, this concern can be traced down to Luther's view that the religious practice of his day was pervaded with a spirit of pelagian "own-works-righteousness" mindset, which also became manifest in the Mass.[58] To combat what he considers as distortion, he deemed it necessary to make a neat distinction between spiritual (interior) and external sacrifices. According to Luther, «we should bring spiritual sacrifices, since the external sacrifices have ceased and have been changed into the gifts to churches, monastic houses, and charitable institutions».[59] Instead of these "external" sacrifices, Luther proposed «to offer ourselves, and all that we have» and «in addition, we are to offer Him praise and thanksgiving with our whole heart, for his unspeakable sweet grace and mercy (…)».[60]

At this point in his argumentation (the second step) Luther extended the scope of the priesthood and its exercise by detaching the spiritual sacrifice of all believing Christians from the Mass, by stating that «such sacrifice occurs apart from the Mass, and should so occur—since it does not necessarily and essentially belong to the Mass, (…)». Although not pertaining to its essence, Luther considered the offering of oneself in the Mass to have a certain added value.[61]

Thirdly, Luther proposed a radical Christ-centeredness, by which he particularly sought to correct the position of the Roman Catholic priests, who seemed to have the exclusive privilege of offering sacrifices and their

---

57 LW 35:98.

58 In fact, concerning the sacrificial element of the H. Mass, mainstream theology at that time was not able to identify the H. Mass with Jesus Christ's sacrifice on the cross. Therefore, it was commonly held that the H. Mass was a new sacrifice in itself, which caused the impression that it was offered *separately* from the sacrifice of Jesus on the cross. Cfr. A. GARCÍA IBÁÑEZ, *L'Eucharistia, dono e mistero, trattato storico-dogmatico sul mistero eucarístico*, Edizioni Università della Santa Croce, Roma 2006, 321.

59 LW 35:98. These sacrifices are spiritual in the sense that they are not physical, like the animal sacrifices performed under the Old Testament. After the sacrifice of Jesus Christ on the cross at Calvary—where he redeemed mankind once and for all—Christians are called to sacrifice "their hearts", in the sense of Rom. 12, 1 where St. Paul urges believers to offer themselves as "living sacrifices". Cfr. BRAVO, *El sacerdocio común en Lutero*, 335-336 and EASTWOOD, *An Examination of Doctrine till Present Day*, 46-53.

60 LW 35:98.

61 Cfr. LW 35:98-99.

claim that they offered Christ in the sacrament.[62] Luther's corrections were twofold: i) as we have seen above, he opened up the exclusive privilege, revindicating the common priesthood, by making a distinction between—and by dialectically opposing—spiritual and external sacrifices; all Christians are capable of offering spiritual sacrifices.[63] Secondly, he directed his proposal for a radical Christ-centeredness to all believers: believers do not present their offerings themselves, but only Christ can offer these sacrifices to God. Luther stated:

> «To be sure this sacrifice of prayer, praise and thanksgiving, and of ourselves as well, we are not to present before God in our own person. But we are to lay it upon Christ and let him present it for us, (...). For this is why he is also a priest (...), because he intercedes for us in heaven. He receives our prayer and sacrifice, and through himself, as a godly priest, makes them pleasing to God».[64]

Luther had problems of how to understand and conceive the relationship between Christ's sacrifice and the offerings of Christians, while ensuring that Christians do not offer anything, but at the same time affirming that they offer themselves and their all, as it becomes clear in the following text:

> «From these words [from the Letter to the Hebrews, Romans and Psalm 110] we learn that *we do not offer Christ as sacrifice, but that Christ offers us*. And in this way it is permissible, yes profitable to call the mass a sacrifice; not on its own account, but because *we offer ourselves as a sacrifice along with Christ*».[65]

---

62 LW 35:94, «Now since almost everyone has made out of the mass a sacrifice which they offer to God—which, without doubt, is the third and very worst abuse—we must clearly distinguish between what we offer and what we do not offer in the mass» and Cfr. 36:51 «It is the common belief that the mass is a sacrifice, which is offered to God. (...). Over and against all these things, firmly entrenched as they are, we must resolutely set the words and example of Christ».

63 LW 35:100, «For they suppose that only the priest offers the mass as a sacrifice before God. Actually, this is done by everyone who receives the sacrament – yes, also by those who are present at the mass but do not receive the sacrament. Furthermore, such an offering of sacrifice every Christian may make, wherever he is and at all times, as St. Pauls says (Heb. 13:15), "Let us continually offer up a sacrifice of praise through Him", and Psalm 110:4 (...). If he is a priest forever, then he is at all times a priest and is offering sacrifices without ceasing before God. But we cannot be continually the same; therefore, the mass has been instituted that we may there come together and offer such a sacrifice in common».

64 LW 35:99.

65 LW 35:99, italics added.

The text is confusing because Luther affirmed simultaneously that "Christ offers Christians" and that "Christians offer themselves" as well. Therefore, he sought to clarify the relationship between the sacrifice of Christians and Christ's heavenly sacrifice by stating:

> «That is, we lay ourselves on Christ by a firm faith in his testament and do not otherwise appear before God with our prayer, praise and sacrifice except through Christ and his mediation. Nor do we doubt that Christ is our priest or minister in heaven before God. *Such faith, truly, brings it to pass that Christ takes up our cause, presents us and our prayer and praise, and also offers Himself for us in heaven.* If the mass were so understood and for this reason called a sacrifice, it would be well. *Not that we offer the sacrament, but that by our praise, prayer and sacrifice we move him and give him occasion to offer himself for us in heaven and ourselves with him.* It is as if I were to say, I had brought a king's son to his father as an offering, when actually I had done no more than induce that son to present my need and petition to the king and made the son my mediator».[66]

Thus, Luther considered the Mass a sacrifice in this Treatise (1520), provided that the proper order of the sacrifice—as understood by him—is respected. Christ acts as a mere agent, who is willing to present the offerings of those who firmly believe in him that he will indeed do so. These offerings happen through personal faith; the confidence that Christ will comply with the promises and indeed does mediate and bring the sacrifices to God and make them agreeable to his Father.

In the Mass, it is not only the priest who offers Christ, but it is also through their faith that all Christians do "offer him". In Luther's words, they «offer Christ, in [the sense] that I desire and believe that He accepts me and my prayer and praise and presents it to God in his own person. And to strengthen this faith of mine, He gives me a token that He will do it. Thus, it becomes clear that it is not the priest alone who offers the sacrifice of the mass; it is this faith, which each one has for himself. This is the true priestly office, through which Christ is offered as a sacrifice to God, an office which the priest, with the outward ceremonies of the mass, simply represents. Each and all are, therefore, equally spiritual priests before God».[67]

According to these texts, Christ continues to offer himself to the Father only in heaven.[68] Here it becomes manifest that there is a separation

---

66 LW 35:99-100, italics added.
67 LW 35:101-102, italics added.
68 Luther seemed to hold the opinion elsewhere that the sacrifice of Christ is limited to

between Christ's earthly sacrifice and his spiritual offering in heaven. The first has ended, while the latter remains in heaven without "coming down to earth". The believers have access to Christ's heavenly offering and can "join" their sacrifices to it directly in spiritual faith. Luther even seemed to make Christ's sacrifice in heaven dependent on the believer's faith and sacrifice, since he considered that «such faith brings it to pass that Christ takes up our cause (…)» and «by our praise, prayer and sacrifice we move him and give him occasion to offer himself for us in heaven and ourselves with him». In this sense, Luther regarded that Christians "offer" Christ.[69]

Not only is there a separation between Christ's earthly and heavenly offering, but Luther also separated the offerings of Christ and those of Christians. Christ does not unite the believers' sacrifices to his own but presents them alongside each other, i.e., together but separately. This implies that Christ makes the believers' sacrifices acceptable to God by virtue of his intercession (his own prayer and offering), which has no intrinsic effect on the offerings of Christians, which remain as they are— that is, corrupted. God considers the believer's sacrifices acceptable only because Christ's sacrifice is acceptable in itself. After all, sacrifices are meant to honour God and are supposed to please the Father, but in Luther's view, the only one who really can do that is Christ, for he is without sin and, therefore, pleasing to the Father. That is why he considered explicitly, «The sacrificial office properly belongs to Christ and is restricted to His person because as the High Priest, he Himself must sacrifice for our sins in order that we may be reconciled to God».[70]

Although, in the spiritual sphere, in heaven, by an act of faith, the believer can be sure that God regards his sacrifices as acceptable in

---

the unique sacrifice on the cross, an event that had ended and completed Christ's redemptive work once-and-for-all. The redemptive work seemed to be continued in heaven only by Christ's intercession of his prayer for us with the Father. In any case, both positions can be made compatible by considering that, according to Luther, Christ's sacrifice only continues in heaven and not on earth. The mass on earth becomes a memorial of Christ's earthly sacrifice on the cross and a non-exclusive occasion for all believers to offer spiritual sacrifices by their faith in Christ.

69 LW 35:103, «I will gladly agree that the faith, which I have called the true priestly office is truly able to do all things in heaven, earth, hell, and purgatory; and to this faith, no one can ascribe too much. It is this faith, I say, which makes us all priests and priestesses. Through it, in connection with the sacrament, we offer ourselves, our need, prayer, praise, and thanksgiving in Christ and through Christ; and thereby we offer Christ to God, that is, we move Christ and give him occasion to offer himself for us and to offer us with himself».

70 LW 13:318.

Christ[71], in the temporal-earthly sphere, however, the contrary seems true. For this reason, Luther also denied the expiatory character of the Mass[72] and excluded from his concept of sacrifice any form of expiation and atonement. Only the earthly once-and-for-all sacrifice of Jesus on the cross has the power to atone for our sins. The believers' sacrifices do not have redemptive value, because Christ has gratuitously won for us our redemption by his earthly sacrifice on the cross, while in heaven he presents the believers' sacrifices separately. In the mass «there is nothing else than the reception and enjoyment of divine grace, promised and given us in his testament and sacrament».[73]

ii) And the real sacrifice?
By framing the relationship between Christ's sacrifice and those of believers like this, i.e., as spiritual in heaven and as opposed to external on earth, where believers merely offer a contrite heart and their own nothingness, Luther encountered some difficulties in explaining the value of the suffering of Christians in the temporal-empirical sphere.

Luther did recognise the existence of a mysterious link between the suffering of Christ on the cross and the suffering of each Christian, when he said: «I believe that He bore His sufferings and endured the Cross for my sake and that of all believers, and, in doing so, blessed all suffering and every cross».[74] Even more, Luther affirmed the close relationship between the sufferings somewhere else, when he stated: «(…) Christ's sacrifice is a

---

71 This leads to strange inner contradiction that Luther regarded the believers' sacrifices *in themselves* without any value, but at the same time denied the identification of Christ's sacrifice with that of the believers, so that they in the temporal-earthly sphere always remain *in themselves* and, therefore, without any value.

72 «It is the common belief that the mass is a sacrifice, which is offered to God. (…). Over and against all these things, firmly entrenched as they are, we must resolutely set the words and example of Christ», LW 36:51. Luther regarded the Mass a sacrifice only with respect to the elements of thanksgiving and praise, i.e., the believer denies himself, for he recognises and praises God and what he has done for us in the gratitude shown. Cfr. voss, *The priesthood of all believers*, 202-203.

73 LW 35:103.

74 *Reformation Writings*, I. 86. Bravo remarks that according to Luther, the offer of oneself is only valid if it is done in continuity with the sacrifice of Christ on the cross, which happens through faith. In faith, suffering gets a positive meaning in the life of a Christian since it is blessed by the suffering of Christ. The suffering is a duty of the believer as a sinner, the negative side of justification, whereas the duty to preach would follow from the fact that he is justified (the positive side of justification). Cfr. bravo, *El sacerdocio común en Lutero*, 337-339. For Eastwood, it is a matter of solidarity: whereas the guilt of one is the guilt of all, also the penance should be done by all. I suffer for another, as St. Pauls urges that «all should bear one another's burden». Cfr. eastwood, *An Examination of Doctrine till Present Day*, 54-55.

living sacrifice, *his body being sacrificed once on the cross and our bodies being sacrificed daily*, a living and holy sacrifice, which is rational service to God (Rom. 12:1)».[75]

The suffering of a Christian is an imitation of Christ's suffering and is necessary for the believer to be identified with him.[76] However, at the same time, Luther strongly insisted that the suffering of a Christian is not the same as Christ's suffering. In one of his sermons on 'the suffering of a Christian', Luther considered: «His suffering is an example, which we are to follow in our suffering. Though our suffering and cross should never be so exalted that we think we can be saved by it or earn the least merit through it, *nevertheless we should suffer after Christ, that we may be conformed to him*. (…). Therefore, each one must bear a part of the holy cross; nor can it be otherwise: St. Paul too says, "In my flesh, I complete what is lacking in Christ's afflictions" (Col 1, 24)».[77]

A little further in the sermon, he argued: «If you are willing to suffer, very well, then the treasure and consolation which is promised and given to you is so great that you ought to suffer willingly and joyfully *because Christ and his suffering is being bestowed upon you and made your own*».[78]

However, although identifying the sufferings, Luther ended his sermon as follows: «(…) you should accustom yourself to distinguish carefully between the suffering of Christ and all other suffering and know that his is a heavenly suffering and ours is worldly, that his suffering accomplishes everything, while ours does nothing except that we become conformed to Christ, and that therefore the suffering of Christ is the suffering of a lord, whereas ours is the suffering of a servant».[79]

In close connection with the moral identification with Christ by following his example,[80] Luther developed the doctrine of neighbour, as discussed, *supra*. The believer is engaged in works of love and sacrifice (offering and serving) which are never directed to God, but only to

---

75 LW 36:201, Italics added.
76 Luther's concept of identification is a moral one and consists in doing God's will by obeying his (impossible) commandments. In fact, also Luther's concept of sacrifice of total self-giving and heartfelt praise and thanksgiving is closely connected to the will of God for each believer. He described the Christian sacrifice as «the offering of oneself and all that we have to be performed under constant prayer that God's will may be done on earth as in heaven (Matt. 6, 10) in order that we may yield ourselves to God's will and that he may make of us as he pleases», LW 35:98.
77 LW 51:198, Italics added.
78 LW 51:199, Italics added.
79 LW 51:208.
80 For Luther, to be a member of the royal priesthood meant to «give myself to my neighbour, just as Christ offered Himself to me», LW 31:367.

humans, which is pleasing to the Lord.[81] As Luther claimed: «Since we are still living here, we should do for our neighbour as God has done us and give ourselves to Him as God has given Himself to us. Thus it is faith that saves us. But it is love that prompts us to give ourselves to our neighbour, now that we have enough. That is faith receives from God, love gives to the neighbour».[82]

In summary, Christians offer spiritual or heavenly sacrifices—as opposed to external or earthly sacrifices—to God. The latter type of sacrifice is not necessary anymore after Christ's earthly sacrifice on the cross, which he has performed and completed once-and-for all. In this way, believers are not presumptuous to think that they give anything to God—they only receive benefits from him. The believers' spiritual offerings consist of oneself (a contrite heart), prayer, thanksgiving and praise.

All believers can offer these sacrifices to God, not by themselves, but exclusively through Christ, who is the only Mediator and High Priest. The way believers offer these sacrifices in and through Christ—and Luther even considered that believers "offer Christ himself"—is by their own personal faith: their confidence that Christ accepts them and their prayer and praise, and indeed will mediate for them and make their sacrifices acceptable before God. Because the emphasis is put on interior faith, believers can bring these sacrifices to God anywhere and anytime, although Luther recognised that it is more appropriate when it takes place with the multitude and in the assembly. The external rite of the mass becomes a non-exclusive token or sign to strengthen the believers' faith in God's promise.

Christ thus continues to intercede for believers only in heaven by the offering of himself and his prayer to God. Although Christ in heaven presents the believers' spiritual sacrifices to God the Father, he *does not unite* these sacrifices to the offering of himself but *he offers them alongside his own offering*. Christ does not exercise his heavenly mediation by identification of the representative (himself) and the represented (the believers), but as a mere agency.[83] The believers' offerings become spiritually acceptable to God by virtue of Christ's heavenly intercession (his prayer and offer), but always remain wretched "in themselves", i.e., in the temporal-earthly sphere. Luther claims that God is, therefore, not really pleased with these sacrifices, and that these sacrifices lack

---

81 voss, *The priesthood of all believers*, 216.
82 LW 30:67.
83 Legally, in civil law, an agent is an intermediary between the contracting parties, but he does not become a contracting party himself.

redemptory value. In the temporal-earthly sphere, believers are called to suffer to be conformed to Christ, but always keeping in mind that there is an abyss between God and humans. They cannot give themselves directly to God, but they should serve and love their neighbours instead.

4.4.4 Other functions

Apart from the three main priestly functions, Luther recognised four other priestly functions, which were formerly exclusively exercised by the clergy, and attributed them to all believers. These functions are administering Baptism, Holy Communion, the power of the keys (Confession) and judging doctrine.

Luther argued that in the case of emergency midwives could baptize new-borns, which implies that they possess common priesthood.[84]

Concerning Holy Communion, each believer has the capacity to celebrate the mass, since it basically contains the commemoration of the promise made by Christ during the Last Supper to forgive our sins. The believer accepts this promise by personal faith—only for oneself and not for others—and which becomes effective by eating the bread and drinking the cup, which are signs of redemption. Each believer can utter the words of the promise.

Luther held that the power of the keys, which he limited to Confession, were given, not only to St. Peter, but through him to the whole community, i.e., to all of us. For him, all believers have to forgive each other their sins, as they all have to practice fraternal correction (cfr. Matt. 18:15-18).[85]

Finally, Luther taught that each believer has the task (right and duty) to judge doctrine. Commenting on the verse of St. Peter (1 Pet. 2:2), "Like new-born babes, long for the pure spiritual milk", he interpreted the milk as the Gospel which has to be given purely and unadulterated to the new-born young Christians.[86] Since the Gospel is «often like the false commodity which is usually sold and an admixture of human doctrines, the milk must be unadulterated».[87] «Consequently, the Holy Spirit wants every Christian to see what kind of milk he drinks; he himself must learn what to think of teachings».[88] In case of an admixture of human doctrines, each believer has the right to denounce the bad practice and try to restore it. Moreover, it is an obligation whose failure could lead to eternal damnation.[89] However,

---

84 Cfr. LW 40:23–24, 41:151; 44:128 and 39:14.
85 Cfr. LW 36:79.
86 Cfr. LW 30:48-49.
87 *Ibidem*.
88 *Ibidem*.
89 Cfr. voss, *The priesthood of all believers*, 206.

after the Peasants' War and the conflicts with the *Schwärmer*,[90] Luther held that this function should only be exercised by the magistrates.[91]

4.5 Relation between Priesthood and ministries

Luther recognised the existence of ministries, which are all equal in dignity (Baptism) and goal (service to the community), for all Christians are priests and called to be servants. It does not matter in which occupation, for no occupation is too low. What is important is the fact that one is called by God.[92] In the words of Eastwood: «believers come under *favor Dei*, the favour of God, which does not and cannot change; it is the functions for which it is bestowed which are different».[93]

Luther reserved the exercise of the more "ministerial" functions—preaching, Baptism and Holy Communion—to the ministers within the community.[94] Although every Christian is a priest, not everyone is allowed to exercise the faculty to preach.[95] The reason for this is practical, for «the people as a whole cannot do these things, but must entrust or have them entrusted to one person. Otherwise, what would happen if everyone wanted to speak or administer, and no one wanted to give way to the other?».[96] For the sake of order in the community, these ministries should ordinarily be exercised only with the consent of the community. The office of preaching and administering sacraments is reserved for those who are called, in the first instance by God (divine vocation), which is then confirmed by the community.[97] By this confirmation, the members of the

---

90 On the relationship between Luther and "radical" Christian groups, whom he labelled "Schwärmer", such as the "Zwickau prophets", "sacramentarians" like Karlstadt, Zwingli, and Oecolampadius, Anabaptists, and Spiritualists, see A.N. BURNETT, *Luther and the Schwärmer*, Chapter VI, n. 38, in: R. KOLB, I. DINGEL, L. BATKA (eds.), *The Oxford Handbook of Martin Luther's Theology*, Oxford University Press, Oxford 2014, 511-521. Burnett shows that Luther shaped significant elements of his thinking, such as the nature of divine revelation; the necessity of trust in the external Word found in Scripture, proclamation, and sacramental forms of the Word; Baptism; the Lord's Supper; and Christology, through engaging the ideas and challenges of these various groups.
91 Cfr. VOSS, *The priesthood of all believers*, 206. Voss refers to LW 14:341.
92 Cfr. EASTWOOD, *An Examination of Doctrine till Present Day*, 13.
93 *Ibidem*, 42.
94 Luther distinguished between "priesthood" (*Priestertum*) and "ministry" (*Ambt*).
95 Cfr. LW 39:154. The way of organising the community was to become a great point of divergence within the protestant movement.
96 LW 39:154.
97 Voss remarks that «Luther originally meant a public call from a congregation, but that after the Peasants' War, Luther limited the right to call a pastor to the nobles and the magistrates». VOSS, *The priesthood of all believers*, 207.

community give their permission and delegate their powers to the minister to preach to the community. Luther explained this by an analogy of ten ambassadors, who choose among themselves one to represent them.

The minister is not "more priest" than the other believers in the community, since all have the same spiritual powers over the Word. Luther affirmed that it is Christ, who speaks through the minister and that the listener should not care about the person of the minister, his defects, etc. The limit is the correctness of doctrine and practice, in which case the Church should act (through suspension and deposition). Luther taught this as follows:

> «You need not care who or how those from whom you receive it are (…). For all of it is given, not to him who has the office, but to him who receive it through this office, except that he can receive it together with you if he so desires. Let him be what he will. Because he is in the office and is tolerated by the assembly, you put up with him too. His person will make God's word and sacraments neither worse nor better for you. What he says or does is not his, but Christ, your Lord, and the Holy Spirit say and do everything, in so far as he adheres to correct doctrine and practice. The church, of course, cannot and should not tolerate open vices; but you yourself be content and tolerant, since you, an individual, cannot be the whole assembly or the Christian holy people».[98]

4.6 Mediation

As explained earlier, due to his specific theological framework,[99] Luther endeavoured to remove and make obsolete as much as possible any form of human mediation of divine realities between God and humans. By situating each believer directly before God the Father, all sacrifices have become obsolete, and intercessory prayer for others tend to become superfluous. After all, redemption is a personal act of faith in the promise to which no human being can contribute. In fact, the whole issue of human mediation tends to become unnecessary, except for teaching and preaching. If there is any form of mediation left, it seems due to the fact that Luther could simply not deny the reality that believers are still travelling in the temporal-earthly sphere—although he tried and even

---

98 LW 39:156.
99 The framework consisting of the intrinsic corruption of human nature, a neat separation and opposition between the spiritual-supernatural and temporal-earthly spheres, a radical and exclusive Christ-centeredness, the theological position that each believer has direct and immediate access to God, and that the believer merely receives benefits from God without "giving" anything back to God.

made such a denial an integral part of his faith—and had to harmonise somehow his faith with that fact. In any case, Luther consistently and systematically minimised the human role in the supernatural sphere.

Keeping the foregoing in mind, Luther's concept of common priesthood contains certain forms of mediation. The believer is a priest and as such, has the capacity, authority and obligation to mediate somehow in Christ between God and humans (descending dimension) and humans and God (ascending dimension).

The descending dimension lies, firstly, in preaching and teaching of the Gospel, God's Word, to fellow humans beings (believers and non-believers). This is not a "special power" of the clergy, but a normal function—right and duty—of each believer as Christian and priest. Secondly, the four priestly functions of administering Baptism, Holy Communion, the power of the keys (Confession) and judging doctrine contain forms of mediation. For example, in Baptism, it is Christ who baptises, but he uses other people to perform the rite.[100] Furthermore, descending mediation becomes manifest in the fact that God acts through the believer in good works and love for neighbour. The good works are a gift from God to the believer and, through the believer, given to the whole fellowship of believers. In this way, God—through Christ and the believer—becomes present in the life of a Christian and the community. The believer, being redeemed, elected and holy, becomes a sign of salvation for other humans.

The ascending dimension consists, firstly, in the fact that believers intercede and pray for each other to God in Christ. Secondly, believers can and should offer themselves up to God, i.e., to bring him spiritual sacrifices of worship, praise and thanksgiving. These acts, however, do not bring fellow humans any closer to God, since these sacrifices always remain separated from Christ's eternal-heavenly sacrifice.[101] For this very reason, they lack any redemptive and supernatural value. In the temporal-earthly sphere, they are—or so it seems—not pleasing to God. Moreover,

---

100 «For the man baptizes, and yet does not baptize. He baptizes as far as he performs the rite: he submerges the candidate. Yet, in one sense, he does not baptize, but only acts on God's behalf, and not on his own responsibility. Hence we ought to understand Baptism at human hands just as if Christ Himself, nay God Himself, baptizes us with His own hands. The Baptism which we receive through human hands is Christ's and God's, just as everything else that we receive through human hands is God's», *Reformation writings*, I.259, quoted by EASTWOOD, *An Examination of Doctrine till Present Day*, 18-19.

101 As we have seen, Christ's earthly sacrifice has ended and can only be commemorated and Christ in heaven presents his own offer to God separately from the believers' sacrifices.

since the sacrifices have to be pleasing to God, and for Luther, a believer, due to his intrinsic sinful nature, cannot please God directly—believers have to give themselves to their neighbour. God is only pleased if believers "sacrifice" themselves to their fellow human beings, and not if they give themselves directly to God. Since there is no identification between Christ and the believer in the temporal-empirical sphere,[102] the latter also does not mediate between God and humans in this sphere.

4.7 Conclusion
Luther regarded as the core of the priesthood common to all believers the offering up of oneself to God and the bringing of spiritual sacrifices, which are pleasant to the Lord (1 Pet. 2:9). Humans become Christians, priests, kings, saints, or members of God's family by Baptism and faith. Christian priests are called to honour and serve God, and in serving and honouring him spiritually, God honours the Christian. That is the greatness of Christian life, where human beings are called to serve him and to sacrifice themselves and pray for others to God. All works of a Christian are priestly, and they can and should become a service and honour to God. All believers have a common dignity (by virtue of Baptism) and only differ as to their functions, which they carry out in this world. For Luther, each ministry—whether in the church or in the world—is a divine gift and call (*Beruf*, vocation), and a service to be rendered to fellow human beings and the community as any other service.

Due to this "joyous exchange", all Christians share equally in *all* possessions of Christ, as Christ shares in *all* the possessions of the Church, including the priesthood and its functions. Since Christians share equally in all priestly functions, all Christians can, in theory, also exercise the more "ministerial" functions, to build up the Christian community, which formerly were reserved only for the ordained clergy. However, for practical reasons, the priestly ministries of preaching and administering sacraments (Baptism and the Lord's Supper) are to be exercised only by those who have been publicly called and confirmed by the community.

At the same time, Luther strongly emphasised that Christ is the *true-and-only* High Priest and Mediator, who has redeemed humanity by his *once-and-for-all* sacrifice on the cross. This earthly sacrifice has ended, whilst Christ continues his priestly office in heaven, i.e., spiritually, to the Father, by his intercession (prayer and self-offering) on our behalf. Through Christ's intercession, God communicates *the fruits* of his

---

102 The spiritual identification between Christ and the believer in the *fröhliche Wechsel* is not enough since Luther maintained it in opposition to an identification in the temporal-earthly sphere.

sacrifice on the cross to humans. All believing Christians, who act with faith in Christ's priesthood and in their own incapacity, are deemed righteous before God. On this ground, believers may appear before God, because Christ bestows upon them the power and the freedom to pray to God directly and to stand before God's face is the prerogative of none except priests.

Although Christ gave all his priestly functions, in principle, to all believers, at the same time, Christ limited the scope of this participation. Firstly, believers principally do not participate in Christ's sacrifice itself, but only enjoy the fruits of that sacrifice. This participation in the fruits of Christ's sacrifice is only in a spiritual way, "by faith", but not in the "temporal-earthly sphere" and the believer's sacrifices do, therefore, lack redemptive value. Believers' sacrifices are to be carefully distinguished and separated from Christ's sacrifice. Man cannot contribute to his own salvation or that of others, but must merely accept, by faith, the free gift of salvation won for us by Christ.

Christians' sacrifices are regarded as positive because they are blessed by Christ, and they are necessary to be conformed to him in a moral sense, and they carry one other's burdens out of solidarity. Believers, however, cannot effectively unite their suffering to Christ's sufferings in the temporal-earthly sphere, for two reasons: i) theological: Christ's earthly sacrifice has ceased, and in heaven, Christ presents the spiritual sacrifices of believers alongside his own offering, and ii) anthropological: humans, although justified by faith in Christ, always remain complete sinners in the temporal-empirical sphere and are, therefore, not capable to do anything good in this sphere, and especially, not able to unite their sufferings effectively to Christ's and to co-redeem with him.

The antithesis between Christ's suffering and that of man is clearly stated by Luther himself in this text: «Christ's merit and sacrifice stands in contradiction to my sacrifice and work. Only one can be valid: either Christ's or my own».[103] It is this dialectical opposition between Christ's and the believers' sacrifices, in Luther's doctrine, which strikes the exercise of the (common and ministerial) priesthood of believers at its root, and cuts it off from the core of Christ's priesthood, which is his eternal-priestly-redemptive sacrifice.

---

103 LW 13:328.

CHAPTER II.
COMMON PRIESTHOOD IN CALVIN

«We do not appear with our gifts in the presence of God without an intercessor. Christ is our Mediator, by whose intervention we offer ourselves and our all to the Father; he is our High Priest, who, having entered into the upper sanctuary, opens up an access for us; he is the altar on which we lay our gifts, that whatever we do attempt, we may attempt in him».[1]

«But now that the sacrifice has been performed, (…), the Lord (…) has given us a table to feast, not an altar on which a victim may be offered; he has not consecrated priests to sacrifice, but ministers to distribute a sacred feast».[2]

1. Relevant elements of Calvin's life, person and theology

1.1 Life and person

Jean Calvin[3] (1509-1564) was born in France in Noyon. His mother was innkeeper, and his father was a notary and court clerk, who intended his three sons to become priests. Although Jean received his tonsure at the age of twelve and studied Latin, he was never ordained to the priesthood, but instead studied liberal arts in Paris and law at the University of Orlèans. Jean studied also in Bourges where he learned Koinè Greek and was influenced by humanism.

During Calvin's years of formation as a student, the Reformation as initiated by Luther was in full swing. Christians were divided, which

---

1 J. CALVIN, *Institutes of the Christian Religion*, Vol. 2, Eerdmans, Grand Rapids 1979, Book IV, Chapter xviii, 618-619.
2 *Ibidem*, 615.
3 General biography on Calvin: W. NIESEL, *The Theology of Calvin*, Grand Rapids Baker Book House, Michigan 1980, T. H. L. PARKER, *Calvin: An Introduction to His Thought*, Geoffrey Chapman, London 1995, B. COTTRET, *Calvin: A Biography*, Eerdmans Grand Rapids, Michigan 2000, A. GANOCZY, *Calvin's life* and W. DE GREEF, *Calvin's writings*, both in: MCKIM, D. K., *The Cambridge Companion to John Calvin*, Cambridge University Press, Cambridge 2004, R. D. LINDER, *The Reformation Era*, Greenwood Press, Westport (Connecticut), London 2008.

meant not only danger to the unity of the Church, but also chaos in the country, with conflicts and persecutions. For Calvin, these were important issues of concern.[4]

In 1533, Calvin experienced a kind of religious conversion, which he has described on two occasions. Although scholars do not agree on the exact interpretation, it appears that this conversion had to do with his breaking with the Roman Catholic Church. This break should not be understood as a separation from the church—Calvin has always denied to be schismatic, because for him, the Church was "the body of believers who placed Christ at its head" and consequently there is per definition only one "Catholic" and "universal" Church—[5] but rather as a specific mission to reform the one church of Christ according to the spirit of the true gospel; a vocation which he gradually over several years came to understand and to accept.[6] In any case, Calvin was later that year caught up in a conflict at the university in Paris where he stood at the side of the reformers; he was forced to go into hiding and finally to leave France in 1534; first, he went to Strasbourg, later to Basel, and finally, he ended up in Geneva.

In 1536, during his brief stay in Basel, Calvin published his main theological work, the Institutes of the Christian Religion (*Institutio Religionis Christianae*), a systematic exposition of the doctrinal Reformed position. This work was the first expression of his theology and he revised it during his whole life.[7] The work was to have a great impact and influence on religious thinking in Europe and worldwide. Calvin also wrote commentaries on most books of the Bible.

In Geneva, where he spent most of his life, Calvin employed great energy and developed into a zealous defender of the cause of the reformers and re-organiser of the local church of Geneva, according to Reformed principles and ideas. The lawyer-theologian worked inexhaustibly as a teacher, pastor, author and "negotiator" with the city council on the reorganisation of the Church of Geneva and its worship.[8] Although not

---

4 Ganoczy remarks that «the conviction that both State and Church need a ruling authority deserving of respect is clearly discernible from time to time in all ecclesiastical and political statements of Calvin's life», GANOCZY, *Calvin's life*, 6.
5 Cfr. *Instit. Vol. 2*, IV, I, 282.
6 Cfr. GANOCZY, *Calvin's life*, 9-10.
7 The version used and quoted mostly in this book is the ultimate authoritative version of 1559 as translated in English by Henry Beveridge (1845) and published in two volumes by Eerdmans, Grand Rapids in 1979.
8 Calvin wrote in this period a catechism which was largely based on Luther's Large Catechism. The first edition was arranged pedagogically, describing Law, Faith and Prayer. Later, in 1542, Calvin rearranged the order for theological motives, describing first Faith, then Law and finally Prayer, Cfr. COTTRET, *Calvin: A Biography*, 170–171.

without difficulties and opposition—Calvin was expelled from Geneva for two years, which he spent working as a minister in Strasbourg with Martin Bucer—he managed by 1541 to completely reorganise the Genevan church according to reformation principles.

Calvin was known as a man of rigorous discipline and with a strong sense of order; with his brilliant organisational skills, he masterfully divided the ministry in his community into four functions: i) pastors to preach and administer the sacraments (Baptism and Supper), ii) doctors to instruct believers in the faith, iii) elders in charge of discipline and iv) deacons to care for the poor. But not only the formal structure of the community had Calvin's attention. His practical interest and organisational skills are well demonstrated by the way he organised all aspects of community life, first in Geneva, but also helping other Reformed communities in Europe.[9]

1.2 Calvin's theological framework and key insights

This section attempts to give a brief overview of Calvin's theological framework and key insights. Since the common priesthood depends on the understanding and exercise of Christ's priesthood and the way humans participate in that priesthood (section 3), it is crucial to look closely to the way Calvin understood, more in general, the relationship between God and humans and how he conceived the believers' communion with and participation in Christ (section 2).

Calvin's theology is heavily influenced by Luther's theological views,[10] but his approach to the theological issues of his days was more distant—less existential—systematic and practical than Luther's approach. Calvin, with his background as a layman, educated in the study of law and jurisprudence, had a keen sense of the practical aspects of the theological discourse. Being aware of the practical difficulties of some of Luther's theological insights, he was able to successfully mitigate in the life of the community some of its problematic aspects, especially with respect of the doctrine of the common priesthood.[11]

Luther's overemphasis of the interior and spiritual aspects of the personal act of faith, the proclamation of the radical equality and the universal priesthood of all believers, had forcefully contributed to chaos

---

9 After his death, various Congregational, Reformed and Presbyterian churches, which took Calvin's theology and ecclesiology as their example and model, have spread throughout the world.
10 Cfr. GANOCZY, *Calvin's life*, 8-9.
11 Luther's views on the universal priesthood had proved difficult in its practical application, Cfr. VOSS, *The priesthood of all believers*, 208.

and disorder both in Church and society. In the wake of Luther's reform emerged radical spiritualist individuals and groups, all claiming to have been enlightened through the Holy Spirit—with or without the aid of Scripture—with true knowledge of God and humans.

In this setting, it is not surprising that Calvin saw it as his primary task to bring law and order in the Reformed church. That Calvin regarded himself God's chosen instrument with due authority to defend divine interests on earth is illustrated by the way he presents himself in the introduction of his *Institutes* to Francis I, the King of France, as «pleading the common cause of all the godly, and therefore the very cause of Christ», and defending «mighty interests as these: how the glory of God is to be maintained on earth as inviolate, how the truth of God is to preserve its dignity, and how the kingdom of Christ is to continue amongst us compact and secure».[12]

Calvin's main interest was to ensure in practice that all humans—or at least the godly—in their lives give the right praise and true glory to God (*pietas*).[13] The "truth of God", according to Calvin, is basically that God is a majestic, heavenly and spiritual being, who must remain in heaven and cannot become part of his earthly creation,[14] for this would be equal to idolatry and hence blasphemous.[15] The distance between God and humans —given the very nature of things—should always be maintained. It is on the basis of this insight that Calvin reformed Christian doctrine and reorganised the right praise by humans to God in a sober liturgy—precisely reflecting this distance—by preserving the order and the proper preaching of the Gospel in the community. Calvin followed Luther in his accusation of Roman Catholic self-righteousness to try to reach salvation

---

12 *Instit.* Vol. 1, 5.

13 According to Hesselink, *pietas* or *true godliness* is a central theme of the *Institutes*. Calvin in this work not only stressed the importance of true knowledge of God and humans, but also the need to put this knowledge into action. The *Institutes* have, therefore, a pre-eminently pastoral character. Cfr. J. HESSELINK, *Calvin's theology*, in: MCKIM, D. K., *The Cambridge Companion to John Calvin*, Cambridge University Press, Cambridge 2004, 74.

14 This becomes manifest, f. ex., in the following reasoning: «And as it is our duty in regard to the other creatures which the divine liberality and kindness has destined for our use, and by whose instrumentality he bestows the gifts of his goodness upon us, *to put no confidence in them, not to admire and extol them as the causes of our mercies*; so neither ought our confidence to be fixed on the sacraments, *nor ought the glory of God to be transferred to them*, but passing beyond them all, our faith and confession should rise to Him who is the Author of the sacraments and of all things», *Instit. Vol. 2,* IV, xviii, 499-500, Italics added.

15 *Ibidem*, xvii, 594, «For what is idolatry if it is not to worship the gifts instead of the giver?».

based on one's own works without Christ, but he was especially sensitive to the Roman Catholic Church's «impious and superstitious worship» in their sacraments.[16] In Calvin's view, humans can worship God spiritually, but not in the temporal-empirical sphere, for their forms of worship are men-made, which means that they cannot be trusted and are "detestable".[17]

Calvin's sense for the practical aspects and his primary concern for an orderly community caused him to shift the attention *within* Luther's framework to repair any deficiencies and to do "damage control". For this reason, Calvin, over time,[18] stressed more the divine side of the relationship between God and humans, in order to counterbalance the risks of an all-determining, purely subjective, act of faith.

Calvin thus also reframed—along the same lines of thought as Luther—the relationship between God and humans by endeavouring in his theology to show and maintain the existence of an infinite abyss between God and humans and to maximise God's role at the cost of the human role in their mutual relationship. Like Luther, Calvin used a dialectical opposition[19] between them, and established a separation between the spiritual-supernatural and the temporal-empirical spheres. The features of the believers' personal act of faith, their direct and immediate eschatological access to God, and their incapacity to give anything back to God, are present in Calvin's theological framework as well.

---

16 Cfr. *Ibidem*, xiv, 505.

17 «We must hold it as a first principle that as often as any form is assigned to God, his glory is corrupted by an impious lie. (…). But God makes no comparison between images, as if one were more, and another less befitting; He rejects without exception, all shapes and pictures, and other symbols by which superstitious imagine they can bring him near to them» and «Being works of man, they have no authority from God (Isa. Ii. 8, 31; vii. 57; Hos. xiv. 4; Mic. v. 13); and, therefore, it must be regarded as a fixed principle, that all modes of worship devised by man are detestable». *Instit. Vol. 1*, I, xi, 91-94.

18 Calvin developed his theological views over time—in part—to defend sound Reformed doctrine responding often *ad casum*, inserting in his *Institutes* theological disputes with f. ex. Osiander, Servetus, (semi)papists, Anabaptists or other radical spiritualists.

19 *Instit. Vol. 2*, III, xv, 94, «What then is our foundation in Christ? Is it that he begins salvation and leaves us to complete it? Is it that he only opened up the way, and left us to follow it in our own strength? (…). Being admitted to participation in him, though we are still foolish, he is our wisdom; though we are still sinners, he is our righteousness; though we are unclean, he is our purity; though we are weak, unarmed, and exposed to Satan, yet ours is the power which has been given him in heaven and in earth (…); though we still bear about with us a body of death, he is our life; *in short, all things of his are ours, we have all things in him, he nothing in us*. On this foundation, I say, we must be built, if we would grow up into a holy temple in the Lord». Italics added.

Yet at the same time, for the sake of order and discipline in the community, Calvin shifted the attention away from the believers' subjective act of faith to the divine side of the relationship, putting all the emphasis on God. It is interesting to note that Calvin explicitly disapproved the method of radical paradox, which does not leave any room for a gradual communion, but implies that the believer receives "all-or-nothing" at once.[20] Calvin, instead, simply ruled out all human initiative in favour of God's all-determining action. Therefore, Calvin stressed God's majesty, his sovereignty, omnipotence and all-encompassing providence in the governance and care of the world and humans' lives. The price Calvin paid for this shift of attention was his teaching on double predestination. Though this doctrine should not be regarded the central theme of Calvin's theology,[21] the overemphasis on divine sovereignty and his omnipotence, while leaving no room whatsoever for human freedom and initiative, led Calvin logically to consider explicitly that humans are predestined to either heaven or hell.

Other aspects stressed by Calvin are the key notions such as the centrality of the humanity of Christ, God's election and vocation of the believers, the imperative role of the Holy Spirit in the believers' faith (teaching) and regeneration (sanctification), the importance of obedience to God's will as manifested through the law, and a strong(er) ecclesiology, stressing in particular the unity and authority of the Church. His religious views are characterised by great seriousness and responsibility for purity and growth of the Kingdom on earth, a sober liturgy and an intense religious life, stressing that the world is the work field of a Christian.[22]

The shift in attention to the divine side in the relationship between God and humans goes hand in hand with an attempt to systematically exclude any human role. Although intentionally Luther basically does the same, he never really succeeded in overcoming the practical problems, since he made the personal act of faith of the believer the very core of his whole theological system. Whereas for Luther it is the certainty of one's salvation which is the decisive factor to rule out any human role, for Calvin, it is moreover the need to bring order and control in the community. However, by framing the relationship between God and humans like this, Calvin followed Luther in establishing a neat separation

---

20 About those who used this method Calvin said: «They tell you, if you look to Christ salvation is certain; if you return to yourself damnation is certain. Therefore, your mind must be alternately ruled by diffidence and hope; (...)». *Instit. Vol. 1*, III, ii, 490.
21 Cfr. HESSELINK, *Calvin's theology*, 83.
22 Cfr. *Instit. Vol. 2*, IV, xiii, 481, 484.

between them, excluding the possibility of any real communion between God and humans travelling on earth.

In the next section, we will investigate in more detail how Calvin conceived the relationship between God and humans.

2. The relationship between God and humans

After having sketched briefly the general framework and some key elements of Calvin's theology, this section attempts to give a closer view of the way he conceived his relationship with God. As in Chapter I, the main theme of this section is the gap between God and humans, which Calvin over accentuated so that it in the temporal-empirical sphere never can be bridged. The following theological insights are discussed: God's glory versus human sin, the role of the law, Christian freedom and God's mercy, God's saving action and the true knowledge of God, the experience of salvation in faith, mystical union and participation in the free eschatological benefits, direct access, and finally, some characteristics of Calvin's theology of the believers' situation in *statu viae*.

1.1 Widening the gap

Calvin accentuated the gap between God and humans by opposing God's majesty to the corrupted human condition, by stressing humans' ignorance and their incapacity to know God, and by opposing God's sovereignty to human initiative.

As for Luther, also for Calvin, God is overwhelming majesty and greatness. God's majesty contrasts sharply man's sinful condition, which is regarded as an absolute obstacle for humans to enter into communion with God.[1] In Calvin, God's majesty is always opposed to "the body", while "the flesh" is expressly distinguished from grace and virtue.[2]

Following Luther, Calvin situated sin at the heart of the human being, in his very nature.[3] Although the point of departure is that God is good and so is his creation, Calvin put so much emphasis on Adam's fall and its effects that he regarded humans by themselves only capable of sinning. Calvin asserted,

> « (…) this perversity [men's nature as a seed-bed of sin] never ceases, but constantly produces new fruits. (…). For our nature is not only utterly devoid of goodness, but so prolific in all kinds of evil, that it can never be idle. Everything in man, from the intellect to the will, from the soul even

---

[1] *Instit. Vol. 2*, III, vi, 3, «It greatly concerns his glory not to have any fellowship with wickedness and impurity (…)».
[2] Cfr. *Ibidem*, IV, xvii, 582.
[3] *Instit. Vol. 1*, II, ii, 246, «We are all sinners by nature, therefore, we are held under the yoke of sin».

to the flesh, is defiled and pervaded with this concupiscence; the whole man is in himself nothing else than concupiscence».[4]

Responding to the argument that natural affections are not to be condemned, because God has created them, Calvin reasserted: «We hold that all human desires are evil, and we charge them with sin not in as far as they are natural [for they are implanted by God the author of nature], but because they are inordinate, and inordinate because nothing pure and upright can proceed from a corrupt and polluted nature».[5]

The sinful condition of man also hinders humans in acquiring true knowledge of God. According to Calvin, all humans are born and live for the express purpose of learning to know God and it is the law of their being to direct all their thoughts and actions of their lives to this end.[6] Some knowledge of God is naturally implanted in the human mind and conscience. There is a common conviction of all humans there is some Godhead[7] and «a sense of Deity is indelibly engraved and inscribed on every heart».[8] Moreover, «His glory is engraved on each of His works».[9] Even more, Calvin held that these perfections are conspicuously manifest in the whole universe, to such an extent that «we cannot open our eyes without being compelled to behold him»[10]. Thus, it is clear «that the Lord has furnished every man with abundant proofs of his wisdom».[11] God should be contemplated in his works, through which he draws us near, becomes familiar, and in a manner communicates himself to us.[12]

Humans, however, do not derive any benefit from these bright manifestations, because we «inwardly suppress them», due to our ingratitude,[13] negligence,[14] vanity and stupidity.[15] Calvin observed «an immense flood of error», comparing «every individual mind with a labyrinth», and that

---

4 *Ibidem*, 216-217.
5 *Ibidem*, III, iii, 518.
6 Cfr. *Instit. Vol. 1*, I, iii, 45.
7 Cfr. *Ibidem*, 43.
8 *Ibidem*, 44.
9 *Ibidem*, v, 51.
10 *Ibidem*, 51.
11 *Ibidem*, 52.
12 Cfr. *Ibidem*, 57.
13 *Ibidem*, 53.
14 Cfr. *Ibidem*, 55.
15 «Great is our stupidity that we derive no benefit from the bright manifestations of God. Our vanity corrupts heavenly truth. We are all like this, that we substitute monstrous fictions for the one and living God, a disease affecting the noblest», *Ibidem*, 59.

almost everyone creating their own God.¹⁶ So much so, that in Calvin's view «there is abundant evidence of the blindness of the human mind».¹⁷

The reason for this blindness of the human mind is to be found in Adam's fall by which mankind as a whole was alienated from God and acquired «an innate love of self».¹⁸ Although this original sin has not completely destroyed our image of God, all that remained is a fearfully deformed, corrupted human nature, «a ruin, confused, mutilated, and tainted with impurity».¹⁹ Through Adam's fall, mankind fell into disgrace and God withdrew from humans the spiritual or supernatural gifts of faith, love of God and to neighbour.²⁰ According to Calvin, humans in this state can never please God.²¹

But besides the contrast of God's majesty and human's corruption and ignorance, Calvin also stressed God's complete sovereignty, omnipotence and all-encompassing providence in the governance and care of the world and humans' lives. God works all-in-all and takes care of everything. Calvin stressed the importance of creation, not only so that "humans may come to know God", but also to control them. God, being the Creator of the whole universe, has established in his creation an "order of nature", determining the exact way how humans should act and behave.²² By accentuating these divine characteristics, Calvin left no room for any human initiative. Humans not only fully depend on God but are wholly determined by the "order of nature", which God has established in his creation.²³

Finally, it should be noted that humans, according to Calvin, are always liable for all their (wrongful) actions. Though they are outside of their control, they nevertheless fall within the scope of their responsibility. As Calvin pointed out, «men's nature is, as it were, a seed-bed of sin, and

---

16 Cfr. *Ibidem*.
17 *Ibidem*, 60.
18 *Ibidem*, II, i, 211, «Owing to the innate self-love by which all are blinded, we most willingly persuade ourselves that (…) man is perfectly sufficient of himself for all the purposes of a good and happy life».
19 *Ibidem*, I, xv, 164-165.
20 Calvin—following St. Augustine—made a neat distinction and separation between spiritual or supernatural gifts and natural gifts. The latter always remain what they are: corrupted. Cfr. *Instit. Vol. 1*, II, ii, 233.
21 *Instit. Vol. 1*, II, ii, 244, «If everything which our mind conceives, mediates, plans, and resolves, is always evil, how can it ever think of doing what is pleasing to God, to whom righteousness and holiness alone are acceptable? It is thus plain that our mind, in whatever direction it thus turns, is miserably exposed to vanity».
22 Cfr. G.H. HAAS, *Calvin's ethics*, in: MCKIM, D. K., *The Cambridge Companion to John Calvin*, Cambridge University Press, Cambridge 2004, 93.
23 Cfr. *Ibidem*.

therefore cannot but be odious and abominable to God. Hence, it follows that *it is properly deemed sinful in the sight of God; for there could be no condemnation without guilt*.[24] Calvin, by attributing guilt to humans, established a principle of strict liability in theology; even without fault, humans are responsible.[25]

2.1 Bridging the gap

2.2.1 True knowledge and faith

Although God has manifested himself evidently in his creation to all humans, this is, however, not sufficient to come to true knowledge of God.[26] Calvin distinguished a twofold knowledge of God, as Creator and as Redeemer. In Christ, God became man to redeem us with the shedding of his blood on the cross.[27] The knowledge of God as Creator is available for everyone (though nobody can make good use of it). God as Redeemer in Christ, however, is only made known to the elect through the Word. Calvin stated: «God, not in vain, has added the light of his Word in order that he might make himself known unto salvation and bestowed the privilege on those who he was pleased [the elect] to bring into nearer and more familiar relation to himself».[28]

The true knowledge of God the Redeemer in Christ only comes to the elect. Like Luther, Calvin was also convinced that humans are justified by faith alone. However, where Luther sees justification by faith as the firm belief that we are redeemed through Christ's sacrifice on the cross, Calvin defined justification as «the acceptance by which God regards us as righteous whom he has received into grace».[29] This definition emphasises God's sovereign and gratuitous election of the believer and downplays the

---

24 *Instit. Vol. 1*, II, ii, 216-217.
25 This can also be clearly seen in the following reasoning: «No believer ever performed one work which, if tested by the strict judgement of God, could escape condemnation; and moreover, that were this granted to be possible (though it is not), yet the act being vitiated and polluted by the sins of which it is certain that the author of it is guilty, it is deprived of its merit», *Instit. Vol. 2*, III, xiv, 81.
26 *Instit. Vol. 1*, I, v, 62, «Creation exhibits so many bright light lamps lighted up to show the glory of its Author, but in vain for us. They are insufficient in themselves to lead us into the right path».
27 «For if, on the cross, he offered himself in sacrifice that he might sanctify us forever, and purchase eternal redemption for us, undoubtedly the power and efficacy of his sacrifice continues without end». *Instit. Vol.2*, IV, xviii, 608-609.
28 *Instit. Vol. 1*, I, vi, 64.
29 PARKER, *Calvin: An Introduction to His Thought*, 97-98.

subjective act of faith; God first redeems humans so that they become righteous, and then he chooses them because they are just.[30]

Nonetheless, Calvin also acknowledged that this true gospel comes to the elect through faith, which is «an enlightenment by internal revelation by God».[31] More specifically, it is the Holy Spirit, who teaches humans and enlightens them inwardly in such a way that they cannot disregard it.[32] Again, to downplay the subjective act of faith, Calvin left humans with no other option than to accept divine teachings.[33] This divine knowledge is superior to any form of human judgement and all natural ways of knowing. The inner teacher, the Holy Spirit must open the way in our minds, since humans are in themselves totally blind and in utter darkness.

Calvin deemed it important to stress that the Spirit also uses—though not exclusively—[34] external means, like Scripture and humans, to proclaim the Word of God. However, it is only the Spirit—and no other—who teaches and provides humans with a firm conviction and a distinct, solid and certain knowledge of God.[35] It thus appears that none can enter the kingdom of God save those whose minds have been renewed by the enlightening of the Holy Spirit.[36]

---

30 The meaning of "justification by faith alone" in Calvin's definition shifts to "the firm belief that I am accepted (or chosen, elected) by God as righteous".
31 Cfr. *Instit. Vol. 1*, I, v, 62, Calvin refers to St. Paul (Heb. xi, 3) who teaches us that we understand by faith. We have no eyes to perceive it until they are enlightened through faith by internal revelation from God.
32 *Ibidem*, vi, 67, «Since men's error is so deeply rooted in human nature, the true knowledge of God has to be implanted in his heart, before error can be eradicated from it».
33 Calvin stated, «(…) he [the Holy Spirit] is the internal teacher, by whose agency the promise of salvation, which would otherwise only strike the air of our ears, penetrates into our minds. (…) faith itself is produced by the Spirit», *Ibidem*, III, i, 466.
34 Cfr. HESSELINK, *Calvin's theology*, 80.
35 *Instit. Vol. 1*, I, vii, 72, «Let it, therefore, be held as fixed, that those who are inwardly taught by the Holy Spirit acquiesce implicitly in Scripture; that Scripture, carrying its own evidence along with it, deigns not to submit to proofs and arguments, but owes the full conviction which we ought to receive it to the testimony of the Spirit. Enlightened by him, we no longer believe, either on our own judgement or that of others, that the Scriptures are from God; but, in a way superior to human judgement; feel perfectly assured (…) that it came to us, by the instrumentality of men, from the very mouth of God».
36 Cfr. *Ibidem*, II, ii, 240.

2.2.2 The role of the law and the gospel

Like for Luther, also for Calvin, the law is a teacher of despair.[37] The law holds forth the promises of salvation and eternal life to all humans and is a guide to show the way to obtain them. However, according to Calvin, it is impossible for humans to observe the law.[38] The law, therefore, serves to render humans "inexcusable" and to make them conscious of their corrupted nature, misery and incapability to comply with its demands.[39] This insight, in turn, leads to despair when humans realise that the only "just" thing to do would be their condemnation.[40] As Calvin stated, «the Law is a kind of mirror: we behold first our impotence, then our iniquity, and finally the curse».[41] He recommends that we should «learn to tremble» and to «consider ourselves to sit before the heavenly Judge, and anxious for our acquittal, voluntarily humble ourselves, confessing our nothingness».[42]

At the same time, Calvin maintained that God, the God of the gospel, in reality, is not like that. The true (faith in the) gospel teaches humans that God does not hold the imperfect obedience of believers against them. The Lord is aware of human misery and a strict application of the law would definitely render all promises fruitless. God, therefore, does not

---

37 Beeke remarks that Calvin viewed the law above all as a guide to the positive expression of the will of God, whereas for Luther the law was primarily negative. Cfr. J.R. BEEKE, *Calvin on piety*, in: MCKIM, D. K., *The Cambridge Companion to John Calvin*, Cambridge University Press, Cambridge 2004, 133.

38 «It is impossible to observe the Law. (...) we shall not find a single saint who, clothed with a mortal body, ever attained to such perfection as to love the Lord with all his heart, and soul, and mind, and strength; and, on the other hand, not one who has not felt the power of concupiscence (...) no saint ever will attain to perfection, so long as he is in the body (...). So long as we are pilgrims in the world, we see through a glass darkly, and therefore, our love is imperfect. Let it, therefore, be held incontrovertible, that, in consequence of the feebleness of our nature, it is impossible for us, so long as we are in the flesh, to fulfil the law», *Instit. Vol. 1*, II, vii, 303-304.

39 *Ibidem*, III, ii, 489-490, «For nothing stimulates us so strongly to place all our confidence and assurance on the Lord as self-diffidence, and the anxiety produced by a consciousness of our calamitous condition. (...) religious fear, which of necessity we must feel whenever coming into the presence of the divine majesty, we are made aware by its splendour of the extent of our own impurity. (...) God trains his people to humility, and curb them by the bridle of modesty, while yet fighting bravely».

40 «The only thing, therefore, remaining for him is, from their excellence [of the promises for those who are obedient to the law] to form a better estimate of his own misery, while he considers that the hope of salvation is cut off, and he is threatened with certain death (...). Therefore, if we look merely to the Law, the result must be despondency, confusion and despair, seeing that by it we are all cursed and condemned, while we are kept far away from the blessedness which it holds forth to its observers», *Ibidem*, II, vii, 303.

41 *Ibidem*, 305.

42 *Instit. Vol. 2*, III, xii, 62.

look to human works, but forgives its deficiencies, accepts them as if they were complete, and gives the believers gratuitously what he has promised.[43] Believers do, therefore, not despair by the threats of God's law implanted in their hearts and their real incapability to comply with it. True faith in the gospel includes the explicit acknowledgement of this fact and thus the rejection of one's own righteousness and merit,[44] they confidently trust in Christ instead, who has done everything for them gratuitously.[45] Moreover, as a consequence of this acknowledgement, Christ, when apprehended in faith, begets in believers repentance[46] through his Spirit and forgiveness of sins.[47]

2.3 Leaping the gap

Similar to Luther, in Calvin's theology believers also leap the abyss, which separates them from God in the temporal-empirical sphere, by a spiritual act of faith uniting them to Christ and bringing them into the direct presence of God the Father. However, whereas Luther seemed more interested in the benefits obtained by the wonderful exchange with Christ,

---

43 Cfr. *Instit. Vol. 1*, II, vii, 303, «For when we have learned, that the promises would be fruitless and unavailing, did not God accept us of his free goodness, without any view to our works, and when, having so learned, we, by faith, embrace the goodness thus offered in the gospel, the promises, with all their annexed conditions, are fully accomplished. For God, while bestowing all things upon us freely, crowns his goodness by not disdaining our imperfect obedience; forgiving its deficiencies, accepting it as if it were complete, and so bestowing upon us the full amount of what the law has promised».

44 *Ibidem*, III, xii, 67, «Therefore, if we would make way for the call of Christ, we must put far from us all arrogance and confidence. (…) When we have entirely discarded all self-confidence, and trust solely in the certainty of his goodness, we are fit to apprehend and obtain the grace of God».

45 *Ibidem*, II, vii, 306. The effect in the children of God [the elect] is not despair, but that «they may take refuge in his mercy, rely upon it, and cover themselves up entirely with it; renouncing all righteousness and merit, and clinging to mercy alone, as offered in Christ to all who long and look for the true faith. In the precepts of the law, God is seen as the rewarder only of perfect righteousness (a righteousness of which all are destitute), and, on the other hand, as a stern avenger of wickedness».

46 Calvin opposed the Catholic doctrine of contrition as a condition for obtaining forgiveness of sins. In his opinion, this doctrine necessarily leads to either despair or hypocrisy, i.e., a merely pretended fear of the justice of God. *Instit. Vol. 1*, III, iv, 536. Calvin's doctrine is «that the soul looked not to its own compunction or its own tears, but fixed both eyes on the mercy of God alone». The believer's contrition, for Calvin, thus becomes tantamount to «recognising his wretchedness, his turmoil, weariness, and captivity (…)». *Ibidem*, 537 and see also *Instit. Vol. 2*, IV, xvii, 598 where Calvin argued that the condition to be in a state of grace to eat worthily the sacrament would mean that nobody could receive the sacrament of the Eucharist.

47 Cfr. *Instit. Vol. 1*, 29.

Calvin highlighted more the communion itself, again turning the attention away from the act of faith of the believing subject. Calvin explicitly put the 'mystical union' between Christ and the believer at the centre of his theology.[48]

2.3.1 Wondrous exchange and benefits

Nevertheless, speaking in terms that remind of Luther's "joyous exchange", also Calvin considered that Christ by virtue of a mystical union conferred upon the believer all his benefits, such as righteousness, divine filiation, direct heavenly access, eternal life, holiness (his strength in us and his riches). Calvin affirmed,

> «(…) we cannot be condemned for our sins, from the guilt of which he absolves us, seeing he has been pleased that these should be imputed to himself as if they were his own. His is the *wondrous exchange* made by his boundless goodness. Having become with us the Son of Man, *he has made us with himself sons of God*. By is own descent to the earth, he has prepared *our ascent to heaven*. Having received our mortality, he *has bestowed on us his immortality*. Having undertaken our weakness, he has *made us strong in his strength*. Having submitted to our poverty, he has *transferred to us his riches*. Having taken upon himself the burden of unrighteousness with which we were oppressed, he has clothed us with *his righteousness*».[49]

Calvin remarked, «as soon as you are engrafted into Christ by faith, you are made a son of God, an heir of heaven, a partaker of his righteousness, a possessor of life, (…) all the merits are Christ's, since they are communicated to you».[50]

2.3.2 Mystical union

Calvin described this union between Christ and the believer in several ways and wordings. The union is "mystical" in the sense that it is an "intimate" relationship between Christ and the believer.[51] It is, furthermore, "wondrous", "real", "interior" and "gradual". As Calvin asserted,

---

48 Beeke calls Calvin's understanding of "communion with Christ" the heart of his system of theology, which shaped his thought on all other issues. Cfr. BEEKE, *Calvin on piety*, 128. According to Garcia, Calvin did not ground good works in imputation or justification (ex sola fide) but in union with Christ. M.A. GARCIA, *Life in Christ. Union with Christ and Twofold Grace in Calvin's Theology*, Paternoster, Milton Keynes 2008, 260.
49 *Instit.* Vol. 2, IV, xvii, 558. Italics added.
50 *Ibidem*, III, xv, 95.
51 Cfr. HESSELINK, *Calvin's theology*, 81.

«believers are really united to Christ and that Christ is not external to us, but dwells in us; and not only unites us to himself by an individual bond of fellowship, but by a wondrous communion brings us daily into closer connection, until he altogether becomes one with us».[52] The believers «cleave to him» and are thus «pervaded with Christ's holiness».[53]

Calvin was aware of the danger of a possible erroneous understanding of deification of humans, confusing them with God on the metaphysical plane. According to Beeke, union with Christ in Calvin's theology is historical, ethical, and personal, but not essential; there is no crass mixture of human substances between Christ and us.[54] In his debate with Osiander, Calvin argued strongly against «an essential inhabitation of Christ within us». Christ, instead, «resides in our hearts», believers are «partners in the gift» and «engrafted into his body», but there should not be a mixture or confusion of divine and human natures.[55]

The effect of the communion is that "Christ's power works in the believer".[56] The elect are raised from the earth to enter into spiritual communion with Christ in heaven, who comes and dwells to the hearts of the elect on earth, so that it may be said that Christ lives and grows in them.[57] This union is life-giving; «because of the fountain of Christ's perfection in our nature, the pious may, by faith, draw whatever they need for their sanctification. The flesh of Christ is the source from which his people derive life and power».[58] Holiness is "the power of Christ" in the believer. Through faith, believers benefit from the holiness of Christ and by some mysterious union participate in that holiness.[59]

---

52 *Instit. Vol. 1*, III, ii, 490-491.
53 *Instit. Vol. 2*, III, vi, 3, «It is important to realise that we do not come into communion with him by merit of holiness (we ought rather to cleave to him, in order that, pervaded by his holiness, we may follow whither he calls)».
54 BEEKE, *Calvin on piety*, 128.
55 *Instit. Vol 2*, III, 46, «Christ becomes ours, the union of the head and members, the residence of Christ in our hearts, mystical union, making us partners with him in the gift, we do not view him as at a distance and without him, but as if we had put him on, and been ingrafted into his body, he deigns to make us one with himself, and therefore we glory in having a fellowship of righteousness with him».
56 «(...), the righteousness of Christ, and thereby life, is ours by communication, (...). Everyone knows that the only mode in which this is done is, when by a wondrous communication Christ transfuses into us the power of his own righteousness, (...)». *Instit. Vol. 1*, II, i, 215.
57 Cfr. BEEKE, *Calvin on piety*, 129.
58 Commentary on John 6:51, cited by BEEKE, *Calvin on piety*, 128.
59 Cfr. *Ibidem*, 127-128.

Although Calvin put the accent on the "mystical union" itself, it must be duly recognised that—within this union—he laid all the emphasis on God's sovereign role to the detriment of the believers' role, whose contribution to the (comm)union is minimised. With regard to God's role he stressed, a) Christ's sovereign humanity as condition for mystical union, and b) the sovereign role of the Holy Spirit. As to the role of believers in this union, he endeavoured to separate Christ's power from the human works. This becomes manifest in the fact that—according to Calvin—firstly, the supernatural powers of Christ in the believer operate parallel to the believers' natural powers given to them in creation, secondly, believers are not healed through this union with Christ, thirdly, his idea of non-meritorious causation, and finally, his doctrine of imputation.

These teachings have direct consequences for Calvin's vision of the Church, sacraments, sanctification, priesthood, etc.

i) God's sovereign role
Ad a) Calvin stressed the facts that Christ took on our human nature in the Incarnation, his Death, Resurrection, and especially his Ascension into heaven, as necessary conditions for the mystical union between Christ and believers.[60] Christ became human to redeem believers by his Death and Resurrection and to elevate them to heaven.[61] By ascending into heaven, he left the elect alone on earth to be bodily present with God the Father. Although Christ is not bodily present anymore on earth among the believers, he fulfils his promise «to be with them until the end of the world» (Matt. 18:20) by directly ruling the earth and exercising his power and efficacy from heaven.[62] Calvin insisted that Christ is also sovereign in his Incarnation and that after his Ascension into heaven his

---

[60] By emphasising—more than Luther—the importance of Christ's Incarnation and humanity as a condition for our redemption, Calvin recognised the redemptive value of the whole life of Christ, whereas Luther's main focus is on the event of the cross. Cfr. HESSELINK, *Calvin's theology*, 86.

[61] *Ibidem*, 81, Hesselink quotes *Instit*. II.12.3: «Our common nature with Christ is the pledge of our fellowship with the Son of God; and clothed with our flesh he vanquished death and sin together that the victory and triumph might be ours».

[62] *Instit. Vol. 1*, II, xvi, 449, «Being raised to heaven, he withdrew his bodily presence from our sight, not that he might cease to be with his followers, who are still pilgrims on earth, but that he might rule both heaven and earth more immediately by his power; or rather, the promise which he made to be with us even to the end of the world, he fulfilled by this ascension, by which his body has been raised above all heavens, so his power and efficacy have been propagated and diffused beyond all the bounds of heaven and earth».

divinity could not be contained in his humanity.[63] In other words, after his Ascension into heaven, Christ is bodily present in heaven and only spiritually present on earth. Christ does not come down to earth, but the Holy Spirit elevates and unites believers in their hearts with Christ in heaven.

Ad b) This intimate union is the consequence of the believer's act of faith in Christ. However, it is also the Holy Spirit, who produces this act of faith in the believers, while the believers' part in this act of faith in Christ is the explicit recognition of their own nothingness and sinful condition in the temporal-empirical sphere.

ii) The minimal human role
Although there exists a communion between the believer and Christ in faith, by which Christ's power works in the believer, at the same time Calvin endeavoured to separate them. This becomes manifest in the following four of Calvin's doctrines.

Parallel operations
According to Calvin, the supernatural powers of Christ in the believer operate parallel to the believer's natural powers given to him by creation. Calvin separated in believers the regenerated and restored supernatural gifts from the human corrupted natural gifts. The supernatural gifts do, therefore, not really inform or transform the natural gifts, but they are exercised and become operative by God parallelly in the believer.[64]

No healing
The elect are not healed through this union. The presence of (the power of) Christ in believers does heal nor elevate their nature but curbs it.[65]

---

63 HESSELINK, *Calvin's theology*, 82 quoting *Instit.* II.13.4: «Even if the Word in his immeasurable essence united with the nature of man into one person, we do not imagine that He is confined therein. Here is something marvellous—the Son of God descended from heaven in such a way that without leaving heaven He willed to be born in a virgin's womb, to go about the earth and to hang upon the cross; yet He continuously filled the world, even as He had done from the beginning».
64 *Instit. Vol. 1*, III, xxiii, 233, «All these, [the spiritual gifts of faith, love, charity, righteousness and holiness] when restored to us by Christ, are to be regarded as adventitious and above nature».
65 Calvin explained that «notwithstanding of the corruption of our nature, there is some room for divine grace, such grace as, without purifying it [human nature], may lay it under internal restraint. God, by his providence curbs the perverseness of nature, preventing it from breaking forth into action, yet without rendering it inwardly pure». *Ibidem*, II, iii, 251-252.

God restrains human corruption inwardly by the power of the Spirit.⁶⁶ Human nature is corrupt to such an extent that it cannot be healed, but God first must "destroy it" and then make a "new nature" instead. In fact, Calvin described the union with Christ itself as «a destruction of our nature»⁶⁷ and held that «part in which the dignity and excellence of the soul are most conspicuous has not only been wounded, but so corrupted, that mere cure is not sufficient. There must be a new nature».⁶⁸ This new nature entails that «God may create new thoughts and new minds, so that we shall have no desire save that of entire agreement with his will».⁶⁹ Despite these statements, it is remarkable that Calvin, distinct from Luther, upheld the doctrine of the resurrection of the body.⁷⁰

The idea of non-meritorious causation
To keep the actions of God and humans separated, Calvin took recourse to the idea of non-meritorious causation. Good works are necessary for salvation and holiness, but according to Calvin this should be understood properly; the good works are a necessary *consequence* of the union with Christ and the sanctification of believers by the Holy Spirit; God is the exclusive cause of the good works in the believer who performs them non-meritoriously.⁷¹

The doctrine of imputation
Not only are the elect just and righteous by imputation,⁷² but also their holiness is attributed to them. By the virtual communion with Christ, humans do not become just in themselves, but the righteousness of Christ is communicated to the believer by imputation «as if it were his own».⁷³

---

66 HAAS, *Calvin's ethics*, 94.
67 «To be ranked among his sons there must be a destruction of our nature. Both of these we obtain by union with Christ. For if we have true fellowship in his death, our old man is crucified by his power, and the body of sin becomes dead, so that the corruption of our original nature is never again in full vigour (Rom. vi. 5,6). If we are partakers in his resurrection, we are raised up by means of it to newness of life which conforms us to the righteousness of God», *Instit. Vol. 1*, III, iii, 515.
68 *Ibidem*, II, ii, 218-219.
69 *Instit. Vol. 2*, III, xx, 191.
70 *Ibidem*, xxv, 271, «We must hold that the body in which we shall rise will be the same as at present in respect of substance, but that the quality will be different; (…). The corruptible body therefore, in order that we may be raised, will not perish or vanish away, but divested of corruption, will be clothed with incorruption».
71 Cfr. GARCIA, *Life in Christ*, 255.
72 In this life the people of God can only obtain righteousness by imputation; God in his mercy regards them as righteous and innocent. Cfr. *Instit. Vol. 2*, IV, xv, 518.
73 «To declare that we are deemed righteous, solely because the obedience of Christ is

In the temporal-earthly sphere, however, human vices are «covered and buried by his perfection»[74] and believers, strictly speaking, always deserve punishment.[75] Since Christ's power in the believers does not really affect them, but works parallel, Christ's holiness is attributed to the believers as if it was their own.

2.3.3 Direct eschatological access
Especially relevant for the common priesthood of believers is their possibility to have "direct access" to the Father and to be able to enter with boldness into the presence of the Lord.[76] Christ, by his Ascension into heaven as man, opened up the access to the heavenly kingdom for all believers. In heaven, he represents us «as it was in our name» and continually intercedes for us with the Father.[77] From his Ascension, it followed «that we are in a manner now seated in heavenly places, not entering a mere hope of heaven, but possessing it in our head».[78]

Since Christ, after his Ascension, is only spiritually present on earth and not bodily, the access to God is also spiritual. The riches, which are treasured up for us with our heavenly Father, become accessible through prayer in which we appear before God, «for there is a kind of intercourse between God and men, by which, having entered the upper sanctuary, they appear before Him and appeal to his promises (…)».[79] However, even standing in prayer before God, believers can only appeal to him for leniency in Christ, for «Christ himself is the only way and the only access by which we can draw near to God, those who deviate from this way, and

---

 imputed to us as if it were our own, is just to place our righteousness in the obedience of Christ», *Ibidem*, III, xi, 58-59.

74 *Ibidem*, 59.

75 *Instit. Vol. 1*, II, xvi, 436, «God abolishes all that evil that is in us, so that we, formerly impure and unclean, now appear in his sight just and holy. (…) The iniquity, which deserves the indignation of God, remains in us until the Death of Christ comes to our aid, and that iniquity is in his sight accursed and condemned, we are not admitted to full and sure communion with God, unless in so far as Christ unites us. And, therefore, if we would indulge the hope of having God placable and propitious to us, we must fix our eyes and minds on Christ alone, as it is to him alone it is owing that our sins, which necessarily provoked the wrath of God, are not imputed to us».

76 *Instit. Vol. 2*, III, xiii, 72, «For, as Paul declares, faith is not true, unless it suggests and dictates the delightful name of the Father; nay, unless it opens our mouths and enable us freely to cry, Abba, Pater. This he expresses more clearly in another passage, "In whom we have the boldness and access with confidence by the faith of him" (Eph. iii. 12)».

77 Cfr. *Instit. Vol. 1*, II, xvi, 450.

78 *Ibidem*.

79 *Instit. Vol. 2*, III, xx, 146.

decline this access, have no other remaining; his throne presents nothing but wrath, judgement, and terror».[80] Calvin found it necessary to point out that believers do have access to God, but they cannot come too close; only Christ presents the prayers of the believer to the Father,[81] while the sinful believers «are standing far off in the outer court».[82] In other words, Christ represents believers, but believers do not represent Christ towards other humans in the temporal-empirical sphere.

2.4 Back in the world
While believers stand directly before God's throne in faith, they are at the same time present in the world. The practical Calvin reminded believers frequently that they are pilgrims on their way to the heavenly kingdom.[83] Christ has done everything to reconcile believers and acquire their salvation, but Calvin understood well that believers—although the Holy Spirit brings them in a wondrous communion with Christ by faith in his power and with Christ's mystical presence in their hearts—do not yet possess the fullness of the spiritual blessings in the temporal-empirical sphere.[84]

Hereunder I will discuss the following characteristics of Calvin's theology of believers' situation in *statu viae*: i) the process of regeneration, ii) the emphasis on the external and visible Church, iii) the believers' election and vocation, iv) no human cooperation, v) human freedom and obedience, vi) the believers' identification with Christ by external cross-bearing, vii) the value of human works and service to God, viii) double predestination, and ix) secularisation.

2.4.1 A process of regeneration
As long as humans are in the corruptible body, they still have to be made in conformity with Christ. In this earthly life, believers have to exercise a

---

80 *Ibidem*, 166.
81 «(…) no prayer is agreeable to God which he [Christ] as Mediator does not sanctify», *Ibidem*, 175.
82 «Christ appears in the presence of God and the power of his death has the effect of a perpetual intercession for us; that having entered into the upper sanctuary, he alone continues to the end of the world to present the prayers of his people, who are standing far off in the outer court», *Ibidem*, 168.
83 E.g. *Instit. Vol 2*, III, x, 31, «To his people, the present life is a kind of pilgrimage by which they hasten to the heavenly kingdom».
84 *Instit. Vol. 1*, II, ix, 365-366, «Christ has not left any part of our salvation incomplete, yet we cannot infer that we are now put in possession of all the blessings purchased by him. Although Christ offers us in the Gospel a present fullness of spiritual blessings, fruition remains in the keeping of hope, until we are divested of corruptible flesh, and transformed into the glory of him who has gone before us».

hopeful faith that the promises are really attributed to them in Christ.[85] In the meantime, God admits believers in a process of regeneration. Calvin held that after their free justification and election, the Holy Spirit regenerates believers, who are adopted children of God, in a gradual process towards holiness. This process of regeneration is analogue to that of creation, for the Holy Spirit "recreates" the lives of the chosen believers so that they become conformed to Christ. According to Calvin, justification—i.e., the free gift of divine filiation—is not the end, but the beginning of Christian life.[86]

The aim of the process of regeneration is real holiness, which is a duty for the believer.[87] Echoing St. Paul, Calvin pointed out that the Holy Spirit progressively makes the believer "a new creature in Christ" and "a holy temple to the Lord" for his glory.[88] In this process, God restores in the elect the spiritual or supernatural gifts[89]—which were withdrawn by Adam's fall— of faith, love of God and to neighbour as well as his election to admit him on the path to holiness.[90] By returning the supernatural

---

85 *Instit. Vol. 1*, II, ix, 366, «Indeed, we have no enjoyment of Christ, unless by embracing him as clothed with his own promises. Hence, it is, that he indeed dwells in our hearts, and yet we are as pilgrims in regard to him, because "we walk by faith, not by sight" (2 Cor. 6:7) (…) in Christ we possess everything pertaining to the perfection of heavenly life, and yet faith is only a vision "of things not seen" (Heb. xi 1)».

86 *Instit. Vol. 2*, III, xi, 37, «Christ is given to us by the kindness of God and is apprehended and possessed by faith, by means of which we obtain in particular a two-fold benefit: first, being reconciled by the righteousness of Christ, God becomes, instead of a judge, an indulgent Father; and secondly, being sanctified by his Spirit, we aspire to integrity and purity of life».

87 *Ibidem*, vi, 3, Calvin considered, «We must be holy, because God is Holy (…). Holiness is our union with God. It is important to realise that we do not come into communion with him by merit of holiness (we ought rather to cleave to him, in order that, pervaded by his holiness, we may follow whither He calls). It greatly concerns his glory not to have any fellowship with wickedness and impurity (…). For what end were we rescued from the iniquity and pollution of the world into which we were plunged, if we allow ourselves, during our whole lives, to wallow in them? (…) The Lord adopts us for his sons on the condition that our life be a representation of Christ, the bond of our adoption».

88 *Instit. Vol. 1*, III, i, 466, «Salvation is perfected in the person of Christ, so, in order to make us partakers of it, he baptises us "with the Holy Spirit and with fire" (Luke iii, 16), enlightening us into the faith of his Gospel, and so regenerating us to be new creatures. Thus cleansed from all pollution, he dedicates us as holy temples to the Lord».

89 Calvin made a neat distinction and separation between these spiritual or supernatural gifts and natural gifts. The latter always remain what they are: corrupted. Cfr. *Instit. Vol. 1*, II, ii, 233.

90 *Ibidem*, «Man, when he withdrew his allegiance to God, was deprived of the spiritual gifts by which he had been raised to the hope of eternal salvation. He is now an exile from the kingdom of God, so that all things which pertain to the blessed life of the soul

gifts, the image of God in his elect is gradually restored.[91] This explains both that there are differences between the elect as to the degree of holiness; some believers have more faith than others, because they have received more light than others,[92] and that believers—while travelling as pilgrims on earth—are always accompanied by their sinful nature (*simul sanctus et peccator*), which serves to keep believers humble and repentant.[93] The continual regeneration takes a lifetime and ends with the believer's death.[94]

2.4.2 Emphasis on the external and visible Church

Calvin endeavoured to give due priority to the Church; the elect form part of a community and their lives of faith, calling and holiness unfold within that community. Calvin tried to bring back order in the Reformed Church and steered a middle course. He striked a balance between, on the one side, the rigid Roman Catholic Church, who claimed exclusive control of grace by their ministerial priesthood and sacraments, and on the other side, anarchical spiritualists like the Anabaptists, who downplayed all exterior forms and relied only on the direct interior efficacy of the Holy Spirit in each believer.[95]

Calvin followed Luther in establishing a neat distinction between a visible and invisible Church, the latter being the "true Church of the elect", which is known to God only. The true Church is small and the godly are few. Only God knows who are mystically united to him and admitted by his secret election into the fellowship of believers. Within this framework, Calvin endeavoured to give an important role to the

---

are extinguished in him until he recovers them by the grace of regeneration. Among these are faith, love to God, charity towards our neighbour, the study of righteousness and holiness».

91 «It pleases God to renew his image in us in degrees, so to some extent there is always a residue of corruption in our flesh, we ought by no means to neglect the remedy», *Instit. Vol. 2*, III, xx, 194.

92 Cfr. *Instit. Vol. 1*, 22.

93 *Instit. Vol. 2*, III, xiv, 80, «Still, however, while we walk in the ways of the Lord, under the guidance of the Holy Spirit, lest we should become unduly elated, and forget ourselves, we have still remains of imperfection which serves to keep us humble: "There is no man that sinneth not," said Scripture (1 Kings viii. 46)».

94 *Instit. Vol. 1*, III, iii, 516, «This regeneration or renewal is not accomplished in a moment, a day, or a year, but uninterrupted, sometimes even by slow, progress God abolishes the remains of carnal corruption in his elect, cleanses them from pollution, and consecrates them as his temples, restoring all their inclinations to real purity, so that during their whole lives they may practise repentance, and know that death is the only termination to this warfare».

95 Cfr. B.C. MILNER, *Calvin's doctrine of the Church*, Brill, Leiden 1970, 190-191.

visible Church on earth, warning that outside the Church there is little hope of salvation so that «it is always disastrous to leave the Church».[96] God has instituted the visible Church in time and space as a necessary instrument for salvation and Calvin emphasised the unity of the Church as "Catholic" and "universal". With these adjectives, he meant that the true Church consists of all the believers who have "Christ as head", who cannot be divided.[97] Since there is only one Christ, there is also only one Church. However, since Calvin moved within Luther's framework of the neat division between the invisible and visible Church, this statement regards only the true invisible Church. It follows that the visible Church cannot have any other head than Christ. For this reason, Christ cannot be represented in the visible Church by humans on earth in his capacity as head. The only and ultimate authority and power rest with Christ, whose authority should be exercised by his Word alone.[98] This implies that for Calvin, there is no external magisterium exercised by humans.

Secondly, Calvin established an absolute correlation of the Spirit and the Word but articulated the sovereign freedom of the Holy Spirit over the external means.[99] Though he spoke of the inward working of the Holy Spirit in the elect, who ordinarily uses ordinary external means, like Scripture, ministry, sacraments and worship of the Church, Calvin held, at the same time, that the Holy Spirit is not bound by these means; he can also work directly in the elect without any external mediation.[100] Yet Calvin duly recognised that the Church is the depository of God's Word,[101] but without acknowledging an external magisterium. Furthermore, Calvin taught that the inward operation of the Holy Spirit concerning the external means is twofold; he discloses the Word in the Scripture (or by other means) and simultaneously he opens believers up to the Word.[102]

Thirdly, apart from stressing the unity of the Church under Christ and the working of the Spirit, Calvin emphasised the ethical role of the Church in the sanctification of the believers. The Church is a mother who guides, nurses and educates her children gradually to a life of perfection in Christ. Therefore, God appoints ministers—pastors and teachers—who should be held in the highest regard, for they—though they do not represent Christ as head—are «invested with divine authority to proclaim the Word

---

96 *Instit. Vol 2*, IV, i, section 4.
97 Cfr. *Ibidem*.
98 *Ibidem*, iii, section 1.
99 MILNER, *Calvin's doctrine of the Church*, 190-191.
100 Cfr. *Ibidem*, 190.
101 Cfr. *Instit. Vol 2*, IV, i, 280-281.
102 MILNER, *Calvin's doctrine of the Church*, 190.

of God».[103] To establish firmly their authority, Calvin deemed it useful for didactical purposes to make the distinction between clergy and laypeople, for he considered: «now discipline depends in a very great measure on the power of the keys and on spiritual jurisdiction. That this may be more easily understood, let us divide the Church into two principal classes –viz. clergy and people. The term clergy I use in the common acceptation for those who perform a public ministry in the Church».[104] This statement seems to be a revision of Luther's position, who had done all he could to abolish the different classes within Christendom. Calvin exalted the ministry, but at the same time, inspired by the state of the primitive Church as described in Scripture, masterfully divided the ministry in his community into four functions—(re)introducing a shared form of authority and leadership: i) pastors to preach and administer the sacraments (Baptism and Supper), ii) doctors to instruct believers in the faith, iii) elders in charge of discipline and iv) deacons to care for the poor.

Finally, Calvin—apart from preaching the Word by the ministers—recognised Baptism and the Supper as sacraments. These sacraments are non-exclusive signs of the power of Christ by which the Holy Spirit strengthens the faith of the believers in the promise. God operates *through* these sacraments but is not present *in* them.

2.4.3 The believers' election and vocation in the world
The concepts of election and vocation in Calvin are closely related and play a central role in Calvin's theology. The believer is chosen from eternity *for* something and *in* something. Calvin's dominating thought is that life is regulated by the calling of God and that all things ultimately must be brought into line with one's calling, with the divine choice.[105] Callings are the distinct modes of life by which God orders society.[106] Living according to your own calling and complying with its proper duties, assures that believers keep the right path and that there is harmony

---

103 Cfr. *Instit. Vol 2*, IV, i, 280-281.
104 *Ibidem*, xii, 453.
105 Cfr. EASTWOOD, *An Examination of Doctrine till Present Day*, 72-73. Eastwood quotes Barkley, who stated: «All men are priests in their daily vocation. All are priests though their duties vary according to their calling. The only real farmer is a Christian farmer, the only real doctor is a Christian doctor, the only real mother is a Christian mother, the only real man is a Christian man, the only real woman is a Christian woman; and so on, covering every detail and aspect and station of life. Apart from Christ, we are not what we ought to be».
106 Cfr. *Instit. Vol. 2*, III, x, 34-35.

in the different parts of life.[107] Even politics Calvin described as a sacred calling.[108] According to Calvin, «(…) in everything the call of the Lord is the foundation and beginning of right action» and «(…) all our actions are estimated in his sight, (…)».[109] Although the calling implies a burden to carry, Calvin pointed out that «it will afford admirable consolation, that in following your proper calling, no work, will be so mean and sordid as not to have a splendour and value in the eyes of God».[110]

Calvin stressed the importance of solidarity between believers. He urged a heartfelt and experiential life of piety, Church discipline and obedience to the law to give glory to God in the world in all activities. Each believer occupies his own place and receives his own gifts to build up the body of Christ.

2.4.4 Without human cooperation
The whole process of sanctification should be fully ascribed to God alone,[111] as can be seen in the following three of Calvin's teachings. Firstly, once the believer is given to understand that he is a child of God, he necessarily finds himself involved in a process of regeneration. According to Calvin, «Faith cannot be apprehended without at the same time apprehending sanctification (…). Christ justifies no man without also sanctifying him. These blessings are conjoined by a perpetual and inseparable tie. Those whom he enlightens by his wisdom he redeems; whom he redeems he justifies; whom he justifies he sanctifies. Though we distinguish between them, they are both inseparably apprehended in Christ».[112]

Secondly, as we have seen, good works in the temporal-empirical sphere are a consequence of the believers' communion with Christ. In fact, God completely "takes over" believers, so that the latter do not act by themselves anymore, for the Holy Spirit is as «the *Hand* by which God exerts his power, because by his divine inspiration he so breathes divine life into us, that we are no longer acted upon by ourselves, but ruled *by his motion and agency*, so that everything good in us is the fruit of his grace,

---

107 Cfr. *Ibidem.*
108 *Ibidem*, IV, xx, section 4.
109 *Ibidem.*
110 *Ibidem*, III, x, 35.
111 *Ibidem*, xv, 96-97, «Regeneration is without exception wholly of God, who made new creatures so that that they pass from the kingdom of sin to the kingdom of righteousness». And, *Instit. Vol. 1*, II, v, 287-288, «(…) the grace of God (regeneration) is the rule of the Spirit, in directing and governing the human will. (…) All the actions which are afterwards done are truly said to be wholly his».
112 *Instit. Vol. 2*, III, xvi, 99.

while our own endowments without him are mere darkness of mind and perverseness of heart».[113]

Thirdly, even their "perseverance" to the end is completely taken out of their hands.[114] The process of regeneration has, therefore, a sure outcome, since God cannot fail.[115] The elect are admitted in this process towards holiness, but Calvin insisted also here on the fact that God realises everything in them; believers "by themselves" are and remain corrupt in all their faculties. Therefore, towards God humans are passive, and they have no influence whatsoever on their justification, election, faith or sanctification. Thus, although the process of sanctification in Calvin is a gradual one, this does not imply that believers in any way take part in their increase of holiness. Since Calvin categorically ruled out all human merit, it is always God who gives believers more faith, more light, more repentance, more good works and perseverance till the end,[116] always without any cooperation on their part, let alone the believers' consent.[117]

2.4.5 Human freedom and obedience

Calvin strongly stressed the ethical aspect of Christian life; it is important that Christian ethical doctrine is put into practice so that it may bear fruit.[118] Calvin is well aware that the law should be respected and kept in

---

113 *Instit. Vol. 1*, III, i, 465.
114 Cfr. *Instit. Vol. 2*, III, xxiv, 246, Christ assured the perseverance of all his elect by his prayer. «It cannot be doubted, that since Christ prays for all the elect, He asks the same thing for them as for Peter –viz. that their faith fail not (Luke xxii. 32). Hence, we infer, that there is no danger of their falling away, since the Son of God, who asks that their piety may prove constant, never meets with a refusal. What then did our Saviour intend to teach us by this prayer, but just to confide, that whenever we are his, our eternal salvation is secure?».
115 Calvin explained, «the moment they [believers] are admitted to fellowship with Christ, by the knowledge of the gospel, and the illumination of the Holy Spirit, their eternal life is begun, and then He which hath begun a good work in them "will perform it until the day of Jesus Christ" (Phil. i. 6)». *Instit. Vol. 2*, III, xviii, 120.
116 «In the elect alone, he implants the living root of faith, so that they persevere even to the end. In the reprobates it is something similar to faith, which God takes away—it vanishes in those who are temporarily impressed», *Instit. Vol. 1*, III, ii 478-479.
117 *Instit. Vol. 1*, II, iii, 260, «We must, therefore, repudiate the oft-repeated sentiment of Chrysostom, "Whom He draws, He draws willingly;" insinuating that the Lord only stretches out his hand, and waits to see whether we will be pleased to take his aid. We grant that, as man was originally constituted, he could incline to either side, but since he has taught by his example how miserable a thing free will is if God works not in us to will and to do, of what use were grace imparted in such a scanty measure?».
118 *Instit. Vol. 2*, III, vi, 4, «The doctrine in which our religion is contained we have given the first place, since by it our salvation commences; but it must be transfused into the breast, and pass into conduct, and transform us into itself, as not to prove unfruitful».

place. Even more, although nobody can, the law should be obeyed by all, for «true worship consists in obedience alone».[119] This statement reveals a dialectical opposition between human works—always the fruit of the believer's own corrupted will—and God's will.[120] Therefore, he considered that «the only legitimate service to God is obedience to his law and the practice of justice, purity and holiness»[121] and «everything requisite for the ordering of a pious and holy life is comprehended in the law. The Lord, the better to dissuade us from devising new works, included the whole of righteousness in simple obedience to his will».[122]

This "simple" obedience to God's will is not so simple in reality, for Calvin duly recognised that the believer—who per definition cannot comply with God's law by himself—«stands greatly in need both of help and incentives».[123] For Calvin, this great help and incentive to comply with the law lies, above all, in the freedom *from* the law and the assurance that the elect are nevertheless agreeable to God. The true gospel of Christ has given believers the freedom from being bound by God's law; «the liberty from terror, consciences being freed from the yoke of the law».[124] Although the law is still in vigour, God will not apply it strictly to his elect, since God the Father knows that they are naturally incapable of fulfilling it and he is pleased by the fact that they acknowledge this explicitly and try to comply with the law anyway.[125] For, according to Calvin, the consciousness that God is propitious to them gives the Christian the freedom and the power[126] to «voluntary obey the law», for now, «they hear themselves invited by God with paternal lenity, they will cheerfully and alertly obey the call and follow his guidance».[127]

It is not surprising that Calvin, apart from "voluntary" obeying the law, also deemed it necessary to argue that it is God who replaces the

---

119 *Instit. Vol. 1*, II, viii, 320.
120 Thus, it becomes clear why Calvin qualified a vote of celibacy as "arrogant"; these men and women promise something which they cannot keep. Cfr. *Instit. Vol. 2,* IV, xiii, 475.
121 Cfr. *Instit. Vol. 1*, II, viii, 318.
122 *Instit. Vol. 2,* IV, xiii, 473.
123 Cfr. *Ibidem,* III, vi, 2.
124 *Ibidem*, xix, 134, «No man will ever willingly set himself to observe the Law who is not persuaded that his services are pleasing to God. The indulgence of God in tolerating and pardoning our iniquities is a sign of paternal favour».
125 Cfr. *Instit. Vol. 1*, III, iii, 510-511.
126 *Instit. Vol. 2*, III, xix, 135, «Christian liberty is in all its parts a spiritual matter, the whole force of which consists in giving peace to trembling consciences, whether they are anxious and disquieted as to the forgiveness of sins, or as to whether their imperfect works, polluted by the infirmities of the flesh, are pleasing to God (…)».
127 *Ibidem*, 134.

believers' will with his own. For not only faith is produced in the believers, but also their will is completely replaced. Calvin held «that the Lord both corrects, *or rather destroys*, our depraved will, and also *substitutes a good will from himself*».[128] His grace produces the will itself.[129] According to Calvin, «God could not more clearly claim to himself, and to deny us, everything good and right in our will, than by declaring, that in our conversion there is the creation of a new spirit and of a new heart. It always follows, both that nothing good can proceed from our will until it be formed again, and that after that it is formed again, in so far as it is good, it is of God, and not of us».[130]

2.4.6 The believers' identification with Christ by external cross-bearing

The life of the believers must be brought «into concord and harmony with the righteousness of God, and so confirm the adoption by which they have been received as sons».[131] Jesus is the example set before the believer to imitate so that his life becomes our life.[132] Garcia signalled the relation in Calvin between the mystical union and the so-called "replication principle" based on his exegesis of Rom. 8:28-30; the Spirit of union replicates in the experience of the faithful what is true of Christ in his own earthly experience, which consists primarily of a transition from humiliation to exaltation, suffering to glory, or obedience and good works to eternal life.[133]

From the perspective of believers, this replication is done by participation in Christ's death on the cross by self-denial and cross-bearing. Although all human works, even by the saints, are—in themselves—always sinful and liable to condemnation,[134] believers are submitted to a constant "purification of self-love", consisting in a continual struggle

---

128 *Instit. Vol. 1*, II, iii, 256, Italics added.
129 Cfr. *Ibidem*, 257.
130 *Ibidem*, 258.
131 *Instit. Vol. 2*, III, vi, 2.
132 A Christian life is a life of holiness and identification with Christ. «A Christian life consists of two parts: i) the love of righteousness; that we may be holy, because God is holy, and because we are united to him, and are reckoned among his people; ii) (…), and that we may be conformed to Christ. A model of this is laid down to us, which we ought to copy in our whole life», *Instit. Vol. 2*, Aphorism 49, 683.
133 Cfr. GARCIA, *Life in Christ*, 255.
134 *Instit. Vol. 2*, III, xiv, 80-81, «What righteousness then can men obtain by their works? The best thing which can be produced by them is always tainted and corrupted by the impurity of the flesh, and has, as it were some mixture of dross in it. (…) Even saints cannot perform one work which, if judged on its own merits, is not deserving of condemnation. If we are estimated by our own worthiness, in everything that we think or devise, with all our studies and endeavours we deserve death and destruction».

against their own natural inclinations by means of mortification of the flesh,[135] self-denial and the exercise of the will to joyfully obey the law of God and thus glorifying him.[136]

The elect have to bear their cross—the outward aspect of the imitation of Christ—[137] and to «humbly embrace it».[138] This is necessary for their salvation and the way to «return to God our Maker, from whom we are estranged, that he may become again our Father».[139] It is God himself, who inflicts his elect with the cross to save them.[140] In this way, the arrogance of believers is repressed, because in the experience of the cross it becomes clear how great their weakness and fragility are.[141] The cross is a mark of discipleship and membership of God's family. Christ gave us an example to follow and Christians must be prepared for difficulties and suffering.

> «(…) Christ calls his disciples when he says, that every one of them must "take up the cross" (Matt. xvi, 24). Those whom the Lord has chosen and honoured with his intercourse must prepare for a hard, laborious, troubled life (…): it being the will of our heavenly Father to exercise his people in this way while putting them to the proof. Having begun this course with Christ the first-born, he continues it towards all his children. (…) Why then should we exempt ourselves from that condition to which Christ our Head behoved to submit; especially since he submitted on our account, that he might in his own person exhibit a model of patience? Wherefore, the Apostle declares, that all the children of God are destined to be conformed to him».[142]

Calvin stressed the importance of patience, consolation, spiritual joy in the carrying of the cross.[143] By Christ's death, the elect obtain several

---

135 *Instit. Vol. 1*, III, iii, 526, «As long as we dwell in the prison of the body, we must constantly struggle with the vices of our corrupt nature, and so with our natural dispositions».
136 *Instit. Vol. 2*, III, xiv, 80, «In the regenerated Christ dwells by means of the Holy Spirit, by whose agency the lusts of our flesh are every day more and more mortified, while that we ourselves are sanctified; that is consecrated to the Lord for true purity of life, our hearts being trained to the obedience of the law. It thus becomes our leading desire to obey his will, and in all things advance his glory only».
137 Cfr. HAAS, *Calvin's ethics*, 95.
138 *Instit. Vol. 1*, II, vi, 293.
139 *Ibidem*.
140 Cfr. *Instit. Vol. 2*, III, viii, 23.
141 Cfr. *Ibidem*, 17.
142 *Ibidem*, 16-17.
143 Cfr. *Ibidem*, 23.

fruits, amongst which «that by fellowship with him he mortifies our earthly members, (…) and kills the old man (…) and bring forth fruit, and that we are buried to sin».[144] It follows that by Christ's death and burial, believers receive the blessings to be delivered from death and the mortification of the flesh.[145]

Furthermore, the elect participate also in Christ's Resurrection in the hope of the benefit of a future life with him, which somehow is already present now. According to Calvin, believers may enjoy earthly blessings, as long as it is used with moderation and a pure conscience.[146]

2.4.7 The value of human works and service to God

Human works do not have any intrinsic, supernatural value, but their whole value in the eyes of God is derived from the obedience which believers show by complying with God's law. For this reason only, God approves of them.[147] Calvin regarded it a gross abuse if the believer does not dedicate the free supernatural gifts to the Giver[148] and to put them at God's service.[149] This dedication to God is done by a pure intention of mind so that all the internal affections of believers are sincerely devoted to God.[150] However, at the same time, Calvin affirmed that also the reprobates—who are withheld the effectual agency of his Spirit—[151] work in the "service of God". The reprobates are not excusable, because they know the content of the law and they enjoy breaching it and, therefore, act selfishly.[152] Nonetheless, although violating the law, Calvin maintained that also the reprobates do "service to God".[153] The same holds true for the

---

144 *Instit. Vol. 1*, II, xvi, 441.
145 Cfr. *Ibidem*.
146 Cfr. *Instit. Vol 2*, III, x, 31.
147 *Ibidem*, xi, 56, «However highly works may be estimated, they have their whole value more from the approbation of God than from their own dignity. (…) It is owing entirely to the goodness of God that works are deemed worthy of the honour and reward of righteousness; and therefore, their whole value consists in this, that by means of them we endeavour to manifest obedience to God».
148 Cfr. *Ibidem*, vii, 8.
149 Cfr. *Ibidem*, 7, «(…) it is the duty of the believers to present their "bodies a living sacrifice, holy and acceptable unto God, which is their reasonable service" (Rom. xii. 1)».
150 Cfr. *Ibidem*, «The great point, then, is, that we are consecrated and dedicated to God, and therefore should not henceforth think, speak, design, or act, without a view to his glory».
151 *Instit. Vol. 2*, III, xxiv, 242, «God also, to display his own glory, withholds from them [the reprobates] the effectual agency of his Spirit».
152 Cfr. *Instit. Vol. 1*, I, xviii, 204.
153 *Ibidem*, 202, «The sum of the whole is this, since the will of God is said to be the cause of all things, all the counsels and actions of men must be governed by his providence;

civil government, which is also an instrument of God. Calvin regarded Church and State as separate entities, each with its own functions, but both in the service of God.[154]

2.4.8 Double predestination

Calvin's effort to exclude systematically any role for humans towards God led to the logical consequence of accepting the doctrine of double predestination. God by his secret counsel chooses whom he wills and rejects others.[155] It is only logical that there can be no election (freely, gratuitously) without its opposite reprobation.[156] Although all people are liable to guilt, «God, as Supreme Judge, acquits freely those who He wants to acquit. The lost are justified before God by the burial of their sins; for (as He hates sin) He can only love those whom He justifies».[157] To these justified, God gives mercy (a contrite heart) whereas in other humans (the reprobates) He hardens their hearts.[158] Only the elect[159] are saved and admitted to the heavenly Kingdom, for they are aware that they have a propitious and merciful Father, who does not strictly apply the law to them.[160]

2.4.9 Secularisation

Calvin's framework reveals a secularised form of theology. Christ remains in heaven and does not come down to earth bodily, but merely spiritually; Christ does really enter in the believers' heart by the power of the Holy Spirit. This power operates parallel in the elect, i.e., without them, who

---

so that he not only exerts his power in the elect, who are guided by the Holy Spirit, but also forces the reprobates to do him service».

154 Cfr. HESSELINK, *Calvin's theology*, 88.
155 Cfr. *Instit. Vol. 2*, III, xxi, 209.
156 Cfr. *Ibidem*, xxiii, 226.
157 *Ibidem*, xi, 49.
158 Cfr. *Ibidem*, xxiv, 240.
159 «As the image of God constitutes the entire excellence of human nature, as it is shown in Adam before his fall, but was afterwards vitiated and almost destroyed, nothing remaining but a ruin, confused, mutilated, and tainted with impurity, so it is now partly seen in the elect, in so far as they are regenerated by the Spirit. Its full lustre, will be displayed in heaven», *Instit. Vol. 1*, I, xv, 165.
160 *Instit. Vol. 2*, III, xi, 47-48, «But as it is too well known from experience, that the remains of sin always exist in the righteous, it is necessary that justification should be something very different from reformation to newness of life. This latter God begins in his elect and carries on during the whole course of life, gradually and sometimes slowly, so that if placed at his judgement-seat they would always deserve sentence of death. He justifies not partially, but freely, so that they can appear in the heavens as if clothed with the purity of Christ. No portion of righteousness could pacify the conscience. It must be decided that we are pleasing to God, as being without exception righteous in his sight».

remain corrupt in all their natural capacities, but are restraint in their sinful actions. Humans by themselves are not capable of doing anything good, and in this frame, they are always acting on their own in the temporal-empirical sphere. Therefore, Calvin made a neat distinction between two kinds of intelligence: knowledge of earthly things and heavenly things. On the one hand, all humans dispose of the natural light of reason, which serves to order the world matters of policy and economy, all mechanical arts and liberal studies. On the other hand, the heavenly things, like the pure knowledge of God, the method of true righteousness, and the mysteries of the heavenly kingdom, are reserved for the elect, who can never make them their own. «The kingdom of God is not earthly and carnal, and so subject to corruption, but spiritual, it raises us even to eternal life (…)».[161]

2.5 Preliminary conclusion

The dialectical and exclusive opposition between God and humans finds its expression in the fact that Calvin situated original sin and corruption at the heart of human nature, attributing guilt to humans in all their actions, which stands in sharp contrast to God's glory and majesty. Although Calvin spoke of a mystical union between Christ and believers in order to bridge the gap between God and humans, but at the same time, he endeavoured to reduce the human role in the relationship with God and to keep Christ and believers in the temporal-empirical sphere separated from each other.

Calvin accepted Luther's principle that believers are saved by faith only, but he is also concerned with the follow-up question of what humans are going to do once they know that they are justified and elected. His answer—which is more than a suggestion—is: to glorify God; everything the elect do should be done for the glory of God and only for the glory of God (*Sola Dei Gloria*). The elect are called to dedicate themselves totally to God by a pure intention of mind. Their calling implies an obligation to respond positively and Calvin frequently emphasised the demanding requirements of this divine election. His religious views are characterised by great seriousness and responsibility for purity and growth of the Kingdom on earth, a sober liturgy and intense religious life, stressing that the world is the work field of a Christian.

The elect are admitted to an ongoing process of regeneration towards holiness. Due to his vision that human beings are totally corrupted, while at the same time called to dedicate themselves totally to God, the focus shifts to external discipline and control. Believers—although unable on

---

161 *Instit. Vol. 1*, II, xii, 429

their own—have the duty to comply with God's law. Since they know that God will always forgive them their imperfections, the elect are free from the terror of the law and its joke. This freedom enables them to obey voluntarily and joyfully God's law now that they know that God is pleased with them. Human works as such have no intrinsic value but are esteemed by God solely if they are done out of obedience. Although Calvin deemed the freedom from the law as a great incentive to comply with the law, he however, also held that God must replace the human will by his own.

In Calvin's mystical union or virtual communion between Christ and the elect in the temporal-empirical sphere, the power of God operates in them, but without their participation. This becomes manifest in the fact that God and human actions seem to run completely parallel. The central notion to describe this virtual communion between Christ and the elect and the communication of the benefit thereof, is the concept of imputation. This works as follows. Calvin, firstly, established a strict liability; all people are liable to guilt, which is naturally imputed to them. The obstacle of their sinfulness seems to prevent humans from entering into communion with God in the temporal-empirical sphere, for God hates sin. Secondly, to let God act and be effective in the temporal-empirical sphere, Calvin used a triple imputation: not only guilt is attributed, but also Christ's righteousness; the quality of Christ's righteousness is ascribed to the elect, who in the temporal-empirical sphere are not righteous, but sinful. To this, he added a third imputation, that of holiness; the glory which Christ gives to his Father is attributed to the elect for Christ's sake. It seems, however, that the gap between God and the elect cannot be really bridged in the temporal-empirical sphere, but only virtually and by imputation.

In the following section, the question will be addressed how the common priesthood fits within this framework.

3. The common priesthood in Jean Calvin

As we will see in this section,¹ Calvin speaks on several occasions and in different wordings, both in his *Institutes* and commentaries, on Christ's priesthood relating it to all believers.² Although Calvin follows the same line of reasoning as Luther, he nonetheless did not articulate this doctrine as Luther did.³ Pont remarks that Calvin did not deal with the common priesthood as a separate doctrine and that it is striking that Calvin discussed the universal priesthood only after having discussed extensively his doctrine on ministry.⁴

In Calvin, the doctrine is much more balanced, firstly, because in his theology he related it explicitly to the threefold office of Christ as Prophet, King and Priest.⁵ Christ performed these three offices for us in a unique way, and believers share somehow in these offices as well. Calvin ranked the office of teaching and preaching, which Luther regarded to be a priestly function, under Christ's prophetical office.⁶ Concerning Christ's royal office, Calvin considered that the eternal sovereignty of the King of Kings (Dan. 2:37) will be shared by those who submit to his rule.⁷ Secondly, Calvin entrenched the doctrine of the priesthood of all believers firmly in his doctrine of election and vocation. Thirdly, as we will see in section 3.5, Calvin was able, in the practical application of the doctrine,

---

1 Bibliography on Calvin's priesthood of all believers: J.R. CRAWFORD, *Calvin and the priesthood of all believers*, «SJT» 21 (1968), 145-157, EASTWOOD, *An Examination of Doctrine till Present Day*, 66-90, A.J. PONT, *Die priesterskap van die gelowiges soos Calvyn dit gesien het*, «Hervormde Teologiese studies» 45 (1989) 451-460.
2 According to Crawford, Calvin accepted without qualification the priesthood of all true believers, CRAWFORD, *Calvin and the priesthood of all believers*, 145.
3 Cfr. EASTWOOD, *An Examination of Doctrine till Present Day*, 66.
4 Cfr. PONT, *Die priesterskap van die gelowiges soos Calvyn dit gesien het*, 451 and 457.
5 Calvin discusses the priesthood of Christ together with the other two offices of Prophet and King in Chapter XV of Book II of the Institutes. Calvin did not invent the theology of the *triplex munus*, for St. Thomas Aquinas already discussed it: *Suma Teologicae*, III pars, q.7, a 8 (Christ Prophet); In Hbr, 3, 1, n.244 (Christ Priest); III pars, q. 57, a. 1 and 6 (Christ King). However, it can be said that Calvin revived it and related it explicitly to the Church. Cfr. EASTWOOD, *An Examination of Doctrine till Present Day*, 66 and F. RODRIGUEZ GARRAPUCHO, *Il sacerdozio comune dei fedeli e la missione della Chiesa: nel Vaticano II e nei dialoghi ecumenici postconciliari.*, in R. GIRALDO, P. SGROI, T. VETRALI (eds.), *Ecumenismo come conversione*, Istituto di studi ecumenici San Bernardino, Venezia 2007, 195-196
6 Cfr. *Instit. Vol. 1*, II, xv, 427.
7 Cfr. EASTWOOD, *An Examination of Doctrine till Present Day*, 67.

to strike a balance between the role of the ministers and that of the laity in the community.

This section follows the same structure as the paragraph on the common priesthood in Luther in Chapter I. First, the fundament of the priesthood will be discussed, followed by the believers' participation in it, then we will deal with its finality, exercise and function, its relationship with the ministries, mediation and, finally, the conclusion.

3.1 Fundament of the priesthood

Like Luther, Calvin referred to Psalm 110, verse 4 ('Thou are priest forever, after the order of Melchisedek") to indicate that Christs' priesthood is perpetual and unique.[8] The core of Christ's priesthood is his priestly sacrifice on the cross, where his blood was shed, being the symbol of expiation.[9] Only by that sacrifice we were saved from sin, and opposing Christ's sacrifice to that of humans, Calvin stated: «For being reconciled to God through the *one only true* sacrifice of Christ, (…). No sacrifice of expiation is wanted; and no one can be set up, without casting a manifest reproach on the cross of Christ».[10]

Since there is only *one* true sacrifice, there is also only *one* High Priest. Calvin emphasised strongly that Jesus Christ is the *only* Mediator capable, because he was free of sin, to redeem humans through a priestly sacrifice. In Calvin's words:

> Christ, «who, free from all taint, by his own holiness, procured the favour of God for us. (…) But because a deserved curse obstructs the entrance, and God in his character of Judge is hostile to us, expiation must necessarily intervene, that as a priest employed to appease the wrath of God, he may reinstate us in his favour. Wherefore, in order that Christ might fulfil this office, it behoved him to appear with a sacrifice».[11]

The person of the priest and his sacrifice have unique features. Calvin stated:

> «But since God under the Law ordered sacrifices of beasts to be offered to him, there was a different and new arrangement in regard to Christ—viz.

---

8 Cfr. *Instit. Vol. 1*, II, xv, 431.
9 Cfr. EASTWOOD, *An Examination of Doctrine till Present Day*, 70.
10 J. CALVIN, *Commentaries on the Epistle of St. Paul to the Romans* (tr. & ed. J. Owen), Calvin Translation Society, Edenborough 1844, 452, Quoted by CRAWFORD, *Calvin and the priesthood of all believers*, 146, Italics added.
11 *Instit. Vol. 1*, II, xv, 431.

that he should be *at once victim and priest*, because no other fit sacrifice for sin could be found, *nor was any other worthy of the honour* of offering an only-begotten son to God».[12]

Calvin wanted to make sure that all rights and honour regarding the priesthood and the priestly sacrifice, belong exclusively to Christ. «There being a change of the priesthood, there must of necessity be a change of law. All the sacerdotal functions were transferred to Christ, and in him fulfilled and ended (Heb. vii. 12). To him alone, therefore, *all the rights and honours of the priesthood have been transferred*».[13] This not only holds true for the Levitical priesthood, but also for the so-called "popish priests", for Calvin continued, «If they [the popish priests] are so fond then of hunting out allegories, let them set Christ before them *as the only priest*, and place full and universal jurisdiction on his tribunal: this we will readily admit».[14] On two other occasions in the Institutes Calvin declared: «the honour of the priesthood was competent to none but Christ, because, by the sacrifice of his death, he wiped away our guilt, and made satisfaction for sin»[15] and «the right and honour of the priesthood has ceased among mortal men, because Christ, who is immortal, is the *one perpetual priest*».[16]

As we have seen with Luther, also for Calvin, Christ continues his redemptive work by interceding for humans to the Father not to pay attention to our sins and wretchedness, for:

« (...) the Lord, by his ascension to heaven, has opened up the access into the heavenly kingdom, (...) Faith perceives that his seat beside the Father is of great advantage to us. Having entered into the temple not made by hands, *he constantly appears as our advocate and intercessor* in the presence of the Father; directs attention to his own righteousness, so as to turn it away from our sins; so reconciles him to us, as by *his intercession* to pave for us the way of access to his throne, presenting it to miserable sinners, to whom it would otherwise be an object of dread, as replete with grace and mercy».[17]

---

12 *Ibidem*, 432, Italics added.
13 *Ibidem*, III, iv, 537-538.
14 *Ibidem*, Italics added.
15 *Ibidem*, II, xv, 431.
16 *Instit. Vol. 2*, IV, xviii, 608, Italics added.
17 *Instit. Vol. 1*, II, xvi, 450, Italics added, Cfr. *Instit. Vol. 2*, III, xx, 166.

And referring to St. John (1 John 2, 1), Calvin remarked that Christ is «*a perpetual advocate, who always, by his intercession*, reinstates us in his Father's favour—a perpetual propitiation by which sins are expiated».[18]

To sum up, Christ is our High Priest, who has redeemed humans with his only priestly sacrifice, by shedding his blood on the cross. His priesthood is perpetual and unique. Since Christ is our only mediator all rights and honour with regard to the priesthood and the priestly sacrifice, belong exclusively to him. Christ continues his redemptive work by interceding for humans to the Father, because he is our perpetual advocate.

3.2 Participation in Christ's priesthood

Although Christ is the true and only priest, who has performed the one-and-only, true sacrifice and continues to intercede for us, Calvin affirmed several times and in different wordings that believers, i.e., the elect, do share in Christ's priesthood as well.

> «For being reconciled to God through the *one only true* sacrifice of Christ, *we are all through His grace made priests*, (…) ».[19]

The priesthood is closely linked with holiness, which is realised if humans are in Christ, for only then we are without sin and able to please the Lord. At the same time, Calvin seemed to show some reservations when recognising that believers—even in Christ—are really holy as can be seen in the following text:

> «Christ now bears the office of priest, not only that by the eternal law of reconciliation he may render the Father favourable and propitious to us, *but also admit us into this most honourable allegiance. For we, though in ourselves polluted, in him being priests* (Rev. i. 6), (…). To this effect are the words of Christ, "For their sakes I sanctify myself" (John, xvii, 19); for being clothed with his holiness, inasmuch as he has devoted us to the Father with himself (otherwise we were an abomination before him), we please him *as if we were* pure and clean, nay, even sacred».[20]

The New Testament also testifies that Christians are priests and kings, with the corresponding honour of these offices. Calvin linked the words of Moses to those of S. Peter when he said:

---

18 *Ibidem*, III, iv, 557, Italics added.
19 J. CALVIN, *Commentaries on the Epistle of St. Paul to the Romans* (tr. & ed. J. Owen), Calvin Translation Society, Edenborough 1844, 452, Quoted by CRAWFORD, *Calvin and the priesthood of all believers*, 146, Italics added.
20 *Instit. Vol. 1*, II, xv, 432, Italics added.

> «Peter elegantly transposes the words of Moses [Exod. xix. 6], teaching that the fullness of grace, of which the Jews had a foretaste under the Law, is exhibited in Christ, "Ye are a chosen generation, a royal priesthood" (1 Pet. ii. 9). The transposition of the words intimates that *those to whom Christ has appeared in the Gospel*, have obtained more than their fathers, inasmuch as *they are all endued with priestly and royal honour, and can, therefore, trusting to their Mediator, appear with boldness in the presence of God*».[21]

And referring to the Book of Revelation, Calvin stated: « (…); he it is, I say, who "hath made us kings and priests unto God and his Father" (Rev. i. 6) ».[22]

Besides holiness, Calvin also linked the idea of the common priesthood to the feature of having "direct and immediate access". In his commentary on the Letter to the Hebrews, he stated:

> «He [the author of the Letter] says, first, that *we have boldness to enter into the holiest* … (a privilege not given to Israel). But now, the case is very different, for not only symbolically, but *in reality an entrance into heaven is made open to us* through the favour of Christ, for *he has made us a royal priesthood*».[23]

The benefits of Christ—including the priestly privilege—are made available to us by the hidden operation of the Spirit.[24] To communicate the blessings which the Father has bestowed upon Christ to us—not for private use, but to enrich the poor and needy—he must become ours and dwell in us.[25] Firstly, Christ becomes ours through faith,[26] but Calvin drew attention to the fact that «all do not indiscriminately embrace the offer of Christ which is made by the Gospel (…)».[27] He proposed «to inquire the secret efficacy of the Spirit, to which it is owing that we enjoy Christ and all his blessings»[28]. According to Calvin, «the Holy Spirit is the

---

21 *Ibidem*, xii, 301, Italics added.
22 *Instit. Vol. 2*, IV, xviii, 618-619.
23 J. CALVIN, *Commentaries on the Epistle of Paul the Apostle to the Hebrews* (tr. & ed. J. Owen), Calvin Translation Society, Edenbourough 1853, 234, Quoted by CRAWFORD, *Calvin and the priesthood of all believers*, 147, Italics added.
24 Cfr. *Instit. Vol. 1*, III, i, 462.
25 Cfr. *Ibidem*, 463.
26 «Faith is the hand of the soul, which receives, through the same efficacy of the Holy Spirit, Christ offered to us in the Gospel». Aphorism 44, in: *Instit. Vol. 2*, 682.
27 *Instit. Vol. 1*, III, i, 463.
28 *Ibidem*.

bond by which Christ effectively binds us to himself».²⁹ «Salvation is perfected in the person of Christ, so, in order to make us partakers of it, he baptises us "with the Holy Spirit and with fire" (Luke iii. 16), enlightening us into the faith of his Gospel, and so *regenerating us to be new creatures*, Thus cleansed from all pollution, he dedicates us as holy temples to the Lord».³⁰

These benefits of the Holy Spirit also include sanctity and divine filiation. «The Holy Spirit is the Spirit of Sanctification and the seed and root of heavenly life in us»³¹ and «is called by the Scripture "the Spirit of adoption" because he is witness to us of the free favour with which God the Father embraced us in his well-beloved and only-begotten Son, so as to become our Father, and *give us boldness of access* to him; nay, he dictates the very words, so that we can boldly cry, "Abba, Father."».³²

To sum up, the elect share in Christ's priesthood. Christ has made them through his grace priests with him because he has sanctified them by his priestly offer; the elect, as far as they are *in Christ*, are, therefore, without sin and can appear directly before the Lord to please him. The elect are united to Christ through the Holy Spirit. Finally, the nature of this mystical union and participation in Christ' righteousness, holiness and priesthood is by a threefold imputation.

3.3 Finality of priesthood

For Calvin, the end of human existence is the glory of God.³³ Also the believers' priesthood serves that end. Calvin considered: «(…), we are all through his grace made priests, in order that we may dedicate ourselves and all that we have to the glory of God».³⁴ The elect have been made priests so that we can «offer ourselves and our all to God, and freely enter the heavenly sanctuary, so that the sacrifices of prayer and praise which we present are grateful and of sweet odour before him».³⁵

3.4 The exercise of the priesthood

The exercise of the common priesthood in Calvin must be seen in the light of his teaching on election and calling, which is closely related to

---

29 *Ibidem*.
30 *Ibidem*, 466.
31 *Ibidem*.
32 *Ibidem*, 464.
33 Cfr. EASTWOOD, *An Examination of Doctrine till Present Day*, 71.
34 J. CALVIN, *Commentaries on the Epistle of St. Paul to the Romans* (tr. & ed. J. Owen), Calvin Translation Society, Edinburgh 1844, 452, Quoted by CRAWFORD, *Calvin and the priesthood of all believers*, 146.
35 *Instit. Vol. 1*, II, xv, 432, Italics added.

holiness.[36] As we have seen, for Calvin, holiness regards all aspects of life, which has to be brought into line entirely with the divine calling.[37] He described holiness and vocation in terms of self-denial, self-sacrifice, the carrying of the cross and a virtuous ascetical life; before believers can dedicate themselves to God, they first must deny themselves. In the Institutes this is expressed as follows:

> «The sum of a Christian life is *denial of ourselves*,[38] of which the ends are four: i) that *we may devote ourselves to God as a living sacrifice*, ii) that we may not seek our own things, but those which belong to God and to our neighbour, iii) that we may patiently bear the cross, the fruits of which are—acknowledgement of our weakness, the trail of our patience, correction of faults, more earnest prayer, more cheerful meditation on eternal life, iv) that we may know in what manner we ought to use the present life and its aids, for necessity and delights (...) that *all things may correspond to our calling*».[39]

Through the mediation of Christ, the elect are purified, sanctified, sprinkled with blood (of Christ); they offer themselves, wholly, in sacrifice, and sacrifice their goods in mutual assistance.[40]

The question arises what the role of the priesthood of the believers is within this general framework of election and holiness, which comprises the whole of Christian life. The common priesthood of the believer becomes manifest in the sense that, for Calvin, *in Christ* the elect are consecrated through the Holy Spirit and, therefore, capable of rendering all their actions pleasing to the Father. This is the meaning of "having direct access to the Father in Christ". In Calvin's words:

> «We do not appear with our gifts in the presence of God without an intercessor. Christ is our Mediator, *by whose intervention we offer ourselves and our all to the Father*; he is our High Priest, who, having entered into

---

36 Cfr. EASTWOOD, *An Examination of Doctrine till Present Day*, 72.
37 Cfr. CRAWFORD, *Calvin and the priesthood of all believers*, 147.
38 *Instit. Vol. 2*, Aphorism 50, Italics added.
39 *Ibidem*, Aphorism 51, Italics added.
40 Crawford affirms that, according to Calvin, Christians are, firstly, by their calling in Christ, consecrated to God and in turn, the Christian is called upon to dedicate his personality to God. To fulfil this, the believer will devote himself, his talents, his property and his all, as a "living sacrifice", in those areas of life where he can best serve God. Cfr. CRAWFORD, *Calvin and the priesthood of all believers*, 147-148.

the upper sanctuary, opens up an access for us; he is the altar on which we lay our gifts, *that whatever we do attempt, we may attempt in him*».[41]

and,

«from this again arises not only confidence in prayer, but also the tranquillity of pious minds, while they recline in safety on the paternal indulgence of God, and feel assured *that whatever has been consecrated by the Mediator is pleasing to him*».[42]

Although this priestly capacity of the elect concerns the offering of all things and actions in Christ, Calvin mentioned more specifically the exercise of their priesthood by offering sacrifices of praise, thanksgiving, and intercessory prayer.[43]

3.4.1 Intercessory prayer

The elect are granted the priestly privilege of prayer, not only to each individual for oneself, but God also allows all to intercede mutually for each other to beseech for each other's salvation, all depending, of course, on the one intercession of Christ.[44] Calvin wanted to secure the absolute glory of God and, therefore, exhorted extensively that the elect cannot call on the saints in their own right and title for assistance, but only in as far they supplicate for us to God through Christ.[45]

Prayer is an act of solidarity among Christians. «All the members of the body of Christ should pray mutually for each other, since the members are mutually sympathetic; if one member suffers, the others suffer with it. And thus the mutual prayers of all the members still labouring on the earth ascend to the Head, who has gone before into heaven, and in whom there is propitiation for our sins».[46] Nevertheless, this intercessory prayer of the elect does not make them mediators, for there is only one Mediator, Jesus Christ.[47]

The summary of prayer is, which has been delivered to us by Christ the Lord and is contained in the Lord's Prayer and the two Tables.[48] From

---

41 *Instit. Vol. 2*, IV, xviii, 618-619, Italics added.
42 *Instit. Vol. 1*, II, xv, 432, Italics added.
43 Cfr. *Instit. Vol. 2*, III, xx, 165 ss.
44 Cfr. *Ibidem*, 167.
45 Cfr. *Ibidem*, 168 ss. It seems that Calvin here failed to understand that a saint is precisely a saint because of his or her communion with Christ.
46 *Instit. Vol. 2*, III, xx, 168.
47 Cfr. *Ibidem*.
48 Cfr. *Ibidem*, Aphorism 59, 684.

the *Our Father*, it follows that we are God's children and that a feeling of brotherly love ought to exist among us.⁴⁹ The First Table is entirely devoted to the glory of God, while the Second Table relates to ourselves and our neighbours.⁵⁰

3.4.2 Spiritual sacrifices
For Calvin, the core of common priesthood is the offering of spiritual sacrifices, which means "spiritual worship" and includes all good works of the the elect, as Calvin pointed out commenting on the words of St. Paul to the Romans and Philippians:

> «Thus Paul beseeches us, by the mercies of God, to present our bodies "a living sacrifice, holy, acceptable unto God", our "reasonable service" (Rom. xii. 1). Here he speaks very significantly when he adds, that this service is reasonable, for he refers *to the spiritual mode of worshipping God*, and *tacitly opposes it to the carnal sacrifices of the Mosaic Law*. Thus to do good and communicate are called sacrifices with which God is well pleased (Heb. xiii. 16). Thus the kindness of the Philippians in relieving Paul's want is called "an odour of a sweet smell, a sacrifice acceptable, well-pleasing to God" (Phil. iv. 18); and thus *all the good works of believers are called spiritual sacrifices*».⁵¹

Calvin had several reasons for opposing the "carnal" to the "spiritual". Firstly, he argued that God is only pleased with spiritual worship because his own nature is spiritual.⁵² Secondly, he regarded the partaking of the flesh in the Lord's Supper a spiritual act rather than a carnal act to avoid "transfusion of substances".⁵³ Finally, due to the believers' unworthiness, humans can never give anything to God, or as Calvin himself put it, «the best and only worthiness which we can bring to God is our own vileness».⁵⁴

---

49 Cfr. *Ibidem,* Aphorism 60.
50 Cfr. *Ibidem,* Aphorisms 61 and 62.
51 *Instit. Vol. 2,* IV, xviii, 618, Italics added.
52 *Instit. Vol. 1,* II, vii, 300, «(...) God did not enjoin sacrifice, in order that he might occupy his worshippers with earthly exercises, but rather that he might raise their minds to something higher. This is clear even from His own nature. Being a spirit, he is delighted only with spiritual worship».
53 Cfr. BEEKE, *Calvin on piety,* 135.
54 «(...) the best and only worthiness which we can bring to God is our own vileness, and, if I may so speak, unworthiness, that his mercy may make us worthy; to despond in ourselves, that we may be consoled in him; to humble ourselves that we may be elevated by him; to accuse ourselves that we may be justified by him; (...) that worthiness which is commanded by God [to have access to the sacred feast], consists especially in faith, which places all things in Christ, nothing in ourselves, and in charity, charity

3.4.2.1 Limitations

All good works of the elect to neighbours are regarded to be a sacrifice to worship God, i.e., to give him thanks and honour. Calvin, however, made a clear distinction between two types of sacrifices: expiatory and eucharistic.[55] The first type is the unique and eternal sacrifice of Christ on the cross to regain the favour of God for the elect.[56] They do not participate in that type of sacrifice, but only in the second type which is meant exclusively to give thanks and honour God, and includes:

> «(…) all the offices of charity, by which, while we embrace our brethren, *we honour the Lord himself in his members*; in fine, all our prayers, thanksgivings, and every act of worship which we perform to God. All these depend on the greater sacrifice with which we dedicate ourselves, soul and body, to be a holy temple to the Lord. (…). This kind of sacrifice *has nothing to do with appeasing God*, with obtaining remissions for sins, with procuring justification, but is wholly employed *in magnifying and extolling God*, (…). From this office of sacrificing, all Christians are called "a royal priesthood", because by Christ *we offer that sacrifice of praise of which the apostle speaks, the fruit of our lips, giving thanks to his name* (1 Pet. ii. 9; Heb. xiii. 15)».[57]

The elect do not expiate for their sins, since «"Christ is the Lamb of God, who taketh away the sins of the world (John i, 29)". He, I say, takes them away, *and no other*; that is, since he alone is the Lamb of God, he alone is the offering of for our sins; he alone is our expiation; he alone is satisfaction. (…) it follows that *we could not be partakers of the expiation accomplished by Christ*, were he not possessed of that honour of which those who try to appease God by their compensations seek to rob him».[58]

3.4.2.2 And the real sacrifice?

Calvin did recognise that the cross continues to be present in the life of the elect. Even more, they must identify themselves with Christ's death on the cross so that its benefits (redemption, sanctification, the priesthood,

---

which, though imperfect, it may be sufficient to offer to God, that he may increase it, since it cannot be fully rendered». *Instit. Vol. 2*, IV, xvii, 599.
55 Cfr. *Ibidem*, 616.
56 Cfr. *Ibidem*.
57 *Ibidem*, 617-618, Italics added.
58 *Instit. Vol. 1*, III, iv, 557, Italics added.

etc.) become effective; there is no redemption or priesthood without identification with Christ's death on the cross.[59] According to Calvin, «There is no access to God *for us or for our prayers* until the priest [Christ], purging away our defilements, sanctify us, and obtain for us that favour of which the impurity of our lives and hearts deprives us. Thus we see, that if *the benefit and efficacy of Christ's priesthood is to reach us, the commencement must be with his death*».[60]

The cross is a mark of discipleship and membership of God's family. Christ gave us an example to follow and Christians must be prepared for difficulties and suffering.

> «(…) Christ calls his disciples when he says, that every one of them must "take up the cross" (Matt. xvi, 24). Those whom the Lord has chosen and honoured with his intercourse must prepare for a hard, laborious, troubled life (…): it being the will of our heavenly Father to exercise his people in this way while putting them to the proof. Having begun this course with Christ the first-born, he continues it towards all his children. (…) Why then should we exempt ourselves from that condition to which Christ our Head behoved to submit; especially since he submitted on our account, that he might in his own person exhibit a model of patience? Wherefore, the Apostle declares, that all the children of God are destined to be conformed to him».[61]

Calvin's position that believers' sacrifices and their imitation of Christ's suffering on the cross are necessary to be saved, but do not have redemptive value, leads to an emphasis on the obligation of cross-bearing as a divine instrument to make the elect in conformity with Christ; the dimension of Christ's invitation to carry his cross *with him* is lost out of sight.

Although Calvin recognised the continuing presence of the cross and sacrifice in the life of the elect, he does not identify cross and sacrifice with the Supper. According to Calvin, it is erroneous to believe that «the Mass is a sacrifice and an oblation for obtaining the remission of sins».[62] Christ's sacrifice does not continue, but the fruits of that sacrifice become available to us in two ways: «For Christ did not offer himself once, in the view that his sacrifice should be daily ratified by new oblations, but that

---

59 Cfr. EASTWOOD, *An Examination of Doctrine till Present Day*, 68.
60 *Instit. Vol. 1*, II, xv, 431-432, Italics added.
61 *Instit. Vol. 2*, III, viii, 16-17.
62 *Ibidem*, IV, xviii, 607.

by the preaching of the gospel and *the dispensation of the sacred Supper, the benefit of it should be communicated to us*».[63]

The Supper is «the memorial from which they [the elect] may learn that the expiatory victim by which God was to be appeased *was to be offered only once*. For it is not sufficient to hold that Christ is the only victim, without adding that his is the only immolation, in order that our faith may be fixed to his cross».[64] But now that the sacrifice has been performed, (…), the Lord (…) has given us a table to feast, not an altar on which a victim may be offered; he has not consecrated priests to sacrifice, but ministers to distribute a sacred feast».[65]

The offerings of the elect during the Supper are the sacrifices of thanksgiving and praise. Calvin affirmed, «this kind of sacrifice is indispensable in the Lord's Supper, in which, while we show forth his death, and give him thanks, we offer nothing but the sacrifice of praise».[66] Although Calvin does not identify Christs' sacrifice on the cross with the Supper, he, however, stated: «And yet we deny not that in the Supper the sacrifice of Christ is so vividly exhibited as almost to set the spectacle of the cross before our eyes, (…)».[67]

According to Hesselink, Calvin maintained that Christ was truly present in the total act of the Supper through the Holy Spirit.[68] Since "Christ's body is in heaven and we are still pilgrims on earth", this gap is bridged "by the miraculous and secret virtue of Christ's Spirit for whom it is not difficult to associate things that are otherwise separated by an interval of space" (Geneva Catechism, Qs. 353-355).[69] Calvin meant by Christ's real presence that Christ's power or energy works in and through the sacrament by the Spirit.

Beeke remarks that Christ's death and resurrection are not ineffective, but Christ applies his salvation to believers for their regeneration.[70] Piety shows the Spirit of Christ is working in us what has already been accomplished in Christ, who administers his sanctification through his royal priesthood to the Church.[71]

---

63 *Ibidem*, 609, Italics added.
64 *Instit. Vol. 2*, IV, xviii, 611, Italics added.
65 *Ibidem*, 615.
66 *Ibidem*, 618.
67 *Ibidem*, 614.
68 Cfr. HESSELINK, *Calvin's theology*, 87.
69 Cfr. *Ibidem*.
70 Cfr. BEEKE, *Calvin on piety*, 128.
71 Cfr. *Ibidem*, and *Instit. Vol 1*, II, xvi, section 16.

3.5 Relation between priesthood and ministries

Each Christian is a priest in Christ. Yet Calvin also recognised ministers within the community. Being a practical man, he affirmed that God uses humans to govern the Church and who declare his will.

> «For though it is right that he [the Lord] alone should rule and reign in the Church, that he should preside and be conspicuous in it, and that its government should be exercised and administered solely by his word; yet as he does not dwell among us in visible presence, so as to declare his will to us by his own lips, he in this (…) uses the ministry of men, by making them, as it were, his substitutes, not by transferring his right and honour to them, but only doing his own work by their lips, as an artificer uses a tool for any purpose».[72]

Calvin recognised on the basis of Scripture the existence of various ministers: «And he gave some, apostles; and some, prophets; and some, evangelists; and some, pastors and teachers; for the perfecting of the saints, for the work of ministry, for the edifying of the body of Christ (…)».[73]

As we have seen, Calvin, with his talent and genius for systematisation and discipline, organised the Church in Geneva establishing four ministries; that of pastor, doctor, elder and deacon,[74] which function as an organic whole, complementing one another and working under Christ.

> «See how all men, without exception, are placed in the body, while the honour and name of Head is left to Christ alone. See how each member is assigned a certain measure, a finite and limited function, while both the perfection of grace and the supreme power of government reside only in Christ».[75]

Calvin held the ministry in the highest regard.[76] «(…) God has repeatedly commended its dignity by the titles which he has bestowed upon it, in order that we might hold it in *the highest estimation, as among the most excellent of our blessings*. He declares, that in raising up teachers, he confers a special benefit on men, (…). He [St. Paul in a passage of the second Epistle to the Corinthians] contends, that *there is nothing in the*

---

72 *Instit. Vol. 2*, IV, iii, 315-316.
73 *Ibidem*, 317.
74 Cfr. CRAWFORD, *Calvin and the priesthood of all believers*, 152-153.
75 *Instit. Vol. 2*, IV, vi, 361.
76 Cfr. CRAWFORD, *Calvin and the priesthood of all believers*, 152.

*Church more noble and glorious than the ministry of the Gospel, seeing it an administration of the Spirit of righteousness and eternal life».[77]

This dignity and special benefit does not imply a fundamental difference between believers. Calvin made a distinction between the ministry (the office) and the person holding the office, who does not speak in his own but only in God's name.

> Calvin stated: «Therefore, it is here necessary to remember, that whatever authority and dignity the Holy Spirit in Scripture confers on priests, or prophets, or apostles, or successors of Apostles, is wholly given *not to men themselves, but to the ministry to which they are appointed*; or, to speak more plainly, to the word, to the ministry of which they are appointed. For were we to go over the whole order, we should find that they were not invested with authority to teach or give responses, save in the name of the Lord. For whenever they are called to office, *they are enjoined not to bring anything of their own, but to speak by the mouth of the Lord*».[78]

The minister is called by God personally and through the elect to a particular office of spiritual responsibility in the Church.[79] Calvin accorded to the congregation of believers certain responsibilities and privileges (doctors, elders, etc.), urging them to undertake these for the glory of God, however, without linking his organisational theories explicitly to the doctrine of the priesthood of all believers.[80] Apart from the role of the laity regarding ecclesiastical discipline (eldership), Calvin strongly favoured active participation of the laity in the community. He saw the possibility of a mutual cure of souls among believers, such as mutual confession, admonition, correction, consolation, and edification, which belong to the normal life of lay believers in the community.[81]

In Calvinism, there is a strong emphasis on personal responsibility, since each individual Christian is obliged to glorify God through his life and work—be it a secular profession or an ecclesiastical ministry—and no one can take the place of another before God, since everyone has to appear personally before God's throne.[82] In this personal responsibility

---

77 *Instit. Vol. 2*, IV, iii, 317-318, Italics added.
78 *Ibidem*, viii, 390, Italics added.
79 It is interesting to note that Calvin considered it an offer of the minister to bring before God the fruits of his service, those souls whom he has led to Christ. Cfr. CRAWFORD, *Calvin and the priesthood of all believers*, 148.
80 Cfr. *Ibidem*, 154.
81 Cfr. *Ibidem*.
82 Cfr. *Ibidem*, 155.

the idea of the priesthood of all believers, though unspecified by Calvin, may be seen to have had a place in his thought.[83]

3.6 Mediation

Calvin put so much emphasis on the unique character of the mediation of Christ, and opposed it to human mediation that it seems there is no room left for humans. For Calvin, humans do not mediate, because only Christ mediates. However, the question has to be formulated differently; to what extent do and can the elect, according to Calvin, *really* (i.e., in the temporal-earthly sphere) participate in Christ's mediation?

Like Luther's concept of common priesthood, Calvin's understanding of priesthood does contain forms of mediation.[84] Each true believer is chosen a priest in Christ with "direct access" to God and, as such, he has the capacity and obligation to mediate between God and humans (descending dimension) and humans and God (ascending dimension).

The descending mediation becomes manifest in the fact that God acts through the elect in all their good works and services to neighbours; the redeemed believer is deemed holy before the Lord, and all his works in Christ are considered as such. In this way, the life of the Christian becomes a sign of holiness and mediates God's goodness to others.[85] However, it should be remembered that Calvin also considered that God uses the reprobates to do him service as well. In any case, believers participate in Christ virtually and by imputation; Christ's power works in them, which is then attributed to them.

The ascending dimension consists, firstly, in the fact that believers intercede and pray for each other to God and, secondly, believers can and should offer themselves up completely to God which means, in particular, to bring him spiritual worship consisting of spiritual sacrifices of prayer, thanksgiving and praise. The core of these sacrifices is self-denial; the offering of a humble and contrite heart. However, at the same time, it has to be recognised that Calvin denied the possibility for the elect to participate in Christ's redemptive sacrifice in the temporal-empirical sphere.

---

83 Cfr. *Ibidem*, 154, Crawford cites A. KUYPER, *Calvinism*, Sovereign Grace Union, London 1937, 83.
84 *Instit. Vol. 1*, III, ii, 473, «Whether God uses the agency of men, or works immediately by his own power, it is always by his word that he manifests himself to those whom he designs to draw to himself».
85 There is also a descending mediation present in the preaching and teaching of the Gospel, God's own Word, to the elect, which is mainly, i.e., the public preaching, reserved to ministers (pastors). However, for Calvin, this is not a priestly function, but a prophetic one.

3.7 Conclusion

In Calvin, the doctrine of the universal priesthood does not play a prominent role but is put at the service of the practical organisation of the community. In view of order in the community, there should be a clear division of functions and responsibilities. Nonetheless, although not prominent, the priesthood of all believers is important for Calvin.

Although Christ is the only real High Priest and our only Mediator, he has made believers virtual priests by Baptism with the Holy Spirit. Since believers have been reconciled to God the Father by the *one-and-only* sacrifice of Christ on the cross, and are full of the Holy Spirit, they are consecrated, chosen and holy. Due to Calvin's framework of dialectical and exclusive opposition between God and humans, everything in their mutual relationship should be ascribed to God and nothing to humans. It follows that God realises everything in the elect without their cooperation. The benefits, including the priesthood, are therefore, not really communicated, but imputed to the elect.

Due to God's favour and calling, the elect are under obligation to respond with a total dedication of their whole person and all that they possess, to glorify and thank God. The priestly privilege is the capacity to appear—in Christ—directly before the Lord and to bring him agreeable and pleasant spiritual sacrifices.

The total dedication to God does not only involve self-denial and a continual struggle against sin but also implies that all works of the elect should become an expression of praise and gratitude to God for their redemption in Christ. The whole of Christian life has to be brought in line with one's divine calling, each one in his own, without overstepping its boundaries.

Besides the offer of oneself, the elect exercise their priesthood in Christ more specifically by offering sacrifices of praise, thanksgiving, and intercessory prayer, which are pleasant to God. Believers pray for each other, beseech for each other's salvation, out of solidarity. Sacrifices of praise and thanksgiving are spiritual worship to God, which comprises all good works of a Christian, and always start with self-denial.

Although Calvin separated the sacrifices and good works of the elect from Christ's sacrifice on the cross, he nevertheless recognised that the cross continues to be present in their lives. The acceptance of the cross is a *conditio sine qua non* to receive the benefits of Christ's sacrifice. Moreover, it is necessary, because God treats members of his family like he treated Christ. The Supper is not to be identified with Christ's expiatory sacrifice, because Christ's sacrifice does not continue. The fruits of that sacrifice become available to the elect by the preaching of the Gospel and the dispensation of the sacred Supper. In the Lord's Supper, which is a commemoration of Christ's death, the elect only give him thanks and offer sacrifices of praise.

CHAPTER III
Reformed common priesthood revisited

This chapter contains an evaluation of the doctrine of common priesthood in Luther and Calvin from a Roman Catholic perspective. Firstly, the theological views of Luther and Calvin are compared by paying attention to some important differences in emphasis, while at the same time presenting the joint framework, approach and views on common priesthood (section 1). Secondly, in section 2, I will evaluate the reformers' views by describing points of connection and divergence with respect to a Catholic understanding of the same. Then, in section 3, some theological implications of the Reformed framework relevant for the common priesthood will be discussed. Finally, to shed light upon the necessary mutual relationship between both ministerial and common priesthoods, some key elements of the Catholic framework in which the common priesthood is understood and exercised will be discussed (section 4).

1. Luther and Calvin compared

This section contains a comparison of the role of the common priesthood in the theological doctrine and spirituality of the two main reformers of the 16th Century: Luther and Calvin. A brief overview of their personalities and motivations is presented, followed by the way Calvin mitigated the role of common priesthood in his theology, as well as an account of their common approach and vision on the mutual relationship between God and humans, while at the same time paying attention to some differences.

1.1 Personalities and main motivation
Luther and Calvin come from different backgrounds and have their own distinct personalities. Luther had been an Augustinian monk, priest and university professor. Due to his rather "volcanic" personality, he could easily fall into extremes: from feeling an intense joy in knowing that he was saved, he could swing to the other side of the pendulum of feeling totally corrupt and liable to condemnation. Understanding this aspect of his personality is crucial in grasping his thought and theological views, because they are shaped on the basis of his personal experiences—his own and that of others. A case in point: he is conflicted in his effort to try

to please God by complying with his law in all its aspects, while at the same time, he is burdened by a sense of failure, of continuously failing to live up to God's demands of perfection. One could surmise that Luther was extremely demanding with himself. This created so much internal tension on him, and so he found a way out of this "desperate situation" through his faith in Christ, who died on the Cross for him personally, and thus, guaranteeing the mercy of God the Father.

On the other hand, Calvin was not a cleric. He was educated as a layman and jurist. He later came into contact with the reformation movement initiated by Luther. It appears that he had not encountered the same intense religious experiences as Luther—the tension between one's effort to comply with God's law and the realization of always failing to live up to it. The decisive experiences for Calvin were rather the deep divisions within Christendom during his time, the situation of his country (France), and the persecution of Christians and friends, whom he knew to be honest and sincere in living their faith. These experience led him to posit that the true religion needs practical leaders to end the prevailing chaos by putting order in the communities and to defend themselves against their opponents—not only what he considered as the "rigid" Roman Catholic Church, but also the "lax" Anabaptists and other radical spiritualist groups.

In this sense, Calvin agreed with Luther that the true religion means God saving man by faith alone. He arrived at this conclusion, not on the basis of his own experiences—as Luther did—but he accepted Luther's teachings. This explains why Luther's writings tend to be more lively and emotional, whereas Calvin's writings are rather more detached and formal. They also differ in the focus of their mission, so to speak: one was more personal-experiential in character, while the other was formal-practical. In other words, Luther's primordial concern was to obtain absolute certainty about his eschatological destiny, while Calvin's main goal was to implement Luther's reform by organising the life of the local community according to these "Reformation" principles.

1.2 Mitigating the common priesthood

Luther's proclamation of the radical equality of all believers, the universal priesthood and his emphasis on the merely interior and spiritual act of faith, had caused practical problems and disorder. The Anabaptists and other spiritual radicals—radicalising Luther's already radical views—completely disregarded all exterior aspects of the Church, Scripture and sacraments in favour of a merely personal, direct and spiritual relationship between God and the believer. In short, the radical equality of all believers and the claim that all belonged to the spiritual estate had become associated with anarchy and chaos.

Nevertheless, Calvin—although he profoundly abhorred chaos and anarchy—did not oppose the revolutionary and utopic ideas of radical equality and universal priesthood (personal, direct and immediate eschatological access to God for all), but rather accepted them. However, in order to safeguard law and order, he encapsulated these doctrines firmly in his teachings on God's sovereign election, vocation, ministry and a stronger external ecclesiology (Church structure and discipline). Calvin's doctrine of the common priesthood thus seems to be more (counter) balanced than Luther's on *at least* the following three points.

i) Calvin made common priesthood an aspect of his doctrine of election and vocation. He put a strong emphasis on the idea that every human being is called by God and assigned a specific task within the community and the world. The believer's obedience to God's will is closely related to complying with one's specific and fixed task, which is ordained by God from eternity. God calls the believer to become holy in *this* place and with *this* task. The common priesthood of believers means that they are consecrated in Christ through the Holy Spirit and, therefore, capable of rendering all actions pleasing to the Father. In Calvin, it is God's election that gives the believer certainty.

ii) Calvin managed in the practical application of the common priesthood, to organise the community in such a way that the priesthood of believers did not interfere with the order in the Church, and at the same time, securing the preaching of the Gospel.[1] Calvin employed great efforts to ensure that the ministry of the Word would be held in the highest regard possible, even making use of, and thus "re-introducing", the distinction between the two classes of clergy and laity,[2] a distinction which Luther had abolished with so much effort and vigour.

iii) Calvin embedded the common priesthood in his theology of the threefold offices of Christ as King, Prophet and Priest. The common priesthood, and thus the equality of all believers, were accepted but at the same time, he regarded the function of preaching to be part of the prophetic office reserved for ministers, and thus removed it as a function of the priesthood of all believers. In other words, while all

---

[1] According to Pont, Calvin developed the thesis of the universal priesthood in such a low-key form to preserve the order in the Church and the prime position of the preaching of the Gospel, PONT, *Die priesterskap van die gelowiges*, 451.

[2] Cfr. *Instit. Vol. 2*, IV, xii, 453.

Christians do participate in Christ's Kingship and Priesthood, not all of them participate equally in Christ's Prophethood.³

1.3 Reframing the relationship between God and humans
As it has been shown, there are clear differences in approach and emphasis on certain doctrinal and spiritual aspects between the two reformers. Nevertheless, Calvin's views on the common priesthood are very similar to Luther's ideas. Both reformers basically follow the same line of thought and way of reasoning. The tendency in their reasoning presuppose and make manifest a common framework within a shared underlying vision and understanding of the relationship between God and the human being. The universal priesthood, where each believer has direct and immediate eschatological access to God the Father in Christ through the Holy Spirit, is at the very core of this framework.

Both reformers stressed the fact that God is absolute majesty, the Creator who cannot be identified with his creation and creatures, and who rules the whole of creation directly from heaven. There is an abysmal gap between God in heaven and humans in the temporal-empirical sphere. For them, this distance should always be maintained. The gap between God in heaven and humans on earth is widened by an over-emphasis on the fallen state of the human condition, which is labelled as "completely corrupted" in his nature due to original sin. In this way, both reformers thus *materially* situated (original) sin at the same level as created human nature itself. In this way, the human (sinful) condition stands in sharp contrast with God's majesty and appears to fully disqualify them from acting in any supernatural relevant way in their current state of travellers in the temporal-empirical sphere.

Both reformers fully ascribed salvation of humans to God alone. Christ and the Holy Spirit bridge the tremendous gap between the Creator and his sinful creatures, the former by his historical salvific act on the cross and continuous intercession before the Father, and the latter by creating a union between Christ and the believers. True knowledge of Christ only comes to humans through the Word and the Holy Spirit teaches humans and enlightens them inwardly in such a way that their minds are completely renewed, i.e., they cannot disregard it. Although

---

3 In any case, both reformers understood the ministry of the Word functionally as the public proclamation of the word and administration of the sacraments and not ontologically in the sense of a special priesthood, while divine institution of the ministry is in no way denied. J. ROHLS, *Das geistliche Ambt in der reformatorischen theologie*, «Kerygma und Dogma, Zeitschrift für theologische Forschung und kirchliche Lehre» 31 (1985), 161.

the Holy Spirit may use external means, such as Scripture and other humans, it is however always the Holy Spirit who guarantees his own teachings to the believer.

For Luther and Calvin, the concept of faith seems to include and require the explicit recognition on the part of believers of their nothingness and sinful condition in the temporal sphere of common life, where the bridge apparently cannot be crossed. Because of the believers' humble confession of faith in Christ and their own incapacity, the Holy Spirit establishes a spiritual communion between them in their hearts. Calvin put this "mystical union" between Christ and the elect at the centre of his theology,[4] whereas for Luther the focus seems to be more on the believer's personal act of faith and the result thereof, that is, the joyous exchange and the communication of the benefits of Christ to the believer.

In the believers' act of faith, the Holy Spirit shows them the true God in Christ through a spiritual encounter. Both reformers made use of a dialectical opposition between the law and the gospel. God apparently uses the law to provoke in humans an act of desperate faith in Christ, in order to show that God the Father is merciful and does not hold their imperfect compliance of the law and imperfect love against them. It appears that Calvin was more aware than Luther of the need, and he endeavoured especially, to uphold the Decalogue by presenting the law as a positive expression of God's will. Due to Luther's theology of the cross and method of radical paradox, he encountered more problems in presenting God's law as positive, for God always manifests himself as exactly opposite to our human way of understanding. Calvin was not aware of Luther's *theologia crucis*.[5] Although Calvin used paradox in his theology, he explicitly warned against the radical "all-or-nothing" approach of Luther which leaves no room for gradual stages and growth in the relationship between God and humans: if believers have faith they are saved and become instantly holy, if there is no faith, condemnation follows.

The "practical" Calvin was apparently able—better than Luther—to create room for the elements of space and time to come into play, and thus for gradual stages and growth, by taking away the radical element in Luther's method of paradox and by considering frequently that believers are pilgrims, who still have to be conformed to Christ during their lives.

---

4 Beeke calls Calvin's understanding of "communion with Christ" the heart of his system of theology, which shaped his thought on all other issues. Cfr. BEEKE, *Calvin on piety*, 128. According to Garcia, Calvin did not ground good works in imputation or justification (ex sola fide) but in union with Christ. GARCIA, *Life in Christ*, 260.

5 Cfr. GARCIA, *Life in Christ*, 258.

However, this difference between the reformers should not be overestimated, because Luther also recognised that believers in the temporal-empirical sphere are travellers on their way to the heavenly kingdom, who still have to be conformed to Christ.

The Genevan theologian took another approach to maintain the distance between God and humans and, at the same time, to virtually bridge it: God's sovereignty. Calvin shifted the attention away from the all-determining subjective act of faith by the believer—so characteristic of Luther's theological views—by putting all emphasis on the divine side of the relationship between God and humans. In Calvin, God is therefore represented, above all, as absolute Sovereign in his capacity as Creator, Redeemer and Sanctifier apparently in opposition to humans, whose role is systematically reduced to nothing. For Calvin, humans are saved, elected and sanctified despite themselves. Also here, we deal with a mere change of perspective and emphasis, for Luther also accepted fully God's sovereignty and omnipotence and endeavoured to reduce humans' role towards God to a minimum.

In any case, both reformers considered that in the spiritual communion believers obtain all the benefits of Christ by a joyful or wondrous exchange, which includes righteousness, divine filiation, certainty, freedom from the law and holiness—and in Calvin's case, being admitted to a process of regeneration. One of the benefits obtained by believers in this spiritual communion is the right and duty to have "direct and immediate access" to God the Father in Christ, a benefit which is closely related to the radical equality of all believers and the common priesthood. In the event of direct and immediate access to God the Father, believers experience the goodness and mercy of God, who, through Christ, is pleased with them and all their actions. Here believers obtain definitive certainty about their eschatological destiny but also come to acknowledge that they, by themselves, are nothing before God and are in no position to give anything back to God in the temporal-empirical sphere.

In this interior experience, the believer is fully united to Christ and receives a new mind and heart. Since they materially situated sin at the level of the created human being itself, both reformers framed redemption of humans by God as a re-creation *ex nihilo*: the human mind and heart must be completely re-created out of nothing and replaced by another mind and heart. However, despite this interior spiritual union, believers in the external sphere of empirical reality remain—and so it seems, should remain—corrupted "in and by themselves", since healing the corrupt nature in this sphere is not possible. Thus, in the temporal-empirical sphere, God operates in parallel to the believer's corrupted nature and being. Hence, their good works are, therefore, not really the believers' works, but are exclusively God's works. At the same time, the benefits they receive in their joyful exchange with Christ—in particular, the freedom from enforcement of the law and the fact that believers have been recreated *ex nihilo* with a new heart and a new mind—enable believers to joyfully and freely comply with the law, and in this way be "obedient" to God's will.

To construe the exterior communion between God and believers in the temporal-empirical sphere, both reformers made use of the (legal) concept of imputation; on the one hand, good works—though not really performed by believers—are attributed to them by imputation; by the merits of Christ's sacrifice on the cross and his continuous intercession, God the Father is willing to attribute Christ's holiness to believers, although in the temporal-empirical sphere they seem not holy, but rather sinful in their very being. On the other hand, at the same time, this sinfulness of the human condition is no longer attributed to believers due to Christ's redemption and God's mercy.

Both reformers maintained that believers must glorify God in and with their whole lives and occupations in the midst of the world, and to offer themselves and all they have as spiritual sacrifices in Christ pleasing to the Lord. Furthermore, they both limited the continuity of Christ's redemptive sacrifice in the temporal-empirical sphere or, as far as Christ's sacrifice is eternal, they excluded the possibility that the sacrifices of Christians are united to Christ's heavenly self-giving to the Father. Believers—although priests in Christ—do not participate in Christ's sacrifice in the temporal-empirical sphere of human experiences. Instead, they give thanks and praise to God for all the benefits they received.

1.4 Preliminary conclusion
In sum, both reformers, in order to safeguard and secure the absolute primacy, sovereignty and glory of God, intended to maximise God's role and minimise that of humans in their mutual relationship. Thus, the reformers reframed the mutual relationship between God and the believer, which they characterised through a) personal faith and election, b) as merely receiving and c) with direct access (common priesthood).

The human being is redeemed by adhering *in faith* to Christ's sacrifice on the cross, which is a divine free gift to which the believer cannot add anything, and—being a priest in Christ—he obtains a right and obligation to immediately appear before the Lord. For both Luther and Calvin, "direct and immediate access" did not simply mean that each Christian can pray to God directly, i.e., without intermediaries, but this feature expresses the eschatological situation that each Christian stands—and has to appear—before God's throne *immediately* to obtain certainty about his salvation; it follows then that each Christian is called to the highest form of contemplation in the world—anytime and anywhere—while standing face-to-face before God, who pronounces his final verdict on the believer.

The motives of the reformers differed: for Luther, it is the personal certainty that is at stake and that is guaranteed by the personal act of faith, and for Calvin—in order to mitigate any possible detrimental effects on the community—it is the emphasis on God's absolute sovereignty, omnipotence and providence in the governance of the world. Thus, Calvin accentuated God's unilateral and gratuitous election and regeneration of the believer within the community and their obedience to the law in order to give glory and proper worship to God in a sober liturgy that reflects the distance between God and humans. At the same time, he downplayed other aspects which he considered problematic, such as the merely subjective act of faith, the radical equality of believers and the common priesthood of all believers. Nonetheless, Calvin accepted—though with a certain reserve and nuance—[6] the direct, immediate and eschatological access of all believers in Christ to God the Father, and their absolute passive role towards God, where they fundamentally lack the capacity and freedom to "give" anything back to God.

---

6 Calvin found it necessary to point out that believers in prayer do have access to God, but not too close; only Christ presents the prayers of the believer to the Father, while the sinful believers «are standing far off in the outer court», *Instit. Vol. 2*, III, xx, 168.

2. Evaluation

This section contains an evaluation of the Reformed understanding and exercise of the priesthood of all believers from a Catholic perspective on common priesthood. The Catholic view is based on the position of the Catholic Church as formulated on and after the Second Vatican Council. First of all, some points of connection will be discussed to be followed by a few points of divergence.

2.1 Points of connection with the Catholic understanding of common priesthood

2.1.1 Christ is the only and true eternal High Priest and Redeemer
The only source of priesthood is Christ, who is the exclusive fundament of all priestly mediation on earth and in heaven. Christ has redeemed humans through the Paschal Mystery—Passion, Death and Resurrection. Furthermore, Christ's priesthood is eternal and he continues his redemptive work in and through the Church.

2.1.2 Greatness of the Christian life in the world
By situating the believer directly before the Lord, where he is deemed righteous, elected and holy, the reformers touched upon the greatness of the common priesthood. In this way, they opened a great horizon of a life of contemplation of every believer in the midst of the world. The reformers intended to elevate ordinary Christians to a higher level of Christian life, by pointing out the importance and beauty of Baptism, through which all humans become equally Christian. All believers belong to the spiritual estate and are called to holiness—it does not matter whether one is shoemaker, pastor, farmer or lawyer. Indeed, all Christians are being called to personal unity with God in daily life in the world, with all their rights and responsibilities, and to offer themselves and all they have as spiritual sacrifices, which are acceptable and pleasing to God; each Christian shares in the priesthood of Christ in order to give all glory to God.

Luther had a point when he reacted against the overstressing of the role of the Roman clergy and the passive laity. Grace is not exclusively distributed by the Roman clergy through the sacraments, all Christians belong to the spiritual estate and are called to the same holiness as the clergy and religious. The ideas of the basic equality of all believers, grounded in Baptism and the universal vocation to holiness have been part of Catholic doctrine but were re-emphasized through a solemn prouncement at the Second Vatican Council.[1]

2.1.3 *The believer's personal encounter with Christ*

The theology of both reformers is Trinitarian: God the Father, the Son Jesus Christ and the Holy Spirit cooperate to redeem human beings. At the same time, they put Christ at the centre of their theology and spirituality. Luther and Calvin strongly emphasised the central role of Jesus Christ in the lives of all believers and the absolute need and importance for them to have a personal encounter and experience in faith with him; each believer can and should directly speak with our Lord in prayer and read the Scripture to hear God's own Word so that they can know and follow Christ. This explains in part the reformers' apostolic zeal, their focus on teaching and preaching and their interest in providing translations of the Bible into vernacular languages—to make the Word of God accessible to each Christian.

The reformers were men with deep religious experience and they emphasised an important insight: that in one's personal experience with God, the believer comes to realise that Christ has died on the cross not in general, but *for him personally*. This insight is not a merely intellectual understanding of a past event, but a *lived experience* with a lasting impact. In this event, Christ becomes present in the life of believers. This encounter invites believers to a continuous conversion—it should be a life-changer.

2.1.4 *The importance of humility*

The reformers had a deep sense of humility and awareness of being nothing before God, who is absolute sovereignty, majesty and mercy. They stressed the fact that humans are in everything—both with respect to creation and redemption—like clay vessels, totally dependent on God. They realised vividly that on their own they can do nothing. Standing before God, humans cannot but be aware of their painful condition as sinners—of having offended the Lord so many times—and their own incapacity to fully comply with God's law. The reformers rightly realised that humans by themselves can only offer to God their misery and

---

[1] The Lutheran-Roman Catholic Commission recently stated: «Not until the Second Vatican Council did the magisterium present a theology of the Church as the people of God and affirm the true equality of all with regard to the dignity and action common to all the faithful concerning the building up of the body of Christ (LG 32)», in: LUTHERAN-ROMAN CATHOLIC COMMISSION, Report *From Conflict to Communion* (2013), no 173, Cfr. LG, Chapter V.

nothingness, begging him for mercy.[2] They highlighted the important and crystal-clear insight that humans can not save, redeem nor justify themselves, but only by and in Christ.

2.1.5 Unconditional love and free gift
The reformers emphasised the believer's personal experience of redemption by God. Through the "joyous exchange", the soul of the believer unites with that of Christ and a spiritual communion takes place. The believer becomes a child of God and due to the merits of Christ, he (sinner) is justified before the Lord and admitted into his presence.[3] Here, God shows in Christ his mercy to human beings. God is a lenient Father who takes into account their weaknesses and who forgives their wretchedness and shortcomings. One of the perennial insights of the reformers is God's unconditional love for sinners. Berndt Hamm forcefully argued that at the centre of Luther's reform stands his new and radical notion of the pure gift of salvation without any human participation, for sinners are unconditionally taken up into salvation by God.[4]

2.1.6 Certainty, freedom and love of neighbour
For the reformers, this unconditional love and acceptance by God is not a merely intellectual concept, rather they emphasised its existential character. A believer should experience "being absolved" by God, the word of forgiveness spoken by God to the believer in Christ, which could be paraphrased as follows: "I love you despite everything". Being children of God and thus loved unconditionally, believers have the absolute certainty of God's favour. God is bound unilaterally by his own promise and not by any human gifts; humans don't have to "buy" God's love.[5]

It is this Word of promise that sets free and relieves believers from their sins. Knowing that God loves them, they are set free to live and to serve, becoming another Christ for their neighbour. This is a great insight, for it is indeed rather difficult to be attentive to others, if one is constantly worried about one's own salvation and if powerful feelings such as fear of rejection, the need for control and lack of certainty have the upper hand. In the words of Moltmann, «the person who is freed from the compulsion

---

2 At the end of his life Luther affirmed with St. Augustine: «Wir sein Pettler. Hoc est Verum, "we are beggars this is true"». WA Tischr. 4, 491; Cfr. CCC no 2559.
3 See also FRANCIS, Encyclical letter *Lumen fidei*, 29.06.2013, no 19-20.
4 Cfr. HAMM, *Martin Luther's Revolutionary Theology of Pure Gift without Reciprocation*, 125-161.
5 Cfr. *Ibidem*, 140.

to perform good works brims over with love, and does every good work spontaneously and unprompted, out of pure thankfulness, (…)».[6] Christians are called to serve and love their neighbours in all they do freely and joyfully, through one's professional vocation in daily life; all acts of a Christian have a priestly character and have somehow the potentiality to be offered to God.

In sum, each Christian by virtue of Baptism is equally a priest in Christ and capable of giving praise and glory to God in all earthly activities by offering themselves and all that they have to the Lord. Thus, all believers somehow share in Christ's priesthood, and whose participation is grounded in a personal and existential encounter with God the Father, in Christ and through the Holy Spirit. The reformers warned against the danger of "own-works-righteousness", the pretension of reaching salvation through one's efforts. Instead, they stressed the importance of humility by recognising one's own miserable condition vis-à-vis God's unconditional love for them. Although humans before God are nothing and can do nothing by themselves, the powerful experience of God's unconditional love sets them free and gives them certainty of salvation. This enables believers to joyfully obey God's will by fulfilling the Decalogue, carrying their cross, living solidarity with and serving their neighbours by teaching and preaching the Gospel, interceding for them in prayer and offering themselves and all they have, as Christ did for us. In this way, they give praise to God and thank him for all gratuitous gifts they received.

2.2 Points of divergence with a Catholic understanding of common priesthood

The reformers—by situating the believer in faith directly before God's throne—touched upon the greatness of common priesthood. However, since the believer does not yet stand directly before the Lord to hear the definitive verdict, the reformers were constraint to put certain limitations on the common priesthood in the temporal-empirical sphere of common life and experiences. Thus, they conditioned the possibilities for the believer to reach full contemplation in the world and to effectively perform spiritual sacrifices agreeable to God. These limitations in the temporal-empirical sphere are: a) the limitation of Christ's priesthood and sacrifice, followed by b) the reformers' attempt to separate Christ's sacrifice from the sacrifices of the believers, c) a shift in focus in Reformation theology from self-giving to self-denial, d) an exclusive

---

6 J. MOLTMANN, *God for a Secular Society: The Public Relevance of Theology*, Fortress Press, Minneapolis 1999, 194.

focus on the world and, finally, e) an oblivion of the believers' task to consecrate the world to God.

2.2.1 Limitation of Christ's priesthood and sacrifice

Both reformers put a limit on the continuation of Christ's priestly office. To understand how Christ, according to the reformers, continues his priestly function after his Ascension into heaven, we have to take into account the separation between the believers' experiences in the temporal-empirical sphere and their seemingly opposite experiences in the spiritual sphere of faith.

In the temporal-empirical sphere, Christ has redeemed humans by his historical sacrifice on the cross. In reality—or in this sphere—Christ is the only Mediator capable, because only he is totally free of sin, to redeem humans, and being the true priest, he has performed the one-and-only true priestly sacrifice on the cross once-and-for-all. Therefore, it is not necessary anymore for believers to sacrifice, or at least, not in the way Christ did. Christ's real sacrifice is over and belongs to the past and collective memory of humans.

In the reformers' spiritual sphere of interior faith, Christ continues his redemptive work by interceding for humans to the Father not to pay attention to their sins and wretchedness in the temporal-empirical sphere. For both reformers, Christ only continues his priestly work on earth directly *in* and *from* heaven, which is accessible for each believer through a personal act of faith by means of the Holy Spirit, who brings the believer in direct contact with Christ on the cross and before the throne of God the Father.

2.2.2 Separation between Christ's sacrifice and the believers' offerings

As a matter of principle, believers do not participate in Christ's sacrifice in the temporal-empirical sphere. The reformers endeavoured to separate the believers' sacrifices from Christ's eternal sacrifice. Although the reformers do speak of "sacrifice" in connection to the priesthood, this is mainly to carefully distinguish the believer's "offering of oneself" from Christ's (real earthly) sacrifice on the cross. Since Christ's sacrifice does not continue in the temporal-empirical sphere, nor are the believers' sacrifices united to Christ's heavenly offering,[7] the believers' sacrifices

---

7 Luther explicitly considered that Christ also continues to offer himself to God the Father in heaven for the believers, but in Luther's own interior experience of his encounter with Christ and direct access to the Father, it seemed that Christ nonetheless did not unite Luther's sacrifices to his own heavenly offering. The reason for this is that Luther "felt" himself and regarded all that he had to offer as completely sinful and thus unworthy to be offered by Christ to God the Father.

become an imitation of a past historical example. These sacrifices cannot be united to Christ's sacrifice in the temporal-empirical sphere, but only in a moral sense of solidarity, and their sacrifices do not, therefore, have any redemptive value. In other words, believers can intercede, give thanks and praise in Christ, but they do not offer their sacrifices in Christ—they "merely" perform these acts as an imitation of his example.[8] It follows that believers, according to the reformers, although "priests" and doing "good works" in Christ, do not enjoy the priestly privilege of being co-redeemers in and with Christ for their sacrifices are separated from Christ's sacrifice.

2.2.3 A shift from self-giving to self-denial

While standing directly before God the Father in Christ, the believer experiences his nothingness and feels that he is not capable of giving anything back to God, other than his own nothingness. Within this frame —which seems to contemplate the believer just by himself—the centre of gravity and attention of the believers' sacrifices shifts from self-giving (love) to self-denial. Since the believer is apparently standing before God on his own, although he does stand next to Christ, he is not capable of giving himself as Christ did, but only to deny himself and trust on the efficacy of Christ's sacrifice and God the Father's promise and leniency.[9] This implies that in the Reformed view, believers not only have nothing to give back to God,[10] but also fundamentally lack any possibility to give anything back to him.

---

8 The reformers employed various arguments to prevent believers from uniting their sacrifices to Christ's sacrifice: i) it is not possible because the sacrifice belongs to the past, ii) believers can't because they are sinful, iii) it is also not necessary anymore for Christ has done it for you, thus iv) it would be ungrateful, blasphemous and even arrogant. These arguments, however, do not seem to hinder the reformers from recognising that believers can be co-operators with God on the level of creation, sharing in his divine creative attributes in the governance and rule of the world. I will come back to this issue hereafter sub e) oblivion of the task to bring back the world to God and in section 3.3: paradoxical anthropology.

9 Hamm describing Luther's experience of God's saving Word as follows: «In the midst of their sin human beings receive God's acquittal: "For me [God the Father] you are for Christ's sake righteous and saved, not simply righteous now and one day saved, but already now—before you have or do anything good and apart from having to provide some ability, gift, merit or satisfaction—I give to you my fullest blessing and accept you into my blessedness. Let it be said to you and trust it!"», HAMM, *Martin Luther's Revolutionary Theology of Pure Gift without Reciprocation*, 142.

10 *Ibidem*, 143.

This shift becomes manifest in the fact that in Reformed spirituality, praise, thanksgiving, intercessory prayer and service to neighbour are considered sacrifices in the sense that these acts necessarily imply acknowledgement of God and neighbour and denial of oneself. However, thanksgiving and praise are acts, which in themselves, are not sacrifices, but rather indicate the purpose or motive of the underlying act of self-giving, that is, gratitude or praise. Self-denial (humility) is a condition for sacrifice (love), but not its essence. It thus appears that in Reformed spirituality, the act of self-denial is seen in dialectical opposition to praising and thanking God, which could be interchanged; in the same act of confessing one's nothingness, the believer praises and pleases God.

Due to the frame that a believer cannot give anything back to God — even not in Christ—love, gratitude and praise seem to be seriously hindered and perhaps even impeded. Recently, Paul O'Callaghan argued, in order to show that grace heals human sinful nature (his deeply rooted ingratitude), that—although according to Lutheran theology humans do not respond to grace by "giving" anything back to God but by being grateful for the gifts received—this response is nevertheless a truly human action, which also can be refused to carry out.[11] It seems to me that the response of gratitude to God's gifts can only be considered a truly human action if humans are deemed capable in Christ—and are at least allowed— to give themselves and their gifts back to God in Christ.

Due to this shift in perspective, mortification and penance in Reformed spirituality are not seen as manifestations of self-giving love, but they are foremostly regarded as the believer's duty as a sinner to struggle against his sinful nature and being in order to comply with the Decalogue, and in this way, obey God's will. Due to the framing that believers are supposed to imitate Christ and to carry the cross albeit separated from Christ and his sacrifice in the temporal-empirical sphere, the meaning of the cross and suffering in the lives of believers is altered. Christ's invitation to become his disciple and to follow him by bearing the cross (cfr. Math. 16:24; Mc. 8:34) is lost out of sight and the focus shifts towards the mandatory character of "cross-bearing" as God's necessary instrument to conform believers to Christ: believers have to endure the cross and suffering to withstand the temptations of the devil to test their faith: it is this faith which saves them.[12]

---

11 Cfr. O'CALLAGHAN, *Luther and 'sola gratia'*, 201.
12 Moreover, this way of framing seems to lead to an inconsistency; after all, the reformers had reproached the Roman Catholic Church for exactly this issue; the allegation that Catholics performed self-righteous works of their own and on their own, thus without Christ. However, by presenting human cross-bearing and suffering in this way,

2.2.4 Exclusive focus on the world

All Christians are equal before God's throne. This claim—without taking sufficiently into account that we are still travelling—has profoundly changed the view of how Christians live the tension between the world (the profane) and God (the sacred). The reformers have tried to eliminate the differences between the different vocations and states of life. Whereas the medieval view had resulted in an equilibrium in the tension between the radical demands of holiness and ordinary human flourishing—people could "travel at different speeds", in various states or walks of life: religious, clergy or lay Christians—the reformers, however, could not agree with this "discrimination", and did away with this order altogether, in favour of lay Christians, who became the model of the saint in the midst of the world.[13]

Thus, the reformers' framework does not provide for the possibility that the believers offer sacrifices directly to God in Christ. The believer can do so only indirectly through service to neighbours, which would be the only way to please the Lord. The reformers thus seem to ignore the order, in the temporal-empirical sphere, suggested by St. Paul in his Second Letter to the Corinthians.[14] This way of framing implies an exclusive focus on the world since according to Reformed doctrine, a believer could not "leave" the world or renounce matrimony (i.e., for sake of the heavenly kingdom) to please the Lord. According to the reformers, God apparently does not or cannot ask this of humans—no doubt related to their view of the corrupt human condition—but God would only sanctify humans directly in the midst of the world. For the reformers, "leaving" the world and renouncing matrimony is ungrateful and a form of escaping the tasks and duties in the world, through which humans cooperate with God's creative power in building up the world.

2.2.5 Oblivion of the task to bring back the world to God

Christ became our priest to reconcile the world with God and to bring it back to God (cfr. Eph. 1:10). Christians somehow participate in Christ's priesthood precisely in order to cooperate with this mission. However, the reformers—despite their exclusive focus on the world and their attempt to "spiritualise" the laity by pointing out that believers are

---

i.e., disconnected from the substance of Christ's redemptive sacrifice, the reformers themselves ran the risk of performing self-righteous works, i.e., on their own without Christ. We will see in section 3 how the reformers dealt with this problem.

13 Cfr. TAYLOR, *A Secular Age*, 45.

14 2 Cor. 8:5, «they [the Churches of Macedonia] gave themselves first to the Lord and to us through the will of God».

co-operators with God in the governance and rule of the world—seem to ignore the task of Christians to perfect the world in Christ and to bring it back to God. Due to their framework in which the believer is situated directly and immediately before God's throne, this aspect of the common priesthood appears to fall outside the scope of their radar.

Both Luther and Calvin recognised that believers—being creatures of God—could cooperate with him on the natural plane of creation but refused to accept any human cooperation with respect to redemption, i.e., on the supernatural plane. This theological position leads to the result that humans can use the gifts of creation to build up the world, but that they cannot give these gifts and the world back to God. Believers, instead, praise and thank the Lord for the gifts of creation they have received, but at the same time, they feel unworthy to give them back to God. It appears that believers work, serve their neighbour and offer spiritual sacrifices not out of love (self-giving), but positively —being justified—out of gratitude and to praise God and, negatively—being a sinner—as self-denial and out of duty of ascetical mortification to comply with the Decalogue (obedience). Work and perfection of creation as such do not have in Reformation theology any sanctifying value.[15] In this spirituality, the focus shifted in the understanding and exercise of the believers' priesthood. Believers use the goods of the world out of gratitude, praise, service to neighbour, or out of mortification, but their priesthood does not include the capacity to bring back the world in Christ to God the Father, and in this way sanctifying the world and themselves.

---

15 The reformers' vision of sanctity and the Christian life of perfection is very much conditioned by the prevailing understanding of (late) medieval vision of holiness; i.e., the religious form and understanding of holiness, though with the great difference that the reformers tried to realise it in the world, instead of leaving it. In any case, the spirituality of the reformers—albeit in the world—is characterised by a religious spirituality, which explains the allegation of Voltaire that the reformers have tried "to turn the whole world into a monastery".

3. Some theological implications of reformed understanding of common priesthood

We have seen some points of connection and divergence between the Reformed and Catholic understanding of common priesthood. This section aims to look deeper into some implications of the particular understanding of Reformed common priesthood as each believer having direct and immediate access to God the Father in Christ through the Holy Spirit. These implications include its eschatological confusion, a turn towards gnostic, situational and relational redemption and priesthood, a paradoxical anthropology and a weak ecclesiology.

3.1 Greatness, but also confusion

The theological manoeuvre of the reformers to grant each believer "direct and immediate access" to God is in part revealing for it shows true things, like the fact that we are all sinners and we totally depend on God, and that all humans are equal when standing before God's throne. However, apart from re-discovering and highlighting the greatness of common priesthood, this manoeuvre also causes confusion and disillusion, simply because believers are not yet standing directly before God's throne to hear God's definitive verdict over their lives and actions. The reformers—especially Luther—are so anxious to hear God's positive and definitive verdict now that they anticipated the particular judgement and the definitive reception of eschatological benefits.[1] In the "direct and immediate access" manoeuvre, the reformers prematurely identified the world (the profane) with the sacred,[2] which resulted in an important shift in focus and attention in the life and spirituality of Christians.

The reformers, by anticipating eschatological redemption in faith, thus "leapt" over the gap between God and the human being. In this way, they ignored and put aside the elements of space and time, which governs

---

1 Cfr. HAMM, *Martin Luther's Revolutionary Theology of Pure Gift without Reciprocation*, 141-142, «At the time of his lectures on Romans (1515-1516), Luther had already broken with this catholic model of the road to heaven and its gradualism. For him, the moment of justification and the moment of acceptance of salvation no longer fall to pieces. Instead, they come together in a single moment, in that he fundamentally rejects the reigning thinking regarding gifts, conditions, and causality. He is now convinced that in justification the final acceptance of the sinner into eternal blessedness has already happened—an unconditional acceptance of human beings apart from any qualities or morality of their sanctified lives».
2 According to Taylor, «the two spheres collapsed into each other». TAYLOR, *A Secular Age*, 266.

the current relationship between God and humans in the timeframe between the Ascension and the Parousia. Consequently, they had to harmonise their experience of "direct and immediate access" in which they transcended time and space *in faith* with *the current empirical reality* in which space and time are not transcended in this definite way.³ They did so by adopting a framework where the spheres of faith and temporal-empirical reality are dialectically opposed to each other and always run merely as parallels, for this manoeuvre can only be conceived in such a framework. For what the reformers deemed impossible in temporal-empirical reality—redemption, certainty and holiness—becomes only possible in an act of (desperate) faith, which is diametrically opposed to our common experience in the temporal-empirical sphere. Calvin, although warning against the method of radical paradox, nonetheless, inherited this framework with these particular features.

The common priesthood understood as the believer's right and duty of direct access to God to hear the final verdict anywhere and anytime—or better, transcending time—provides a hermeneutical key to the whole of Reformation theology. The latter can be summarised by the reformers' effort to bring all revealed eschatological truths—like the radical equality of believers, final judgement, the promise of salvation and holiness—in line with the current experience of believers who are still on their way, while downplaying as much as possible the *reality* of the elements of space and time.⁴ Losing the *reality* of space and time out of sight results in a continuous tension and confusion in Reformation theology between the theological position of eschatological redemption ("we are already standing before the Lord") and being caught up by the empirical reality of our present condition as travellers on earth, where believers do not yet stand before the Lord in this definitive way ("we are not there yet"). Though this eschatological confusion is reflected in the whole of Reformation

---

3 It must be stressed that the crucial point here is not so much whether believers, while travelling in space and time, have access to God (cfr. Eph. 2:18), but the reformers claim that this access is direct, immediate and definitive.

4 For instance, Luther's doctrine of neighbour and the reformers' teaching on Christ's exclusive once-and-for-all sacrifice on the cross, seem to relate to the idea that humans don't give anything to God, but only receive. The idea of radical equality of all believers, which is fundamental in Reformed ecclesiology, is based on the "direct access" feature. The doctrine of *simul iustus et peccator* follows logically from Luther's position that a human being is redeemed, while standing before God's throne, firmly believing in Christ's gratuitous one-and-only sacrifice. Also, the problematic issue of human freedom in Reformation theology and Calvin's doctrine of double predestination appears to be linked to their theological position that believers "already stand before God's throne". Finally, in this framework, the priesthood runs the risk that its missionary aspect in the temporal-empirical sphere is lost out of sight.

theology, it becomes particularly manifest in the their understanding of common priesthood as direct and immediate eschatological access to God, which is not only an illustration and reflection of its eschatological confusion, but it is precisely the main cause of it.

3.2 Gnostic, situational and relational redemption and priesthood
Whereas Descartes with his famous formula *cogito, ergo sum*, sought to establish a firm basis—beyond any doubt—for true knowledge in subjective reason, Luther tried the same for the knowledge of his salvation in faith: "I believe, therefore, I am just (and priest)". By framing the issue of his salvation and priesthood in this way, the centre of gravity shifted, and the attention turned away from the underlying substance of the objective redemptive act, i.e., Christ's sacrifice, to the believer's act of faith, i.e., the subjective experience of being redeemed. Although Calvin put the focus on God's sovereign unilateral election and sanctification of the believer, and thus the believer's experience of being elected and admitted into God's favour, for both reformers redemption takes place pre-eminently in the interior mindset of the believer. Here he hears God's definitive Word directly and immediately, re-creating in him a new mind and heart *ex nihilo*.

3.2.1 Gnostic redemption
The nature of this redemption is private interior knowledge and has thus a gnostic character. The so-called external means of written Scripture and preaching by humans are merely instrumental since ultimately, it is the Holy Spirit who guarantees his own teachings to the individual believer. The reformers used—explicitly (Luther) or implicitly (Calvin)—as an epistemological tool to leap the gap and to obtain the privileged knowledge of one's eschatological salvation the method of radical paradox. To leap back, or better, forward towards "true spiritual reality", the reformers thought it necessary to frame redemption as a re-creation out of nothing by God's Word, and thus equating theology of creation with soteriology. Redemption and priesthood in Reformation theology is—and has to be by its very nature—a hidden and interior reality only known to God and "visible" for the faithful eyes of the individual believer.

3.2.2 Situational redemption
The reformers framework of redemption in a personal and direct encounter with the triune God led to a change of perspective from ontological to situational priesthood. For the reformers, the believers' experience of being redeemed or elected is realised, above all, in the event of their direct access to God the Father, in Christ, by the Holy Spirit. It is

in this spiritual and interior experience that believers learn directly and definitely from God the Father, in Christ, by the Holy Spirit that God is well pleased with them and that believers are freed, not from their sins, but from their concerns and worries about their eternal well-being despite their sins. It is also in this event that believers exercise, or rather experience, their priesthood; looking at Christ, believers *feel* that God the Father is pleased with them and is willing to accept their unworthy offerings, so they can "offer themselves and all that they have" to God the Father.

In the reformers, the centre of gravity and attention concerning the priesthood of believers shifted away from Baptism towards the event of direct access. The reformers seem to ground the redemption and priesthood of believers, ultimately not on the objective reality of Christ's incarnation, his priesthood and sacrifice, or in the believer's baptism—though they recognised all these realities and events as necessary conditions—but in last instance, they appear to be grounded in the event of their spiritual direct access to God, which is by definition, situational and experimental. Only in this particular experience, believers obtain their certainty and thus their yearned freedom—they feel God's favour and trust on God's mercy in Christ.

However, in this same experience of standing directly before a judging God, the reformers felt and experienced that their human sinful *reality as such* remained unaffected, and for this reason, they deemed themselves unworthy of identification with Christ in the temporal-empirical sphere. As a result, the reformers obtained in anticipation only a certain psychological certainty of their eschatological redemption. Thus, in the sphere of temporal-empirical reality, believers must recognise over and over again that they are *not* capable of offering themselves and their human temporal affairs to God. It appears that the reformers, to obtain spiritual relief, were, so to say, forced to let temporal-empirical reality go. The believers' priesthood in Reformation theology thus appears to be merely spiritual and interior; it happens foremost in the believers' mind and it seems to be at odds and in continuous tension with its exercise in the temporal-empirical sphere where only Christ exercises directly from heaven his true priesthood.

3.2.3 Relational redemption
This change of perspective from ontology to situational experience becomes also manifest in the fact that Luther regarded "justification" and "priesthood" as relations of the believer with God, which ultimately depend on the believer's faith. Luther had no problem in affirming that

"he who does not believe, is no priest".⁵ For him, believers *are* "just" and "priests" because God *considers* them as such, notwithstanding the continuing presence of sin in the their life, but without recognising that God's consideration—or grace—really affects the *relational being* of humans in the exterior sphere of earthly human experience—through Baptism humans really become children of God (Cfr. 1 John 3:1-2). For Luther, it seems that faith, righteousness, priesthood and divine filiation do not pertain to the being of humans, but that he regarded these realities as merely relational, changeable and unstable, at least on the part of the human being.⁶

Although Calvin tried to counterbalance the merely subjective act of faith by accentuating God's sovereign election and sanctification of believers, he does not seem to overcome the problem. In Calvin, God's election and grace do not really affect believers either—other than that it is supposed to give believers eschatological certainty—but God operates in parallel with them, the result of which (good works) is then attributed to believers as if it were theirs. For Calvin, the power of God thus really acts in and through humans, but it appears difficult for humans to express this reality of divine election and action in the temporal-empirical sphere in more objective terms.

3.3 Paradoxical anthropology

The event of direct access also determines the Reformed vision on anthropology, which could be qualified as paradoxical. On the one hand, Reformation theology has an extremely weak vertical anthropology (towards God), while at the same time, a strong horizontal anthropology (towards neighbour). In the relation towards God, humans are nothing and they can

---

5 This seems contradictory but is merely paradoxical. It is the perspective of the observer that changes. The believer is seen in two distinct perspectives of relation. If a human being looks at himself and contemplates his earthly situation through the eyes of the merciful God, who always grants forgiveness, the human being is just. If, on the other hand, the human being looks at himself just with his own eyes, without taking into account the merciful God, he sees his earthly situation, which is characterised by sin and wretchedness. These two perspectives of the relation between God and humans are really opposed to each other; they differ like day and night on earth (the same earth, but with or without light of the sun), but it only considers the subjective human side of the relationship between God and humans, and ignores the divine side.

6 Cfr. WA Tischr., n. 11, 1652, 3175, 3734, 4655. Cfr. WA 56: 442, «Man is always in non-being, in becoming to be, in being, always in privation, in potency, in actualising, always sinning, in justification, in justice, i.e., always a sinner, always penitent, always just (Semper homo Est in Non Esse, In Fieri, In esse, Semper in privatione, in potentia, in actu, Semper in peccato, in Iustificatione, In iustitia, i.e., Semper peccator, semper penitens, semper Iustus)». See also BRAVO, *El sacerdocio común en Lutero*, 307.

do nothing, but only receive. This is an essential part of the Reformed act of faith and a requirement for the believers' spiritual communion with Christ and direct access to God the Father. Luther explicitly held that Christ precisely in faith becomes present and taught the communion by a joyful exchange. However, his specific understanding of faith as mere humility seems to seriously hinder the believers' communion with Christ and their exercise of the priesthood in the temporal-earthly sphere.[7]

Furthermore, the weakness of humans towards God is enhanced in the event of direct access to God. Conceiving God's sovereignty in opposition to—and thus at the cost of minimising—the believers' role in their mutual relationship, necessarily resulted in the reformers' doctrine of direct access. As we have seen, the reformers minimised humans' role by situating sin at the heart of the human condition, making them corrupted in all their faculties. The reformers formally recognised that the human being is good in the temporal-earthly sphere, because the whole of creation with the human person at the top, was created by God, "who saw that everything was very good" (Gen. 1, 31). However, they also maintained that humans, due to their fall, practically lost their image of God and are, therefore, not capable by themselves of doing anything good.[8] This move led paradoxically to the doctrine of direct access, for only if each believer has direct access to God in Christ, he does not depend on any other (sinful) human being or any of his unstable human realities, such as the Church.

The sinful human condition is thus a *conditio sine qua non* for spiritual communion and direct access to God in Reformation theology. For this reason, it appears that for the reformers, God cannot heal human beings from their sins in the temporal-empirical sphere, since in that case, the

---

7 This might be one of the reasons that the claim of the so-called Finnish Luther school (Mannermaa, Saarinen, c.s.), who endeavours to show that Luther's insistence on "Christ present in faith" (*In ipsa fides Christus adest*) entailed a "real-ontic" indwelling of Christ in faith and unity between Christ and the believer (a real deification), encountered resistance and is regarded controversial among Lutherans, especially in continental Europe. Cfr. V-M KARKKAINEN, "*By the Washing of Regeneration and Renewal in the Holy Spirit*": *Towards a Pneumatological Theology of Justification*, 317, in: H. MARSHALL, V. RABENS, C. BENNEMA (eds.), *The Spirit and Christ in the New Testament and Christian Theology*, W. B. Eerdmans, Grand Rapids, Michigan/Cambridge 2012 (303-322) and also R. SAARINEN, *Justification by faith. The view of the Mannermaa School*, 255, in: R. KOLB, I. DINGEL, L. BATKA (eds.), *The Oxford Handbook of Martin Luther's Theology*, Oxford University Press, Oxford 2014, 254-264.

8 This implies that the reformers attributed—not formally, but materially—to humans the superhuman power to make human nature (their being and person) itself intrinsically corrupt, ruling out human freedom. Also, for this reason, they had to fall back on and invoke a proper act of divine re-creation *ex nihilo* to resolve the theological problem they had created.

believer would lose his direct access to God. This paradoxical line of reasoning only makes sense and can be understood properly in a framework which is based on a dialectical opposition between God and human beings, where the opposition and distance should always be maintained in the temporal-earthly sphere so that the gap which separates God from humans could be leapt merely spiritually.

The result—which is paradigmatic for the relationship between God and human beings in Reformation theology—is a combination of an intrinsic sinful human being who stands directly before God, who in turn pronounces his *final* judgement on the believer. This combination of theological views weakens Reformed vertical anthropology further, since in this setting and frame there is no room at all for real gradation and growth in holiness towards God, neither is there any room for human freedom or initiative, nor can the believer at the moment of particular judgement give anything (back) to God, other than his contrite heart.[9] Time has simply run out and space has vanished since God's judgement is regarded to be final—to obtain eschatological certainty—and diametrically opposed to our human experiences on earth; in faith, human sin becomes God's glory.

Instead, as we have hinted upon several times, the reformers took recourse to their strong theology of creation framing the "healing" of the believer in the spiritual sphere as a divine act of re-creation out of nothing and—at least for Luther, also explicitly out of its opposite—God recreates the minds and hearts of the believers and gives them completely new minds and hearts. This way of reasoning seems to confirm the impression of a dualistic view in Reformation theology. In this way, the reformers could maintain that God heals humans in the true spiritual, interior reality and gives freedom and certainty, while in the current empirical, external sphere believers remain complete sinners. In this latter sphere, believers are free to use the gifts of creation to serve their neighbour imitating Christ, thus forging a strong horizontal anthropology towards their neighbour. However, because salvation is so deeply hidden away in the interior mind and heart of believers *and* their contrary earthly experiences always remain sinful, human beings in the external-empirical

---

9 Though it seems that Luther's radical theology of gift implies that the believer in this situation cannot even give God a contrite heart but can only trust upon Christ's work and God's promise. Cfr. HAMM, *Martin Luther's Revolutionary Theology of Pure Gift without Reciprocation*, 142, «For the certainty of the salvation in faith can and must stand not on the inner dimensions of the human being, which are always unstable, under attack and unworthy of all God's gifts, in particular not upon so-called "true contrition" but upon the unassailable, unmistakable external dimension of the promise of forgiveness coming from the oral and written gospel and the sacraments».

sphere seem not worthy to be in communion with Christ. Yet here believers have to serve their neighbours in accordance with God's law.

3.4 Weak ecclesiology

The paradoxical move of diminishing the human role by granting believers everything directly and immediately, led to another paradoxical result. Instead of reinforcing the believers' relationship with God, it contributed to a weak ecclesiology. This weakened ecclesiology becomes manifest in the fact that each believer exercises priesthood, standing alone before God where he has to admit that he cannot be in communion with Christ in the temporal-empirical sphere. As a consequence of this position, believers are also hindered in mediating divine realities in the latter sphere to their neighbours.

3.4.1 No real communion in the intermediate time
The Church on earthly pilgrimage becomes merely a group of believers who jointly profess that Christ has done everything and that the believer, both individually as well as collectively, cannot do anything but trust in the salvation realised by Christ. The believers in the congregation are "sharers" and "joint owners" of all the goods it possesses merely in a spiritual and psychological way, while in the empirical-earthly sphere the goods are virtually present under the promise of salvation; the church is reduced to a congregation of people who firmly hold on to this promise in the future.

The congregation of believers appears, therefore, to be characterised by non-communion with God in the actual historical sphere. Due to the reformers' framework of conceiving communion with God in Christ in an exclusively internal and spiritual manner, they appear to have lost him in the reality of common life and experience. Thus, in Reformation theology, God operates in humans, but without really healing them and without their cooperation. On the supernatural plane, humans cannot do anything for each other. Even more, the essence of their faith seems to be that to be "justified" and to become "holy", they have to continuously recognise with an increasingly deeper awareness that they cannot do anything for their fellowmen in relation to God.

3.4.2 No human mediation of divine realities
Although the reformers intended to elevate and "spiritualise" ordinary lay Christians by giving all believers direct access to God in their normal lives in the world, at the same time, they "put" these Christians in the temporal-earthly sphere at a greater distance from God. Not only because the channels of sacramental grace were cut short, but above all, because

the world from now on has to be identified with the sacred, which eventually led to the latter's loss. This seems paradoxical, because, at first sight, it appears that God is brought nearer, for the Holy Spirit is supposed to *directly* dispense his grace and sanctify the people in the world; God would distribute grace equally to all believers in the world anywhere and anytime without intermediaries.[10] In reality, however, the Holy Spirit simply does not dispense his grace like this (cfr. Acts 2, 1 Cor. 12).

The eschatological confusion becomes manifest in the tension between the simultaneous dignity of humans and their sinful nature in the reformers' vision on human mediation of salvific grace. On the one hand, both reformers strongly emphasise the *true and only* mediation and priesthood of Christ, apparently leaving no room for human participation, but on the other hand, they paradoxically appear to extend mediation to all Christians, that is, all believers can and should teach, pray for one another, forgive sins and offer spiritual sacrifices by serving their fellowmen.

The challenge for the reformers was how to conceive that grace could be transmitted by a sinful human being (though deemed holy at the same time) in the temporal-earthly sphere to other humans. And their solution seems to be that believers *as sinners*—thus in the temporal-empirical sphere—do not mediate divine grace to others. They only "mediate" as far as they are redeemed or holy, i.e., in the spiritual sphere of interior faith where God is working directly in them. Humans, justified by faith or election, are worthy as recipients and possessors of grace but do not mediate the means of salvation (salvific grace) to other humans, for that is the sole prerogative of Christ. It is, therefore, always and only, God who directly acts in and through believers, who, being redeemed, elected and made holy, become a sign of salvation and holiness for other people. It is in this sense that Reformed Christians can be said to "mediate" between God and other human beings.

Whereas, the Catholic Church specifically upholds the doctrine of *ex opere operato*—so fiercely criticised by Luther—in order to safeguard and secure the sacramental presence of Christ in the Church and the

---

10 This theological position mixes up the reality of believers in *statu viae* with their eschatological destination since it ignores the fact that the profane and the sacred are only to be identified fully at the end of times. Until then there are no persons, places and times, which are intrinsically "sacred"; these realities are only "sacred" in as far as they are dedicated to God and have become signs of our encounter with him. Cfr. E. CASTELLUCCI, *Sacerdozio*, in: G. CALABRESE, P. GOYRET, O. PIAZZA (eds), *Dizionario di Ecclesiologia*, Città Nuova, Roma 2010, 1239.

distribution of grace by potential sinful humans to other human beings,[11] the reformers paradoxically—as a logical consequence of the doctrine of direct access—extended this kind of functional or instrumental mediation to all believers in all circumstances. Calvin explicitly held that "God makes humans his substitutes, who only do God's own work by their lips, as an artificer uses a tool for any purpose". And Luther, with respect to Baptism, maintained that it is Christ himself who acts through humans. Also, with regard to service and good works rendered to neighbours, it is God who directly performs in and through believers these services and good works. Consequently, the reformers attributed the same degree of certainty to grace distributed in the sacraments to all believers who exercise their profession in the world as a service and perform good works to their neighbour.[12]

3.5 Preliminary conclusion

In sum, the common priesthood understood as the event and experience of each believer having direct eschatological access to God in Christ shows a dualism in the believer's relationship with God. On the one hand, the spiritual sphere of experiences in faith where communion and the event of direct access take place in the interior mind and heart of the believer, and on the other hand, the temporal-empirical sphere where the believer seems to experience the contrary, where humans do not have to be, and cannot be, in communion with Christ. It appears that the reformers endeavoured to always maintain and foster this dualism.

By giving this kind of direct and immediate access to all, the earthly Church on a pilgrimage to heaven runs the risk of being without specific purpose and mission. Due to the position that God directly distributes grace equally to all believers, a principle which radically determines reformative ecclesiology, all human mediation of divine realities has become *functional* or *instrumental*. Human beings—since they in the temporal-empirical sphere always act on their own—do not play any *constitutive* role in the building up of the Church, for only Christ builds up the Church directly, i.e., using human beings but without them.

---

11 After all, this doctrine—in which faith is supposed—expresses the reality that in the liturgy certain acts have God Himself as subject, and not only the Church; Christ is acting through the ministerial priest (words and gestures) to render Himself present in the Church, a "power" which the priest does not have by himself, but a prerogative given to him by God due to his special configuration with Christ. Cfr. ccc no 1128.

12 Faith is supposed to be present in the believer. The issue of certainty of grace is being shifted to the question of certainty of faith in the case of Luther: how do I know that I really believe? And election in the case of Calvin: how do I know that I am really elected?

The reformers' framework of the relationship between God and humans does not only make the sacrifice obsolete ("we are already in heaven for free by only believing") but also intercessory prayer for others tend to become superfluous—after all, redemption is a personal act of faith in the promise to which no other human being can contribute. As a matter of fact, the whole issue of human mediation (sacrificing and intercessory prayer) becomes unnecessary, except for teaching and preaching, which is directly done by God instrumentally in and through believers, i.e., without them. Believers do serve their neighbours as Christ did for them, but this fraternal service seems to be seriously hindered if they must continuously acknowledge that they cannot be in communion with Christ in the temporal-earthly sphere.

4. Key elements of a catholic understanding and exercise of common priesthood

We have studied the notion and implications of common priesthood in Luther and Calvin, which is a horizontal priesthood exercised by each believer on earth in God's direct heavenly presence, without an essentially distinct ministerial priesthood, as maintained in Catholic theology. A study of the current Reformed and Evangelical positions on common priesthood falls without the scope of this book, but it is presupposed that the reformers' basic framework and lines of thought in the 16th century still stand today among many Evangelical and Reformed denominations, and can be found even among Catholics. In order to clarify the importance of the relationship between the common and ministerial priesthoods, this section presents some key elements of Catholic doctrine—especially since the Second Vatican Council[1]—that are relevant for a proper understanding and exercise of these two forms of participation in Christ's priesthood by believers in God's Church on earth.

The key elements to be discussed are, firstly, some epistemological and anthropological principles, followed by the importance of the intermediary space and time, the notion of the Church as a family-community and, finally, some issues related to the exercise of the double form of participation in Christ's priesthood by believers in the temporal-earthly sphere. The identified elements are not dealt with in an exhaustive or definitive way. However, these themes are relevant and could even open horizons in the ecumenical dialogue on a common understanding of a doctrine of the Church.

4.1 Some epistemological and anthropological principles

4.1.1 Open, inclusive and fruitful

As a matter of principle, God's revelation and his action in the world and humans' reception of divine realities should be regarded as positive, inclusive and fruitful.[2] From a Catholic perspective, the interior, spiritual sphere of faith and the external sphere of temporal-empirical experience are not supposed to be separated but are essentially open and ordained to

---

1 Cfr. LUTHERAN–ROMAN CATHOLIC COMMISSION, Report *From Conflict to Communion* (2013), no 90, «While the Council of Trent largely defined Catholic relations with Lutherans for several centuries, its legacy must now be viewed through the lens of the actions of the Second Vatican Council (1963-1965)».
2 Cfr. O'CALLAGHAN, *Luther and 'sola gratia'*, 195.

each other and are supposed to have a fruitful mutual relationship. The spiritual sphere, i.e., God's grace, can and should be allowed to penetrate the temporal-empirical sphere, so that humans and their human realities can be "attracted" by God and be "directed" towards God, by "purifying" them and "elevating" them to the divine life.[3]

4.1.2 Principle of continuity and unity
It is thus important to recognise—besides a certain discontinuity and transformation—a unity and continuity between creation, redemption, sanctification, and the final restoration so that we are always dealing with the same underlying reality, which is transformed into something new. Therefore, it is not necessary—as the reformers alleged—that God should totally renew the human mind and heart with an act of creation *ex nihilo*. God's redemptive and sanctifying work, as well as the mysterious renewal of the universe at the end of time, can be regarded as a new creation.[4] However, it should not be understood—like the reformers did, apparently to circumvent a communion between Christ and the believer in the temporal-empirical sphere—as a creation *ex nihilo*, which is the specific act of God's creation of the world out of nothing at the beginning of space and time.[5] The specific finality of the act of redemption and final restoration, however, is to make clean, purify, heal, support, and elevate the stained, wounded and fallen *existing* creation, and not to introduce a second perfect creation alongside the first corrupted creation.[6]

4.1.3 Moderate paradox
The epistemological principle that God manifests himself *always* in an opposite and contrary form to human understanding needs to be nuanced. Luther had a point when he put Christ's cross at the centre of his theology, for the Paschal Mystery illuminates all earthly existence in a most definite way. Luther was also right when he pointed out that it is rather difficult to grasp for the human mind that the cross is, in reality, an

---

3 FRANCIS, Encyclical letter *Lumen fidei*, 29.06.2013, no 15, «Christian faith is thus faith in a perfect love, in its decisive power, in its ability to transform the world and to unfold its history. "We know and believe the love that God has for us" (*1 Jn* 4:16). In the love of God revealed in Jesus, faith perceives the foundation on which all reality and its final destiny rest». Cfr. CCC no 1129.

4 *2 Pet.* 3:13; *Rev.* 21:1, «a new heaven and a new earth». See also VATICAN COUNCIL II, past. const. *Gaudium et Spes*, 7.12.1965, no 39 and FRANCIS, Encyclical letter *Lumen fidei*, 29.06.2013, nos 4; 19; 26.

5 Cfr. CCC no 296.

6 Cfr. *Ibidem*, no 1047.

act of love. There is certainly room for paradox in theology,[7] but as Calvin rightly alerted, this should not be a radical paradox in which all opposites can be simply exchanged by a mere subjective act of faith. God does challenge human pettiness and worldly standards to make room for another vision that transcends our mere human vision, but he does not continuously play a game of hiding in opposite forms to humble human intellect and to test our faith.[8] There should be both continuity and discontinuity between the old and new vision in faith of divine, earthly realities.

Luther's problem here—and not so much Calvin's—is reductionism, for God did not *exclusively* reveal himself in Christ on the cross, but rather his whole life—before and after his Resurrection—is a revelation of God and relevant to us.[9] By putting Christ's cross in the centre of his theology and leaving the rest of Christ's life in the background, Luther ran the risk of placing Christ's cross in a vacuum. For if God's way of reaching humans is limited to a radical paradoxical event on the cross, and humans can know God only "from the cross", how could human beings ever be drawn towards the cross? How can humans be convinced—against all their sin and tendency to pervert everything automatically into its opposite—that Christ's cross (and Resurrection) is actually a positive experience?

4.1.4 Christ's Incarnation as a positive and effective event
God does not show himself only in a dialectic way and contrary to human understanding.[10] The event of Christ's Incarnation should not be interpreted as an antagonism between God and humans, as if God became man just to "eliminate human realities" or to "unmask them as false", but rather to unite the divine and the human, purifying and elevating the latter, in order to incorporate it into the former—firstly, in his Person itself (the Incarnation), secondly, in his Person in relation to the world

---

7 Jesus made use of paradoxes, for example, Matt. 10:39, Mc. 9:35, 10:31, Luke 18:14 or 2 Cor. 12:10.
8 Cfr. CCC no 154, «Trusting in God and cleaving to the truths he has revealed is contrary neither to human freedom nor to human reason». A 20th-century spiritual author has put it as follows: «Let us marvel at the lovable paradox of our Christian condition: it is our own wretchedness which leads us to seek refuge in God, to become "like unto God". With him we can do all things». J.M ESCRIVÁ DE BALAGUER, *the Forge*, Scepter, London New York 1988, n. 212, 92.
9 Cfr. VATICAN COUNCIL II, dogm. const. *Dei Verbum*, 18.11.1965, no 4; Cfr. CCC. nos 606-607.
10 Besides a moderate paradox, Catholic theology employs the analogy to express and clarify the difference as well as the similarity between God and humans in Christ.

(Redemption), and thirdly, sacramentally, in his Person in the Eucharist.[11] The same holds true for the sanctifying action of the Holy Spirit in the world and in the believers. God's grace really affects believers and the supernatural does penetrate and interact with the natural sphere.[12]

This way of framing makes it possible to recognise that the whole life of Christ is relevant to us both in theory and practice. What is perhaps most striking about the earthly life of Jesus Christ is precisely the normality and the humanity of it—yet being God, at the same time divine—; his birth[13] and the thirty years before he started his public ministry, when he showed himself in an ordinary family life as a child.[14] In his public life, he also showed himself to his disciples—and through the Gospel to us as well—in his glorified state on Mount Tabor,[15] and after his death on the cross, his Resurrection and appearances to his disciples.[16] Jesus performed miracles, but he spent most of his earthly existence as a carpenter in relative anonymity.[17] All these events, which attempt to show *both* Christ's humanity *and* divinity are meaningful events for us today as well.[18]

The encyclical letter *Lumen fidei* frames the relation between faith in Christ and our human reality and experiences as follows:

«To enable us to know, accept and follow him, the Son of God took on our flesh. In this way, he also saw the Father humanly, within the setting of a journey unfolding in time. Christian faith is faith in the incarnation of the Word and his bodily resurrection; it is faith in a God who is so close to us that he entered our human history. Far from divorcing us from reality, our faith in the Son of God made man in Jesus of Nazareth enables us to grasp reality's deepest meaning and to see how much God loves this world and is constantly guiding it towards himself. This leads us, as Christians, to live our lives in this world with ever greater commitment and intensity».[19]

---

11 Cfr. CCC no 460.
12 Cfr. *Ibidem*, no 702; «(…), the joint mission of the Father's Word and Spirit remains *hidden*, but it is at work». See also nos 1092 and 1104.
13 It is true, as Luther asserted that also Christ's Incarnation, as the Creator that has become a human being, is a paradoxical event. Cfr. LW 5:218-224 and ALTHAUS, *The Theology of Martin Luther*, 179. However, this event should be interpreted as a successful attempt to bridge the gap between God and humans in the temporal-empirical sphere, and not as a mere manifestation of the gap or the human inability to cross it.
14 Cfr. Luke 2:51.
15 Cfr. Math. 17:2, Marc. 9:2-7 and Luke. 9:29.
16 Cfr. Marc. 16:9-14 and Jn. 21:2 and 21:14, Acts 1:3.
17 Cfr. Math. 13:55.
18 Cfr. CCC nos 516-518.
19 FRANCIS, Encyclical letter *Lumen fidei*, 29.06.2013, no 18.

4.1.5 God respects and assists humans

As a matter of principle, it should be duly recognised that humans are *capax Dei*, i.e., capable of knowing God by creation and revelation and responding to him positively with their whole being—reason, will and heart—because God *gave* this capacity *to* them.[20] God wants to be discovered by humans, without imposing and forcing himself upon them. In this regard, it is of utmost importance to affirm that i) morality is situated on the level of human actions and not on the ontological level of their being, ii) humans are free beings capable of giving meaningful responses to God, and that iii) sin weakens human freedom but does not annul it.

i) The level of morality

The Reformed approach and line of reasoning in which the external, earthly sphere of human experiences as such appears to be equated with sin and wretchedness should be reconsidered. Morality is situated at the level of the *qualitas* of the human acting. Sin and virtue are a (dis)quality or (dis)value of human acts and not ontological categories of the human being itself.[21] This becomes plainly clear if we consider that the morally wrongful act (sin) has an opposite, the morally virtuous act, and admits gradations—a human act can be morally better or worse. If sin were an ontological category of the human being itself, the opposite would be impossible, nor would be any gradations.[22] In fact, the opposite of "being" would be the logical concept of "non-being", since one can not speak of "more or less being".

The Reformed line of reasoning implies a complete identification of the person (his being) with his actions. In such a case, human "contrition" or "conversion"—a radical or small change of life—seems to become impossible, because such human attitude always requires taking a distance from one's own actions.[23] Though there obviously exists a very close mutual relationship between the person and his acts—a person who

---

20 CCC no 52, «God, who "dwells in unapproachable light", wants to communicate his own divine life to the men he freely created, to adopt them as his sons in his only-begotten Son (1 Tim. 6:16; cfr. Eph. 1:4-5). By revealing himself God wishes to make them capable of responding to him, and knowing him, and of loving him far beyond their natural capacity».

21 On ontological qualitative values see D. VON HILDEBRAND, *Christian Ethics*, D. McKay Company, New York 1953, 129-139.

22 *Ibidem*, 135-136.

23 As a matter of fact, Reformation theology does not recognise the possibility of true human contrition. For this reason, both reformers took the position that this cannot be asked and required of humans since contrition is only unilaterally given to them by God. Cfr. hamm, *Martin Luther's Revolutionary Theology of Pure Gift without Reciprocation*, 142.

commits sins becomes a sinner—it would be erroneous to completely identify them. Hence, it should be possible to distinguish the person from his actions, without separating them.

ii) Man can give meaningful responses to God
Humans are created as free beings, who have been granted their own autonomy, which is proper to that of a redeemed creature. This is not an absolute, but relative autonomy, though a *real* one and it consists in the capacity, with their whole being (mind, will, heart, soul and body), to take their own meaningful stances towards God and others: veneration, faith,[24] (dis)obedience, love, hate, joy, contrition,[25] forgiveness, hope, gratitude, a moral choice (sin or good works), etc. These human responses to God and neighbour are only possible and meaningful if humans are really free beings with their own relative autonomy.[26] The granting of this human autonomy to be exercised in the intermediary time and space is not at odds with God's sovereignty and majesty, but rather a manifestation of it.[27]

iii) Freedom and sin
The fall of humans did not affect them in their being, their human nature as such, but in the quality and harmony of their relationship with God, others and the world. Humans chose freely to turn away from God from being "friends" to "enemies" and to live their lives, i.e., to be and act, without God.[28] Fortunately, humans do not have the capacity to make their own person, nature and being, "intrinsically" corrupt in the same way that they cannot undo their creaturely status. Humans can ignore, refuse or abuse the gifts of creation and redemption, but they cannot undo them, nor can they make them intrinsically corrupt.

The main theme of Christian freedom is thus the capacity of believers to choose God with their whole being. The exercise of their freedom is damaged and influenced by sin, which turns them into slaves, but the

---

24 Cfr. CCC no 1102.
25 Contrition is both a grace of God *and* an adequate human response to his own faults and sins involving his intellect, will and—above all—his heart. Cfr. D. VON HILDEBRAND, *Fundamental Moral Attitudes*, trans. A. M. Jourdain, Longmans, Green and Co., New York 1950, 26.
26 Cfr. GS 17.
27 Only in a framework where God and humans are considered dialectically opposed to each other, the granting of real autonomy to humans would be regarded as problematic with respect to God's autonomy.
28 Cfr. CCC nos 398-400.

capacity to return to God is not annulled by it.[29] Sin is thus a weakening of the capacity to respond adequately to God. Christ did not only restore the human being's broken relationship with God, but he also reinforced it, since «we already glory in the "liberty of the children of God"».[30] God "attracts" and "draws" humans patiently, always respecting their autonomy.[31] This interaction between God and humans is a great and wonderful mystery of Christian life.

4.2 The intermediary time and space
The project of the reformers shows, above all, the utmost importance of respecting the intermediary space and time. By their claim that each believer has direct and immediate access to God and thus anticipating eschatological realities, the reformers gave a preview of the greatness of what has yet to come, and in a certain way is already present in the Church. In this preview, they opened a great horizon for Christians by pointing out that all Christians are priests, who can and should follow and imitate Christ in the midst of the world by offering all their daily activities to God. However, due to lack of patience and ignoring the *reality* of the elements of space and time, which give perspective and relief to the Christian life, the reformers—especially Luther, but Calvin as well[32]—overlooked or downplayed the role of Christians on earth, who are living in the intermediary time and space, and in particular, their role of mediating the means of salvation by participating in Christ's redemptive sacrifice and their task of perfecting the world in Christ and to bring it back to God.[33]

4.2.1 God's salvific plan
The congenial tension between God (the sacred) and the world (the profane) is part of our human, earthly situation. This follows from the fact that God is holy, while the world has not yet arrived at that blessed state, but still has to become holy. In order to achieve this, God has designed and put into action his salvific plan, according to divine pedagogy and didactics.[34] Key points of this divine plan of reconciliation

---

29 Cfr. *Ibidem*, nos 1730; 1739.
30 Cfr. Rom. 8:21; CCC no 1741.
31 Cfr. *Ibidem*, no 160; 1742; John 12:32.
32 Although Calvin acknowledged gradual stages in the process of holiness and stressed frequently the fact that believers are pilgrims on their way to heaven, yet he attributed the gradual stages in their sanctification unilaterally to God and he did not give full content and meaning to the role which they are supposed to have in God's salvific plan.
33 Cfr. GS 58 (4).
34 Cfr. CCC no 53; St. IRENAEUS, *Adv. haeres.* 3, 20, 2: PG 7/1, 944.

are the Incarnation, the Paschal Mystery, the Ascension, Pentecost and the Church. God carries out his salvific plan both *outside*—transcending space and time—since it has an eternal origin and destiny, as well as *in* space and time, for the object of salvation and union is the created world, which also consists of free subjects. God, somehow—both acting from outside and from within the subject—invites all people to freely unite to, and to participate in, the Paschal Mystery in order to give glory to God.[35]

4.2.2 Already, but not yet

Christ has anticipated the eschatological event by his Incarnation, his whole earthly life culminating in the Paschal Mystery, Resurrection and Ascension into heaven. In this way, Christ has reconciled heaven and earth[36] and radically eliminated the distinction between the sacred and the profane. This means that in Christ, i.e., those who are in Christ, all human activities can be sanctified and can become a meeting point of heaven and earth. In Christ, and through the Holy Spirit, God the Father can be praised everywhere on earth (cfr. John 4:23). However great this truth may be and crucial with respect to the exercise of common priesthood, this elimination of the distinction between sacred and profane does not apply automatically, as it were, by divine decree, because humans are free and autonomous beings in space and time. The congenial tension between the sacred and the profane—although the two in principle have been reconciled in Christ and are, therefore, no longer a dichotomy—remains present until the definitive realisation of God's plan by the mysterious renewal of humanity and the world at the end of times.[37]

4.2.3 Layered structure

The intermediate time and space are characterised by a wonderfully "layered" structure, according to God's pedagogy and corresponding to human nature and being, in which the Christian life unfolds. This layered structure becomes manifest in creation,[38] the stages of revelation[39] and the economy of redemption and salvation.[40] This frame allows for real gradual stages and growth in the process of sanctification in the temporal-

---

35 Cfr. VATICAN COUNCIL II, Const. *Sacrosanctum Concilium*, 4.12.1963, 5.
36 Cfr. Isa 45:8; Ps 85:12.
37 Cfr. GS 39; CCC no 1042-1043; J. MARTÍN GÓMEZ, *Sacerdocio común-sacerdocio ministerial*, Instituto Superior de Estudios Teológicos San Ildefonso, Toledo 2008, 13-15; ESCRIVÁ DE BALAGUER, *Christ is passing by*, Four Courts Scepter, Dublin 1982, no 112, 154.
38 Cfr. CCC. nos 342-343.
39 Cfr. *Ibidem*, no 54-65.
40 Cfr. SC 2; CCC. nos 759; 874 ss; 1324.

empirical sphere. Thus, although God can and should be praised by humans everywhere on earth, the privileged place to worship and to encounter God are church buildings, which are especially dedicated to God and humans for this purpose.[41] Other elements of this layered structure are the liturgy[42] and consecrated persons.[43] In order for the profane to become sacred, certain places, times and persons are "separated" from the world in order to be "consecrated" (ordained to God in a special way), and then, "put back" at the service of God in the world,[44] in view of the mission to bring back the world to God and to sanctify the profane by dedicating it to God. This dedication is performed in the liturgy and daily life and has both an interior aspect (acts of will, intellect and heart) as well as an exterior aspect (the offering to God through words and actions).

4.2.4 The access to God
The claim that each believer has spiritual, direct access before God's throne should be nuanced, simply because believers in *statu viae* do not yet stand before God's throne in the sense the reformers proposed, i.e., to hear God's definitive verdict about one's eschatological destiny. The current relationship between God and humans is characterised by the elements of space and time, where humans still have a real role to play. Believers do have access to God in prayer[45] and the sacraments, but this access is not *per se* direct and not yet definitive.[46]

In the time-lapse between Ascension and the Parousia, i.e., the "time of the image", Christ becomes present in various ways: the Word, prayer, life of the saints, our neighbour—especially in the poor—and the Liturgy, most eminently in the Eucharist, which is Christ's eternal sacrifice (self-giving) to the Father and to humans[47]. This new phase of the history of

---

41 Cfr. CCC no 2691.
42 SC 2, «For the liturgy (…) is the outstanding means whereby the faithful may express in their lives and manifest to others the mysteries of Christ and the real nature of the Church».
43 Cfr. CCC. no 917.
44 This "putting back" is not always a physical "putting back". Nonetheless, the different vocations in the Church are to be considered an enrichment of the community where everyone is called—each one in his own way—to serve God and neighbour. Consecrated persons do not stand above or outside the community but form an integral part of it. Cfr. CCC no 814.
45 CCC no 2565, «(…) Thus, the life of prayer is the habit of being in the presence of the thrice-holy God and in communion with him». See also nos 2609 and 2781.
46 Cfr. *Ibidem*, no 1026.
47 Cfr. LG 48; SC 7; CCC no 1373.

salvation is called "the sacramental economy".⁴⁸ The modality of presence of Christ is characterised not by an "immediate" or "direct" contact with him, like the historical experience of the Apostles who could touch Christ, but by a "mediate" contact through his ecclesial Body, which are concrete persons and in an eminent way the Eucharist, where Christ by the Holy Spirit "comes down" in order to "take the believer up".

The sacramental economy makes possible the mysterious communion between God and humans. It guarantees that God can remain God, the omnipotent Creator and totally transcendent Being, and yet at the same time can enter into our world, becoming part of our reality in space and time, offering himself to humans to give them the opportunity to give themselves and their realities with and in Christ to the Father by the Holy Spirit. In this way, a full communion between God and humans is established while God remains God and humans remain human, yet in a mysterious communion with each other, so that they in the temporal-earthly sphere already participate in divine life, so that it can be said that in the heart of a person in grace lives the Holy Trinity (cfr. Jn. 14:32; Eph. 3:17).

4.3 A family community

For a proper understanding and exercise of any form of priesthood of believers, it is of utmost importance to grasp the nature of the communion between God and the believer. In what way are believers identical to Christ so that they can be said to be *in Christ* and participate meaningfully in his priesthood? It is far from easy to grasp the precise nature of the relationship and communion between God and humans.⁴⁹ According to the Council document on the Constitution of the Church, *Lumen Gentium*, the Church is the mysterious community of the triune God and humans.⁵⁰ The Council Fathers recognised that the Church forms a complex reality, since in it coalesces both divine and human elements. It developes both inside time *and* transcends time, connecting heaven *and* earth ("already there, but not yet"). It is both visible *and* invisible, stable *and* dynamic, equal *and* diverse, hierarchical *and* charismatic.⁵¹ Furthermore, the letter *Communionis Notio* of the Congregation of the

---

48 Cfr. CCC nos 1076–1109.
49 For example, I refer to the ongoing debate by Lutheran theologians on the nature of the spiritual communion and the presence of Christ by faith as proposed by the earlier mentioned Finnish Luther School (Mannermaa). But the exact nature of the Church is also a hotly debated issue among Catholic theologians.
50 Cfr. LG 2; CCC no 760.
51 Cfr. LG 4; 8.

Doctrine of the Faith, indicates that «the concept of communion is very suitable for expressing the core of the Mystery of the Church, and can certainly be a key for the renewal of Catholic ecclesiology».[52] Though complex as it may be, it might be argued that as conditions for a meaningful understanding and exercise of common priesthood by believers, there should be between God and humans, at least, i) a real spiritual communion, ii) a stable community and iii) a dynamic communication with mutual giving and receiving.

4.3.1 Real spiritual communion
For (com)union between God and humans, it should be duly recognised that the communion and identification between Christ and the believer is both a spiritual identification *and* a real one.[53] As stated ealier, the temporal-empirical sphere of our common experiences and the spiritual sphere of our experiences of faith do not run parallel to—and are not supposed to be separated from—each other but are essentially ordained and open to each other. The spiritual, more specifically the Holy Spirit, penetrates the temporal-empirical sphere to elevate it so that the same reality of our common experiences becomes spiritual, while at the same time remaining in and part of the temporal-earthly sphere. That God's action in the world is effective implies and requires—due to the very nature of God and humans—that God's action in the world is in part hidden *and* in part visible, external to humans and experienced already in this temporal-empirical sphere.[54] Christ's Incarnation and humanity teach us that for humans to become divine, we have to be very human.[55] The spiritual identification with Christ in faith is a *conditio sine qua non* for communion with Christ on earth, but it is seriously impeded when it is understood as a parallel experience, or—even worse—in opposition to

---

52 CONGREGATION FOR THE DOCTRINE OF THE FAITH, Letter *Communionis Notio*, 28.5.1992, no 1.
53 Cfr. H.U. VON BALTHASAR, *Karl Barth: Darstellung Und Deutung Seiner Theologie*, Hegner, Köln, 1962, 396.
54 Cfr. CN 4: «Ecclesial communion is at the same time both invisible and visible. As an invisible reality, it is the communion of each human being with the Father through Christ in the Holy Spirit, and with the others who are fellow sharers in the divine nature, in the passion of Christ, in the same faith, in the same spirit. In the Church on earth, there is an intimate relationship between this invisible communion and the visible communion in the teaching of the Apostles, in the sacraments and in the hierarchical order. By means of these divine gifts, which are very visible realities, Christ carries out in different ways in history his prophetical, priestly and kingly *function* for the salvation of mankind (LG 25-27). This link between the invisible and visible elements of ecclesial communion constitutes the Church as the *Sacrament* of salvation».
55 Cfr. ESCRIVÁ DE BALAGUER, *Christ is passing by*, no 109, 152.

an earthly-temporal identification. In such a case, spiritual identification would obviously not be sufficient to make the believer's identification with Christ, and thus his communion with God, complete. God's grace effectually changes the relationship with humans in the temporal-empirical sphere, and not merely and exclusively in the believer's head by a subjective act of faith in a paradoxical divine act of recreation *ex nihilo*.[56] To put it differently, if God *considers* a human being just, then that human being *is* just, albeit still *in statu viae* in the temporal-earthly sphere. The same holds true for the priesthood and divine filiation.

4.3.2 Stable community
Fortunately, the communion between God and humans does not only depend on the believer's interior experience—which according to the reformers themselves is always unstable and under attack—but also requires a stable external structure, which has God as author and origin.[57] The Scripture, in revealing the inner nature of the Church, represents and describes the Church through various complementary images (sheepfold, flock, vineyard, building, temple), none of which completely exhausts its essence.[58] St. Peter refers to the believers and their priesthood as "living stones" who form part of a "spiritual building" (cfr. 1 Pet. 2: 4-5). St. Paul connects the common priesthood with the image of Christ's Body, using as analogy the human body to explain that although the Church forms as one body in Christ, yet the members receive different spiritual gifts and functions to cooperate organically with each other (cfr. Rom. 12). In *Presbyterorum Ordinis*, the Council Fathers related the priesthood common to all believers to the image of the Church as the People of God.[59]

In any case, the Church is not only the Body of Christ or the People of God, but also God's family.[60] The image of the Church as the family of God may shed some light on various dimensions of the mutual relationship between God and the believers as well as within the community of believers. These dimensions are in particular relevant for a correct

---

56 Calvin, although he put all the emphasis on God's election to redemption and regeneration, reasoned in the same line.
57 Cfr. CCC no 765.
58 Cfr. LG 6; CALABRESE, *Comunione*, in: G. CALABRESE, P. GOYRET, O. PIAZZA (eds), *Dizionario di Ecclesiologia*, Città Nuova, Roma 2010, 283.
59 VATICAN COUNCIL II, Decree *Presbyterorum Ordinis*, 7.12.1965, no 2, «All belonging to this people [the People of God], since they have been sanctified by the Holy Spirit, can offer themselves as a "sacrifice, living, holy, pleasing to God" (Rom 12:1)».
60 Cfr. Mt. 12:49; Rom. 8:14-16; 1. Cor. 4:15, Gal. 3:26; Eph. 1:5; JOHN PAUL II, Apostolic Exhortation *Familiaris Consortio*, 21.11.1981, no 15; CCC nos 764; 1655.

hermeneutics and exercise of the common priesthood: the ontology of relations and the basis of the equality and hierarchy among the believers. In order to understand properly these dimensions, it is worthwhile to analyse the metaphysical structure of the community of believers with God, that is, the Church as family.[61]

i) Ontology of relations
Humans are relational beings. Their essence and identity is based on, and shaped by, their relationships with God, other human beings and the world.[62] This network of communitarian and interpersonal relationships provides the framework in which human lives and existences unfold.[63] Following the logic of the layered structure, there exists a hierarchy of relationships with different levels (ontological, existential, psychological) depending on the subject, the object and the content of these relationships.[64]

Some relations, like the primordial relation between God the Creator, and humans as his creatures, are given and belong to the constitution of the human being. They determine the identity and essence of the person in a certain definite way. This metaphysical bond between the Creator and his creature cannot be undone. It forms the basis for all other relationships: being creature, man, woman, father, mother, child, Christian, priest, friend, citizen, worker, owner, etc. All these qualitative relations are a determination of humans and their existence in a particular way. These specific determinations depend on humans in various ways and degrees. An exhaustive analysis is beyond the scope of this book, but here it suffices to note that not all qualitative relations are situated on the same level and do not possess the same rank in the hierarchy of relationships, like relations of friendship, work (employer-employee) or to one's property (ownership). These relations, though important, do not determine the identity of the person in an essential way, but more superficially.

The initial—or progressive—identification of humans with God in Christ happens through Baptism, which has a twofold effect. By Baptism, a human being becomes a Christian—a redeemed creature—who is not only restored in the initial friendship with God, but also become part of

---

[61] For a general philosophical account of the metaphysics of community I refer to the work of VON HILDEBRAND, *Gesammelte Werke IV, Metaphysik der Gemeinschaft, Untersuchungen über Wesen und Wert der Gemeinschaft*, Verlag Josef Habbel Regensburg, 1975. Von Hildebrand deals with the Church as the Body of Christ and not from the perspective of family of God (p. 287-294).
[62] Cfr. *Lumen fidei*, nos 38-39.
[63] Cfr. *Ibidem*, no 40.
[64] According to St. Augustine there exists a hierarchical order of love, the *Ordo Amoris*. Cfr. *De Civitate Dei*, XV, 22.

God's family, the Church.⁶⁵ In fact, Christ, the Son of God, by becoming human himself has raised human nature to a divine level and—by the very fact of his Incarnation—has united himself in some fashion with every human being.⁶⁶ By his Incarnation—and the human response by Baptism—Christ has elevated the human being from the status of creature and raised him to a higher level of relation: being a child of God (divine filiation). This identification is an ontological configuration in man's relationship with God. Thus, it is not a change in "the human being as such", but an essential change in the relationship between God and humans; from fallen creatures to redeemed creatures and children of God.⁶⁷ A baptised person belongs to God the Father in Christ by the Holy Spirit and is "consecrated" and "ordained" to God in a unique way,⁶⁸ though this communion can have various degrees of perfection.⁶⁹

ii) The family structure
As requirements for a stable communion as family, there should be both radical equality between the subjects as well as an essential difference. This equality and difference are shown in the relationship *between God and humans* as well as in the mutual relationship *between believers in statu viae*, i.e., the earthly Church. The equality and difference are given in Christ. God, in Jesus, Son of God, became human, took our nature and became one of us, our brother, equal in everything, except for sin.⁷⁰ The event of Christ's Incarnation is the basis of a radical equality between God and humans and makes a real and stable communion between God and humans possible even in the temporal-empirical sphere.⁷¹ The essential difference is given in the fact that Christ is God, the Second Person of the Trinity.

Baptism thus establishes a stable community between Christ and human beings, which has an objective structure with horizontal and

---

65 Cfr. CCC no 1267; See also VATICAN COUNCIL II, Decree on ecumenism *Unitatis Redintegratio*, 21.11.1964, no 2, «It is thus, under the action of the Holy Spirit, that Christ wills his people to increase, and he perfects his people's fellowship in unity: in their confessing the one faith, celebrating divine worship in common and keeping the fraternal harmony of the family of God».
66 Cfr. GS 22(2).
67 *Lumen fidei*, no 42: «Christ's work penetrates the depths of our being and transforms us radically, making us adopted children of God and sharers in the divine nature. It thus modifies all our relationships, our place in this world and in the universe, and opens them to God's own life of communion».
68 Cfr. CCC no 1269.
69 Cfr. LG 14; UR 3.
70 Cfr. CCC no 469.
71 Cfr. *Ibidem*, no 460.

vertical dimensions.⁷² The horizontal dimension includes relations between humans, for all Christians are children of God—in Christ and by the Holy Spirit—and the vertical includes relations between humans and God, who is our Father. However, the ecclesial community, with its interpersonal family relations, is richer than this. After all, the vertical relationship between humans and God has a horizontal dimension in Christ (brotherhood), while at the same time, the horizontal relationships between believers have vertical dimensions in Christ as well (representing the Father as pastor, teacher and priest). Thus, between God and humans there exists both a radical equality and an essential difference in Christ. This also holds true for the mutual relations between Christians, which are not merely horizontal, but have at the same time a vertical dimension, for God has structured the (visible) community of humans and God, the Church, also as a family.

In other words, the radical equality of believers[73] is not situated in the common priesthood—or in an experience of direct and immediate access to God—but is primarily situated at a deeper level of relationship—that of divine filiation. All Christians, through Baptism, belong to God's family and are equally adopted children of God the Father, in Christ, the Son, by the Holy Spirit.[74] Christ, being the only begotten Son of God, Christians are then referred to as "sons in the Son".[75] Only in second place, also based on their configuration with Christ through Baptism—and Confirmation—Christians participate and share in the prophetical, priestly and royal functions of Christ within the community.[76] This participation is equal in the sense that all Christians enjoy the priestly privilege of offering themselves and all their human activities in Christ by the Holy Spirit to the Father. Moreover, by being in communion with Christ in their daily activities, all Christians bring God to the world and to other humans,

---

72 Cfr. CN 3.
73 CCC no 872 (CIC, can. 208; cfr. LG 32): «In virtue of their rebirth in Christ there exist among all the Christian faithful a true equality with regard to the dignity and the activity whereby all cooperate in the building up of the Body of Christ in accord with each one's own condition and function».
74 Cfr. *Ibidem*, nos 1265; 1267.
75 Cfr. GS 22; Rom. 8:15; Gal. 4:6 and 1 John 3: 1-2.
76 CCC no 871 (CIC, can. 204, §1; cfr. LG 31): «The Christian faithful are those who, inasmuch as they have been incorporated in Christ through Baptism, have been constituted as the people of God; for this reason, since they have become sharers in Christ's priestly, prophetic, and royal office in their own manner, they are called to exercise the mission which God has entrusted to the Church and fulfil in the world, in accord with the condition proper to each one». Cfr. CCC no 1268; A. ARANDA LOMEÑA, *El sacerdocio de Jesucristo en los ministros y en los fieles. Estudio teológico sobre la distinción «essentia et non gradu tantum»*, «Scripta Theologica» 22 (1990/2), 403.

where they are his witnesses and co-operators, each in one's own state and activities, which are equally valuable in the eyes of God.

At the same time, the ministerial priest participates within God's family also in an essentially different way in the priesthood of Christ. Without ceasing to be and to exercise the common priesthood, he has been chosen and constituted by God within the community to represent Christ sacramentally to build up God's family on earth. To understand its structure better, we could draw an analogy, *mutatis mutandis*, with a human natural family. Woman and man, equal in dignity as human beings, yet essentially distinct in their women- and manhood, united by marriage in an indissoluble and exclusive bond, participating in God's creative power, become father and mother of their child.[77] Their parenthood presupposes their humanity and does not imply that they cease to be children themselves. The horizontal relation of equality between spouses creates a vertical one, that between father/mother and son/daughter. Parents and their children are equal in their humanity and divine filiation, yet essentially different in their mutual relationships (woman–, manhood and filiation). To be fruitful, it is necessary that there is *both* a radical equality *and* an essential complementary difference between the spouses.[78] By analogy, the same holds true for the spiritual fruitfulness of the ecclesial community, i.e., common and ministerial priests are *both* radically equal in their filiation, while *at the same time* essentially distinct in their relationship with God.[79]

In Catholic theology, nobody is considered owner of grace and no believer can distribute grace to himself,[80] as nobody is owner of life or is able to transmit life to others just by oneself. At the same time, each Christian has an absolute necessity of receiving God's grace. The sacramental economy—which always presupposes a context of faith in the Trinitarian God, his grace, and humility on the part of the believer—is precisely the expression of the fact that grace comes to the believer from outside of him, from God, but through other believers.[81] This, of

---

[77] Cfr. Gen. 1:27; CCC n. 369-371 and GS 12(4), stating: «Their companionship produces the primary form of interpersonal communion».

[78] Cfr. CCC no 372.

[79] Cfr. LG 10.

[80] The requirement of apostolic succession (cfr. Jn. 20: 21-32; CCC no 1087) should also be seen in this context.

[81] *Lumen fidei*, no 41: «Those who are baptized are set in a new context, entrusted to a new environment, a new and shared way of acting, in the Church. Baptism makes us see, then, that faith is not the achievement of isolated individuals; it is not an act which someone can perform on his own, but rather something which must be received by entering into the ecclesial communion which transmits God's gift. No one baptizes

course, does not exclude the possibility that God operates directly in the believer without cooperation of other believers. However, it does provide certain sacramental channels of "guaranteed" grace—even if administered by sinful men—to the faithful in order to sanctify God's family. This enables them to become holy and to "distribute" God's grace in their daily lives and occupations, where they become effective witnesses of Christ to the world and his co-operators to bring the world back to God.

4.3.3 Dynamic communication
The Church is thus a stable community with an objective structure, but is also called to a more intense union and communion with Christ and each other. Community, communion and communication are not only divine gifts but also tasks.[82] To understand properly the dynamic character of humans' communion with God at the existential level, it is worthwhile to consider the following three aspects: i) a human being's real capability to cooperate with God, ii) God's respect of human freedom, and iii) the path of spiritual growth.

i) Real human cooperation
Real communication between God and humans presupposes not only that God gives himself to humans in the temporal-earthly sphere, but also that humans are capable of really giving "something of their own" to God, albeit something which was given to them by God first.[83] Humans have received all of God gratuitously in creation, including their own being, as well as the fruits of redemption. In this sense, believers do not have any merit.[84] They do not "produce" creation, nor the fruits of redemption, but receive all freely from God as redeemed creatures to administer, cultivate, restore and transmit the fruits and communicate them freely to others in the temporal-empirical sphere. This is real human cooperation with God on the supernatural plane, which cooperation *itself* is also an unmerited gift to humans through God's grace.[85]

ii) God's respect for human freedom
God for his part does all he can to help humans, while at the same time,

---

himself, just as no one comes into the world by himself. Baptism is something we receive».
82 Cfr. CCC no 820.
83 Cfr. *Ibidem*, no 1333.
84 *Ibidem*, no 2007, «With regard to God, there is no strict merit on the part of man. Between God and us there is an immeasurable inequality, for we have received everything from Him, our Creator».
85 Cfr. CCC nos 2008-2009.

he always respects the current status of believers travelling in space and time towards the meeting from face-to-face. God has "committed himself" to help humans (their salvation and sanctification) and does not abandon them halfway. God «desires all men to be saved and come to the knowledge of the truth» (1 Tim. 2:4). For this reason, believers may assume that God does everything possible to assist humans—the Incarnation, the Paschal Mystery and Ascension of Christ, Mary as mother of God and mother of all Christians, the Church, grace, the assistance of the Angels, the example and intercession of the saints, etc., are all manifestations of God's good intentions with humans.

At the same time, it should be duly recognised that God always respects his own creation—God's Incarnation itself is a superb manifestation that God takes seriously and respects it—and wants humans to freely choose to be in (a fuller) communion with him. God has thus created humans in his own image, as free beings, capable of choosing for him—obviously always presupposing God's grace—[86] to cooperate with him in the temporal-empirical sphere. God always acts in such a way that he does not force himself upon humans (cfr. Luke 24:28). Christ shows himself and is present in the Eucharist under a veil[87] and the Holy Spirit teaches humans divine realities in such a way that they can ignore these teaching or prove to be slow learners (cfr. Luke 24:25). There is a limit on human freedom as well; humans can never undo their metaphysical condition of being God's creature. In this sense, humans will always be bound to their Creator, who through Christ and by the Holy Spirit always invites humans to (a fuller) communion with him.[88]

iii) The path of spiritual and real growth
This frame of dynamic communion and its sacramental nature makes it possible to grasp the fact that sanctification is a spiritual and gradual process within the temporal-earthly sphere. In this sphere not only God, but also humans—endowed with intellect, will and heart—play a decisive role, not because they are so good "by themselves", but because God has

---

86 Cfr. *Ibidem*, nos 1730; 1741-1742.
87 Cfr. *Ibidem*, no 1404.
88 *Lumen fidei*, no 45: « In the celebration of the sacraments, the Church hands down her memory especially through the profession of faith. The creed does not only involve giving one's assent to a body of abstract truths; rather, when it is recited the whole of life is drawn into a journey towards full communion with the living God. We can say that in the creed believers are invited to enter into the mystery which they profess and to be transformed by it».

given them this role and does not cease to offer his assistance to them to perform it.[89]

Communion and freedom as gift and task entail the continuous renewal of humans' desire and effort to be in an increasing communion with Christ.[90] It seems that the reformers precisely denied the possibility for humans to have this "pure intention", since they think that humans always act sinfully and automatically pervert everything, looking egoistically for their own interests.[91] Indeed, by giving themselves or something back to God, they do not—or should not—do so primarily with the intention of "saving themselves" or "earning a (heavenly) reward", but rather do so primarily because God invites them and they freely decide to do so out of love. However, it should also be duly accepted that God consequently gives believers a compensation on earth and in heaven (cfr. Math. 19:23-30; Ephes. 6:7), which is also a divine gift that should be accepted with gratitude.

Nonetheless, faith and experience also teach us that our freedom is wounded and hurt by original and personal sin.[92] Sin damages the relationship with God at the existential level. As pointed out earlier, humans choose to turn away from God—from being "friends", they become "enemies". Although a relation of human friendship can be terminated by a unilateral decision of one of the friends, God on his part did never consider humans his "enemies".[93] God—due to the facts of the case and because he takes his own creation seriously—could not consider humans his friends either. In any case, although humans' rejected God, he did not leave them totally onto themselves. As stated before, in his plan of salvation, God decided to reinforce his community with humans to the level of divine filiation.[94]

Christians will always remain children of God, whatever they do. The objective structure of the community cannot be undone. However, this does not mean that each child automatically lives and behaves like a good child and friend of God.[95]

Although human freedom is restored by and in Christ, our human condition and exercise of our freedom remains fragile and needs to grow

---

89 Cfr. VON BALTHASAR, *Karl Barth: Darstellung Und Deutung Seiner Theologie*, 386.
90 CCC nos 825; 2784: «The free gift of adoption requires on our part continual conversion and *new life*. (...)».
91 Cfr. HAMM, *Martin Luther's Revolutionary Theology of Pure Gift without Reciprocation*, 136 and 139.
92 Cfr. CCC no 405.
93 Cfr. *Ibidem*, no 410.
94 Cfr. *Ibidem*, no 412.
95 Cfr. BENEDICT XVI, Encyclical letter *Spe salvi*, 30.11.2007, no 24.

into an ever deeper and more intense communion, a process characterised by falling and getting up (cfr. Proverbs 24:16).[96] The risks inherent to human freedom should not be a cause for anxiety[97]—and even less for the rejection of freedom—but filial confidence (Cfr. Rom. 5: 3-5).[98] Christians know that they are children of God, who always helps them and is always prepared to forgive sins, because he is—as the reformers rightly asserted—keeper of his promises and merciful. However, he is merciful not in the sense that he attributes holiness where there is none, but in the sense that he, being a loving Father, corrects, heals, purifies and elevates *existing* human beings really to divine life, already in the temporal-earthly sphere of common experience.[99]

This divine wish and plan imply the possibility that humans can choose, at the existential level, "to leave" the communion of life and love at any time, and "return" to it,[100] as is made clear in the parable of the prodigal son (Luke 15:11-24).[101] Humans, *in statu viae*—including believers—do, therefore, not yet have absolute certainty about their eschatological destiny.[102] Uncertainty belongs to the human condition as travellers. The pilgrim does not know for sure whether he will arrive at his destiny. Faith tells the believer—as the reformers again rightly asserted—that God is a loving Father, who does everything to establish an intimate communion with him in faith and in the temporal-earthly sphere of common experiences. This gives believers a deep security and a serene hope as children and pilgrims that they will arrive at their final destiny.[103]

---

96 Cfr. FC 18 and 19. John Paul II speaks here of a natural family forming a community of persons, but the same holds true for the Church. See also K. RAHNER, *Gerecht und Sünder zugleich*, «Schriften zur Theologie» 6 (1965), 274-276.

97 "Despair" should be clearly distinguished from "humility" as a response to the human fallen condition and the experience of one's own incapacity to choose and perform the moral good. Both attitudes are human responses to the same reality, but whereas despair is the result of the fact that a person focuses excessively on one's incapability, the humble person considers this same fact in the light of God's goodness, truth and love. In any case, despair is not to be recommended, also because God forbade it in his First Commandment. Cfr. CCC no 2091.

98 Cfr. *Ibidem*, no 2734.

99 Cfr. VON BALTHASAR, *Karl Barth: Darstellung Und Deutung Seiner Theologie*, 396-397.

100 Cfr. *Ibidem*, 391.

101 The reformers, though they were right that faith is a *conditio sine qua non* for one's salvation and that ultimately "everything depends on God", denied that God gave humans a real role in their mutual relationship, even to such an extent that a human being at the existential level—so to speak—could "make it and break it".

102 Cfr. RAHNER, *Gerecht und Sünder zugleich*, 268-269.

103 Cfr. FRANCIS, Apostolic exhortation *Gaudete et exultate*, 19.03.2018, no 125.

God in is plan of salvation, has designated a function to (original) sin, concupiscence and human fragility. These realities in some way belong to, and have a role to play, in God's plan of love. Salvation is not limited to an instantaneous moment, but in some way continues to happen in time, so that humans could unite themselves to Christ's sacrifice on the cross in the holy Mass.[104] The Catholic Church considers original sin even optimistically in a positive light qualifying it as a *felix culpa* in the hymn *Exultet* in the Pascal Virgil; Adam's guilt is said to be fortunate because it deserved such a great Redeemer.

The testing, i.e., the fact of being tempted, forms part of the Christian life.[105] Self-righteousness, a temptation for all—Catholics and Protestants alike—is not taken away by introducing a practical dualism in theology, denying human freedom and real cooperation. Good works are both of God *and* the believer together, each in their own way and manner.[106] Only if the good work is considered a theandric action, which is somehow both divine and human,[107] gratitude or ingratitude becomes possible and meaningful; acknowledging God's gifts received to be really fruitful or to hide the talent in the ground (Cfr. Math. 25:14-30). From the testimonies of the saints it becomes clear that a saint, the more he or she experiences God's love, the more he or she feels sinful. The saints are perfectly aware that their response to God's love is imperfect, that they totally depend on him in everything and that their role in God's project is minimum, though real in Christ.[108]

The human-sinful condition and fragility as such are not an obstacle to be in communion with God.[109] Our failures and sins do not separate us

---

104 Cfr. CCC no 618.
105 Cfr. *Ibidem*, no 396.
106 Cfr. FRANCIS, *Gaudete et exultate*, no 56.
107 A theandric action does not mean—as Paul O'Callaghan rightly observed—that God's action is to be "added" to or "combined" with human action as if the final result might be the sum total of the action of the Creator and his creature, as if God contributed 90% and humans the other 10%. Cfr. O'CALLAGHAN, *God and Mediation*, 15 and *Luther and 'sola gratia'*, 196.
108 CCC no 2011, «The saints have always had a lively awareness that their merits were pure grace». As examples, we can mention Teresa de Lisieux and Alfonso María de Liguori, Cfr. G. IAMMARRONE, *Il dialogo sulla giustificazione: La formula 'simul iustus et peccator' in Lutero, nel Concilio di Trento e nel confronto ecumenico attuale*, Edizioni Messaggero, Padova 2002, 81; 124; 152.
109 Or as a 20th-century spiritual author put it: « (…). Your wretchedness is not an obstacle but a spur for you to become more united to God and seek him constantly, because He purifies us». ESCRIVÁ DE BALAGUER, *Furrow*, Scepter, London, New York 1987, no 134, 66.

permanently from Christ, for if the sinner is contrite,[110] he is allowed into communion again and able to really cooperate with Christ carrying the cross, loving and repairing for his sins and that of others. Thus, temptation and sin present themselves as phenomena, which can and should be overcome with God's grace, since Christ died to liberate humans from sin and to elevate them to the condition of children of God. The main theme of Christian freedom is not "being free from worries about one's eschatological destiny", but their real capability of choosing to be in communion with God, and thus live a life of love.

In short, the reformers have a point when they asserted that (i) (original) sin is a reality which defines our human condition on earth, (ii) God has justified humans in Christ and that they are lost when they only look at themselves, without counting on God, and (iii) for humans it is not always possible to respond to God's love as they should, i.e., totally. However, all this is no reason to be sad, but on the contrary, a reason to fight and struggle out of love, trusting that God helps humans and forgives them always whenever they ask for it.

4.4 The exercise of the priesthood in the temporal-earthly sphere
The exercise of the priesthood by believers in the temporal-earthly sphere depends, above all, upon Christ's priesthood and sacrifice. Christ continues his priesthood and sacrifice in the temporal-earthly sphere through believers, who are sacramentally united to him and who have their own role to play in this sphere.

4.4.1 Christ eternal priesthood and sacrifice
Christ is our High Priest, who has redeemed us with his whole life and especially in the Paschal Mystery once-and-for-all to give the whole of creation back to God.[111] After his Ascension into heaven, Christ not only continues to exercise his office as Mediator and Advocate before God by interceding for humans with the Father, but he also continues to give and offer himself to the Father and to humans. [112] The Paschal Mystery is an action carried out by Jesus Christ, who is God and human and has, therefore, this double dimension; this action is simultaneously divine and

---

110 Contrition is both a grace of God *and* an adequate human response to his own faults and sins involving his intellect, will and—above all—his heart.
111 JOHN PAUL II, Encyclical letter *Ecclesia de Eucharistia*, 17-IV-2003, no 8: «The Son of God became man in order to restore all creation, in one sublime act of praise, to the One who made it from nothing. He, the Eternal High Priest who by the blood of his cross entered the eternal sanctuary, thus gives back to the Creator and Father all creation redeemed».
112 Cfr. CCC no 662.

human with all its implications. Among others, the Paschal Mystery takes place both within time and out of time, or to put it differently, it transcends time.[113]

4.4.2 Continuity of Christ's heavenly priesthood and sacrifice on earth

Christ's one-and-the-same redemptive earthly sacrifice on the cross and his heavenly offering to God the Father by the Holy Spirit, continues to be present on earth in the life of Christians.[114] Due to their configuration with Christ through Baptism and Confirmation, Christ becomes present in their lives. The Church, i.e., the whole community of the baptised, participates really in Christ's sole eternal priesthood and sacrifice.[115] All family members possess a common priesthood, which is the capacity to unite one's daily sacrifices and sufferings to Christ's one-and-only sacrifice.[116]

4.4.3 Sacramental union and double participation

The privileged way in which the believer's offerings are united to Christ's offering, is sacramentally in the Eucharistic celebration,[117] which is not only the preaching of the Word and anamnesis of the Paschal Mystery, but also the most eminent actualisation of Christ's eternal sacrifice,[118] where believers have the privilege to unite effectively—out of love—their daily spiritual sacrifices to Christ's sacrifice.[119] Thus, Christ does not stay in heaven to receive believers' spiritual sacrifices to present them *alongside* his own offering to the Father, but Christ comes down to earth by the Holy Spirit and through the ministerial priest to render his eternal sacrifice present in space and time in the offerings of bread and wine.[120] This sacramental presence of Christ in the ministerial priest and in the bread

---

113 Cfr. *Ibidem*, nos 1085, 1364 –1369.
114 ESCRIVÁ DE BALAGUER, *Christ is passing by*, no 103, 146.
115 Cfr. LG 10;34; PO 2 .
116 Cfr. LG 10; CCC no 1141.
117 PO 2: «Through the ministry of the priests, the spiritual sacrifice of the faithful is made perfect in union with the sacrifice of Christ».
118 Cfr. CCC nos 1104–1107.
119 Cfr. SC 9-12; 14; CCC no 1350: «The presentation of the offerings at the altar (…) commits the Creator's gifts into the hands of Christ who, in his sacrifice, brings to perfection all human attempts to offer sacrifices».
120 Cfr. CCC no 1367. About the different views and explanations of the real presence of Christ in the Eucharist, I will just remark here that *the* difference between the doctrines of transubstantiation, consubstantiation and virtual presence seems to boil down to the following: Christ's self-giving to the Father and to humans in the temporal-empirical sphere (cfr. CCC n. 1375–1376). The Eucharist is—analogue to Christ's Incarnation—God's "commitment" to humans and the world by becoming part of it Himself.

and wine in the temporal-empirical sphere are necessary conditions so that the believers' sacrifices can be completely united to Christ's sacrifice.[121] All believers—including the ministerial priests—exercise their common priesthood to the glory and honour of God by sanctifying themselves and all their daily occupations, i.e., by offering them in Christ to the Father by the Holy Spirit.[122] By being in communion with Christ, all Christians bring God to the world and to other humans, where they are his witnesses and co-operators, each in his own particular state and activities.

The exercise of common priesthood in the temporal-earthly sphere should be distinguished from its exercise in heaven. All Christians in heaven and purgatory still somehow participate in Christ's priesthood and sacrifice, although not in the same way as on earth. At the same time, in heaven, ministerial priests will cease to exercise their specific ministry, though they remain as ministerial priests.

The Catholic vision allows for complementary and different vocations within the Church as to their position and task in the world. Laypeople are especially called by God to sanctify the world and worldly activities "from within",[123] whereas religious are specifically called to testify before the world of its eschatological and definitive end in heaven.[124] Nonetheless, all believers, each in their own way and equally valuable in the eyes of God, work in the service of God and each other to build up his Church and the kingdom of God on earth.

4.4.4 A real human role

The frame is thus a community of life and love, joint mutual self-giving, which requires that humans are free beings, who are capable to give "something of their own" to God, albeit something which was given to them by God first. Salvation or sanctification is not an automatic process but requires the free and real cooperation of humans in time and space, because God never imposes himself, but always respects human freedom, which is a divine gift as well (as is faith and election). Humans thus offer

---

121 BENEDICT XVI, Apostolic Exhortation *Sacramentum Caritatis*, 22-11-2007, no 47, «(…) in the bread and the wine we bring to the altar, all creation is taken up by Christ the Redeemer to be transformed and presented to the Father. In this way, we also bring to the altar the pain and suffering of the world, in the certainty that everything has value in God's eyes. The authentic meaning of this gesture (…) enables us to appreciate how God invites man to participate in bringing to fulfilment his handiwork, and in so doing, gives human labour its authentic meaning, since, through the celebration of the Eucharist, it is united to the redemptive sacrifice of Christ».
122 Cfr. PO 5.
123 Cfr. GS 54.
124 Cfr. LG 44.

real things in Christ spiritually—i.e., through the Holy Spirit—which are agreeable to God.[125] Believers offer themselves and their day-to-day activities which means that human reality is purified, directed and elevated to God.[126]

The reformers do have a point when they stated that a human being on his own is "nothing at all" and can do absolutely nothing supernaturally relevant towards God. However, the recognition of this fact (humility or self-denial) is a condition for self-giving (love)—self-denial is not the end-station, but the point of departure. Humans are never completely on their own. In and with Christ by the Holy Spirit, they can work for God and perform miracles in the sphere of temporal-earthly reality. It seems that the reformers were not able to grasp the fact that humans with God's assistance and grace can cooperate in the sanctification of the world and of themselves.

In a strict sense, humans "add" nothing to the Paschal Mystery, which is perfect in itself, because of the priest (Jesus Christ), the sacrifice (the humanity of Jesus Christ) and the result (salvation of the human race) are all perfect and complete.[127] However, it is not a question of perfecting what is already perfect. What matters is that humans—willingly—can and may participate in the Paschal Mystery, conforming their lives to Christ's. Then believers will be co-redeemers with and in Christ, not because they are so good, but because God is.[128]

All believers share in Christ's priesthood—besides the offering of the daily activities—also by intercessory prayer to God the Father. In this respect, it is relevant to consider that the ecclesial community is not limited to the earthly pilgrim Church, but also includes the heavenly Church.[129] Believers, therefore, can also pray to saints, who intercede for

---

125 Thus, when St. Peter and St. Paul speak of *spiritual* sacrifices and offerings (1 Pet. 2:5, Rom. 12:1, 15:16), they do not exclude the *real* offering, but they presuppose it. Cfr. A. VANHOYE, *Sacerdotes antiguos, sacerdote nuevo según el Nuevo Testamento*, Ediciones Sígueme, Salamanca 2002, 281.
126 CCC no 1109: «The Church, therefore, asks the Father to send the Holy Spirit to make the lives of the faithful a living sacrifice to God by their spiritual transformation into the image of Christ, by concern for the Church's unity, and by taking part in her mission through the witness and service of charity». See also CCC no 1129.
127 CCC no 1322; CCC no 2100: «The only perfect sacrifice is the one that Christ offered on the cross as a total offering to the Father's love and for our salvation. By uniting ourselves with his sacrifice we can make our lives a sacrifice to God».
128 Cfr. *Ibidem*, nos 1091; 1460; 1508; 1521.
129 CN 6: «In its invisible elements, this communion exists not only among the members of the pilgrim Church on earth, but also between these and all who, having passed from this world in the grace of the Lord, belong to the heavenly Church or will be incorporated into it after having been fully purified. This means, among other things, that there

them not because of "their own merits", but because of their communion with Christ.

4.5 Conclusion

According to Catholic understanding, humans in the temporal-earthly sphere are capable—despite their misery and weaknesses—to be in sacramental communion with Christ. In this way, they are able to participate in his priesthood as free beings who are able to give adequate human responses, including contrition, to divine-earthly realities. The community of the Church has also a family structure: the relations between God and believers as well as among the earthly community have both horizontal and vertical dimensions, which are necessary, amongst other reasons, to render Christ's eternal priesthood and sacrifice present on earth and to make the exercise of common priesthood by all believers possible.

The reformers stressed the capacity of each believer to appear in faith directly before the Lord's throne in heaven to hear his definitive verdict, while at the same time emphasising that they are not worthy to offer anything to God and perform any good works by themselves. This way of framing implies that the temporal-earthly sphere with its layered structure is set aside: every believer is equal and equally priest before the Lord. Consequently, in this view, although touching upon the greatness of the common priesthood and holiness in the midst of the world, believers seem to have no possibility—both in the temporal-empirical and heavenly spheres—to join their works, sufferings and human realities to Christ's sacrifice. Instead, the reformers stressed the incompatibility of Christ's work and sacrifice with any human works and sacrifice, in order to avoid any possible pride, arrogance and ingratitude on their part. It follows that the focus and attention in the understanding and exercise of the priesthood by all believers shifted towards humility, self-denial and thanksgiving. The reformers' basic framework in the 16th century still stands today among Evangelical and Reformed denominations.

The Catholic and Reformed frameworks differ in their basic concepts and attitudes, such as the way and nature of the believers' access to God, human freedom and capacity to give adequate responses to divine

---

is a *mutual relationship* between the pilgrim Church on earth and the heavenly Church in the historical-redemptive mission. Hence the ecclesiological importance not only of Christ's intercession on behalf of his members, but also of that of the saints and, in an eminent fashion, of the Blessed Virgin Mary's. *Devotion to the saints*, which is such a strong feature of the piety of the Christian people, can thus be seen to correspond in its very essence to the profound reality of the Church as a mystery of communion».

realities, the consequence of sin on human freedom, the need for absolute eschatological certainty in relation to filial confidence, the possibility for believers to be in communion with Christ in the temporal-earthly sphere with its layered structure and the family structure of the Church. All these themes, ways of reasoning and underlying lines of thought—considered in their mutual relationship—are important to include in and deal with during ecumenical dialogue in order to arrive at a satisfactory result. Truly, the greatness of the common priesthood of all believers could be a leading and unifying motive in ecumenical dialogue.

CONCLUSION

In this book, we have studied the common priesthood in Reformation theology and spirituality to shed light upon and to clarify the relationship between common and ministerial priesthoods—understood as being essentially distinct from, and mutually ordained to, each other—as maintained in Catholic doctrine. At the same time, we have tried to identify relevant elements, which might contribute to the ongoing ecumenical dialogue.

The priesthood of all believers is a central theme in Reformed doctrine and spirituality since it lies at the very basis of the Reformed framework and understanding of the relationship between God and humans. The reformers, in order to safeguard and secure the absolute primacy, sovereignty and glory of God, endeavoured to maximise God's role and subsequently minimise that of humans, in their mutual relationship. They characterised this apparent imbalance by the believer's experience of a) personal faith and election, b) being on the receiving end and c) direct access to God (common priesthood). The relationship between God and humans is, therefore, conceived as dialectically opposed, while at the same time, exclusive.

Luther stressed the radical equality of all believers, which he related to the priesthood. He claimed that all believers, by faith, are equally "priests" before God. He placed this claim—priesthood of all believers—in the believers' experience of personal redemption and their direct and immediate access to God. To obtain absolute certainty about his definitive eschatological destiny, Luther made a substantial leap—disregarding the gap of time and space—by and in an act of faith to anticipate God's final verdict. He affirms that God tells each believer personally his final verdict in a direct encounter. Ultimately, it is in *this* particular and personal experience that the believer obtains psychological certainty and freedom from the law—feels God's favour and may trust on God's mercy, in Christ.

The common priesthood does not have the same role in Luther and Calvin. Luther's initial proclamation of the radical equality of all believers led to chaos and anarchy. Calvin observed that phenomenon, and intended to safeguard law and order in the community. In order to mitigate any possible detrimental effects on the community, Calvin put all the emphasis on God's absolute sovereignty, omnipotence and providence in the governance of the world. He accepted the direct, immediate and eschatological access of all believers in Christ to God the

Father through the Holy Spirit, but highlighted God's unilateral gratuitous election and regeneration of believers within the community, and downplayed Luther's mere subjective act of faith, the radical equality of believers and, thus, the common priesthood. In fact, to explain the order and organisation in the community, Calvin even used the "Catholic" distinction between "clergy" and "lay people", albeit merely in a functional sense. In any case, he continued to work within Luther's framework.

Be that as it may, both reformers used their personal experience of direct access to God as a paradigmatic model of the common priesthood in the temporal-earthly sphere. The affirmation that all believers belong to the spiritual estate and are radically equal before God led to the disappearance of the hierarchy—in terms of both holiness and authority—in the temporal-earthly sphere, where believers are still travelling towards heaven.

This way of framing had a double and simultaneous effect: the rediscovery of the greatness of the common priesthood, while at the same time, a limitation of the believers' common priesthood in the temporal-earthly sphere. One the one hand, it proclaims that every Christian has to be holy and is called to the highest form of contemplation in the midst of the world, while standing before a judging God, and on the other hand, that each Christian possesses the same authority and responsibility, to be exercised in midst of the world in all their activities. Both reformers regarded the core of common priesthood as the offering of oneself to God and of spiritual sacrifices, which are pleasing to the Lord (1 Pe 2, 9). All believers have a common dignity (by virtue of Baptism) and only differ as to the function, which they exercise in the world. For the reformers, each ministry is a calling, a gift and a service, as any other service. This means that there are no fundamental differences as to the persons who exercise the different ministries, nor as to the content of these ministries. Whether one is a shoemaker, a lawyer or a pastor, everyone equally honours God in their own duties. This is the greatness of common priesthood and Christian life in Reformation theology.

Notably, the reformers believed that, while standing directly before God in a spiritual encounter, humans experience themselves to be completely sinful and unworthy, that is, they are nothing before God, and they cannot give anything back to God, but can only receive God's grace freely. Although the reformers regarded the core of common priesthood as the offering of oneself to God and of spiritual sacrifices, which are pleasing to the Lord, they were at the same time constrained to limit the believers' priesthood in the temporal-earthly sphere. They limited the continuity of Christ's redemptive sacrifice in this sphere and excluded the possibility that the sacrifices of Christians could be united to Christ's heavenly self-giving to the Father. Believers—although priests in Christ—do not have the privilege of participating in Christ's sacrifice in the temporal-earthly sphere of human experiences. The believers' sufferings and actions are to be carefully distinguished and separated from Christ's sacrifice and work, which has redemptive value. It is this **dialectical opposition** between Christ's sacrifice and human action in Reformation theology, which strikes the exercise of the (common and ministerial) priesthood of believers at its root, and it appears to cut it off from the core of Christ's priesthood, which is his eternal priestly redemptive sacrifice.

Moreover, this way of framing also implies a separation of the believers' experience of faith and their experiences in the sphere of the here and now, where believers obtain psychological certainty of their definitive eschatological salvation and freedom from the law, but have to acknowledge with an ever-increasing awareness their nothingness and sinfulness. The reformers, in their experience of direct access before God, seem to equate humans and their mundane realities in the temporal-earthly sphere with sin and sinfulness. Thus, in this sphere of common experiences, believers must admit continuously that they cannot give anything back to God, and that there is no need to do so. In this line of reasoning, an eschatological confusion and tension in Reformation theology becomes manifest and hinders the exercise of the common priesthood by believers in the temporal-earthly sphere, where believers still have a role to play, but apparently cannot be in communion with Christ for they are—or so it seems—completely sinful. This implies, moreover, that the sphere of the believers' personal life of piety and relation with God remains separated from their action within the world. In the former sphere, believers have direct access to God, while in the latter sphere, there are only motives for distraction and contrition, for this sphere is completely dominated by selfishness and sin. In this frame, believers are internally divided—experiencing something like a spiritual schizophrenia—as their lives consist of certain acts, which are deemed holy, and other acts, which are deemed superfluous or morally evil. Both types of acts coincide in the lives of Christians, but without mutually influencing each other.

In Luther and Calvin, we can thus observe three major changes of perspectives concerning the priesthood and sacrifice. Firstly, a change of perspective from ontological to situational priesthood; secondly, a change as to the content and exercise of the priesthood; and thirdly, as to the concept of sacrifice.

a) The believers' priesthood is ultimately situated in their subjective experience of the act of faith, in which they are redeemed and find themselves before the Lord receiving all graces directly. In Calvin, the focus is laid upon God's election of the believer, and the exercise of their priesthood in the direct presence of the Lord.
b) The content of the priesthood of all believers shifts from participation in Christ's sacrifice itself to merely enjoying spiritually the benefits of Christ's sacrifice (redemption, justification and holiness). The spiritual priest, justified by faith, is only worthy as a possessor of grace, but he does not mediate the means of salvation to other men in the temporal sphere—for that is the sole prerogative of Christ. In this framework, all human mediation of divine realities becomes merely *functional* or *instrumental*; humans—since they always act on their own in the temporal-earthly sphere—do not play any *constitutive* role in the building up of the Church, for only God builds up the Church directly. Furthermore, in the exercise of the priestly functions, the emphasis shifts to preaching and teaching (for Calvin, a prophetic function). The first and most important priestly task of a believer is to preach and teach the great wonders of God to others to stimulate them to follow Christ's example and to love one's neighbour, followed by priestly intercession (prayer) for each other to God, and service to neighbour (that is, not directly to God) in all aspects of life.
c) The concept of sacrifice changes: thanksgiving, prayer, praise and service to neighbour are considered sacrifices because the believer acknowledges God and denies himself. The essence of sacrifice shifts from the act of self-giving (love) to God and fellowmen to the act of self-denial (humility) by the believer. The latter attitude becomes the maximum expression and response of the human being before God. It seems, therefore, that believers—as priests—give thanks, glory and praise to God, above all, by denying themselves and not by giving themselves to God in Christ.

A (common) priesthood, which is detached from its source—that is, Christ's substantial eternal sacrifice—becomes vulnerable to other interpretations in order to give it content, which, however, do not reflect the essence of priesthood, but rather only an aspect of it, as manifested in the following examples: priesthood regarded as "exercising pastoral authority" (T. Wengert) or as "service to neighbour" (H. M. Barth) or as "being witnesses of Christ" (K. Barth) or "being active as volunteer in the community" (cfr. W. Hering). These views are not completely wrong. They are just reductionist and, therefore, incomplete. They are wrong only in so far as they pretend to state and claim the entire essence of priesthood.

***

The Catholic framework tries to strike a balance and harmony in the relationship between God and humans, where the common priesthood—at least in theory—could be exercised by all believers in Christ to its fullest potential, that is, rendering Christ present in their own lives and daily activities, offering their lives and activities in Christ, and bringing back the world to God. At the centre of this framework stands Christ's eternal priesthood and sacrifice to God the Father and to humans, the Eucharist. This heavenly offering needs a double form of participation in Christ's priesthood by believers in order to be actualised on earth in the spatial-temporal sphere. In this way, all believers can join Christ's eternal sacrifice in a privileged way in the Liturgy and in all daily activities in the world.

At the basis of a Catholic understanding of common priesthood stands the affirmation that God's revelation and his action in the world, and humans' reception of divine realities, are positive, inclusive and fruitful. God gave humans the capacity to know him through creation and Revelation, and to respond to him positively with their whole being—reason, will and heart. God gave this capacity to them freely to be used for and with him. Humans are thus free beings capable of giving meaningful human responses to God. Though this capacity is weakened by sin, freedom is not annulled by it. God wants to be discovered by humans, without imposing himself upon them, for he always respects human freedom.

There is thus room for a moderate form of paradox in Catholic theology. God does challenge our pettiness and worldly standards to make room for a vision that transcends our mere human vision, but he does not continuously play a game of hiding in opposite forms in order to humble our intellect and test our faith. There is both continuity and discontinuity between the old and new visions of faith in divine and earthly realities. There should also be room for analogy in theology, which makes it possible to pay attention to the difference between God and humans, as well as what they have in common.

The interior spiritual sphere of faith and the external sphere of temporal-empirical reality are not supposed to be separated from, or merely run parallel to, but are essentially open to, and ordained to, each other. Although God's action and those of humans are incommensurable, in Christ's Incarnation, God has united himself somehow with all human beings. Jesus Christ has redeemed us with his whole life. The event of Christ's Incarnation is a successful fruition, uniting the divine and the human, purifying and elevating the latter, to incorporate it into the former—firstly, in his Person itself (Incarnation), secondly in his Person in relation to the world (Redemption), and thirdly, sacramentally, in his Person in the Eucharist.

There is also a unity and continuity between creation, redemption, sanctification and the final restoration, such that we are always dealing with the same underlying reality, which is transformed into a new creation. The specific finality of the act of redemption and final restoration, however, is to make clean, purify, heal, support, and elevate existing creation, which is stained, wounded and fallen.

Christ has anticipated the eschatological event by his Incarnation. His earthly life culminated in the Paschal Mystery. In this way, he has radically eliminated the distinction between the sacred and profane. However, the latter does not apply automatically, as it were, by a divine decree, because humans remain free beings in space and time.

The intermediate time is characterised by a wonderfully "layered" structure, according to God's pedagogy, and corresponding to human nature and being, in which the Christian life unfolds. In the time-lapse between Ascension and the Parousia, i.e., the "time of the image", Christ becomes present in various ways—in the Word, at prayer, in the life of the saints, in the Liturgy, and most eminently, in the Eucharist, which is Christ's eternal sacrifice to the Father and to human beings. This new phase of the history of salvation is called the sacramental economy, where the modality of the presence of Christ is characterised not by an "immediate" or "direct" contact with Christ, but by a "mediate" contact with his ecclesial Body through the Holy Spirit. Here, Reformed and Catholic teachings have a point of connection, because both recognise the Holy Spirit as the one who establishes a bond of union between the believer and Christ. This sacramental-economical system respects human nature, being and freedom. and at the same time, it makes communion between God and human beings in the temporal-earthly sphere already possible, while God remains God and humans remain human, yet already participating in divine life.

The pilgrim Church in the temporal sphere is also structured organically as a family community. This community creates the conditions for a meaningful exercise of common priesthood by all believers, for it makes possible between God and humans a real spiritual communion, a stable community, and a dynamic communication with mutual giving and receiving.

The radical equality of believers is not situated in the common priesthood—or in an experience of direct and immediate access to God—but it is primarily situated at a deeper level of relationship, that of divine filiation. All Christians, through Baptism, belong to God's family and are equally adopted children of God the Father, in Christ, by the Holy Spirit. Based on their configuration with Christ through Baptism—and Confirmation—Christians participate and share in the prophetical, priestly and royal functions of Christ within the community. This participation is equal in the sense that all Christians enjoy the priestly privilege of offering oneself and all their human activities to the Lord. Moreover, by being in communion with Christ in their daily activities, all Christians bring God to the world and to their fellow human beings, where they are his witnesses and *co*-operators, each in their own particular state and activities, which are equally valuable in the eyes of God. Yet, at the same time, there is also an essential difference in the sense that Christ—to "come down" and "take creation up"—makes specific use of some community members, who are sacramentally configured with him in a more specific way, through the ministerial priesthood. Therefore, both common and ministerial priesthoods bring about a radically equal *filiation* to God, while at they same time, the *relationship* with God that is brought about by the common priesthood is essentially distinct from that of the ministerial priesthoods.

The sinful condition and fragility of humanity as such are not an obstacle to be in communion with Christ in the temporal sphere. Human failures and sins do affect negatively the quality of one's relationship with God. However, this relationship can always be restored through contrition and asking God for forgiveness. The believer is then allowed to enter into communion once again, and he is re-enabled to cooperate with Christ through carrying the cross of daily life, loving others through Christ, and making reparation for his sins and that of others. Temptation and sin can and should be overcome with God's grace, since Christ died to liberate humans from sin and to elevate us to the condition of children of God. The main theme of Christian freedom is not being free from worries about one's eschatological destiny, but man's real capability of choosing to be in communion with God, and thus, live a life of love.

In sum, Christ is the eternal High Priest who exercises his office as Mediator and Advocate before God by interceding for humans to the Father, and he continues to give and offer himself to the Father and to humans. Christ's one-and-the-same redemptive earthly sacrifice on the cross and his heavenly offering or self-giving to God the Father by the Holy Spirit continues to be present on earth in the life of Christians. All Christians possess a common priesthood, which is the capacity to unite one's daily sacrifices and sufferings to Christ's one-and-only sacrifice. Christ does not "stay" in heaven to receive believers' spiritual sacrifices to present them *alongside* his own offering to the Father, but he comes down to earth, using the ministerial priesthood and by the Holy Spirit, to render his eternal sacrifice present in the temporal-spatial sphere in the offerings of bread and wine. All believers exercise their common priesthood for the glory and honour of God by sanctifying themselves and all their daily occupations, i.e., by offering them in union with Christ and his sacrifice to the Father by the Holy Spirit. Thus, the Reformed understanding of common priesthood without the ministerial, implies that Christ does not "come down" to earth, but instead that every believer has to "go up" to heaven in order to appear before God's throne, where the believer and all his actions are deemed righteous and holy by virtue of Christ's priesthood (his intercession and sacrifice).

The frame is thus a community of life and love, joint mutual self-giving, which requires that humans are free beings, who are capable of giving "something of their own" to God, albeit something which was given to them by God first. The recognition that believers in Christ can give themselves and their worldly realities back to God should not be considered as "buying" God's love or grace. God's unconditional love is a given. However, this does not mean that salvation or sanctification would be an automatic process. Precisely because God is Love, he never imposes himself upon humans, but he always respects their freedom, requiring their free and real cooperation in time and space, in carrying out with his divine work in them.

BIBLIOGRAPHY

Primary sources

CALVIN, J., *Institutes of the Christian Religion Vol. 1-2*, Eerdmans, Grand Rapids 1979

------------, *Commentaries on the Epistle of St. Paul to the Romans* (tr. & ed. J. Owen), Calvin Translation Society, Edenborough 1844

------------, *Commentaries on the Epistle of Paul the Apostle to the Hebrews* (tr. & ed. J. Owen), Calvin Translation Society, Edenborough 1853

LUTHER, M., *D. Martin Luthers Werke*, Weimar 1883-1929, Weimarer Ausgabe, WA

------------, *Luther's Works*, Jaroslav Pelikan and Helmut T. Lehmann (eds.), 56 vols., Concordia, St. Louis and Fortress, Philadelphia 1955-1986

------------, *Reformation Writings of Martin Luther*, Bertram Lee Woolf (ed. and tr.), Lutterworth Press, London 1952

Specific studies on the Reformed common priesthood

BARTH, H.M., *Einander Priester sein. Allgemeines Priestertum in ökumenischer Perspektive*, Vandenhoeck & Ruprecht, Göttingen 1990

-----------, *«Il sacerdozio universale» secondo Martin Lutero*, Rivista di studi ecumenici, anno VI/1 (1988) 9-31

BRAVO, F., *El sacerdocio común de los creyentes en la teología de Lutero*, Editorial ESET, Vitoria 1963

CRAWFORD, J.R., *Calvin and the priesthood of all believers*, «Scottish Journal of Theology» 21 (1968) 145-157

EASTWOOD, C., *The Priesthood of All Believers. An Examination of the Doctrine of All Believers from the Reformation to the Present Day*, Epworth, London 1960

GOERTZ, HÄRLE, SCHRÖER, *Priester/Priestertum. II. Allgemeines Priestertum*, in Theologische Realenzyklopädie, Bd. 27, 1997, S. 402–413.

VOSS, H.J., *The priesthood of all believers and the mission Dei: A canonical, catholic and contextual perspective*, Wheaton, Illinois 2013

VOSS, K.P., *Der Gedanke des allgemeinen Priester- und Prophetentums. Seine gemeindetheologische Aktualisierung in der Reformationszeit*, Brockhaus, Wuppertal 1990

PONT, A.J., *Die priesterskap van die gelowiges soos Calvyn dit gesien het*, «Hervormde Teologiese studies» 45 (1989) 451-460

Documents of contemporary magisterium

VATICAN COUNCIL II, Const. *Sacrosanctum Concilium*, 4.12.1963
VATICAN COUNCIL II, Dogm. Const. *Lumen Gentium*, 21.11.1964
VATICAN COUNCIL II, Decree *Unitatis Redintegratio*, 21.11.1964
VATICAN COUNCIL II, Dogm. Const. *Dei Verbum*, 18.11.1965
VATICAN COUNCIL II, Past. Const. *Gaudium et Spes*, 7.12.1965
VATICAN COUNCIL II, Decree *Presbyterorum Ordinis*, 7.12.1965
CONGREGATION FOR THE DOCTRINE OF THE FAITH, Letter *Communionis Notio*, 28.5.1992
JOHN PAUL II, Apostolic exhortation *Familiaris Consortio*, 21.11.1981
JOHN PAUL II, Encyclical letter *Ecclesia de Eucharistia*, 17.IV.2003
BENEDICT XVI, Apostolic exhortation *Sacramentum Caritatis*, 22.11.2007
BENEDICT XVI, Encyclical letter *Spe salvi*, 30.11.2007
FRANCIS, Encyclical letter *Lumen fidei*, 29.06.2013
FRANCIS, Apostolic exhortation *Gaudete et exultate*, 19.03.2018

Other sources

ALTHAUS, P., *The Theology of Martin Luther*, Fortress Press, Philadephia 1966
ARANDA LOMEÑA, A., *El sacerdocio de Jesucristo en los ministros y en los fieles. Estudio teológico sobre la distinción «essentia et non gradu tantum»*, «Scripta Theologica» 22 (1990/2) 365-404
ARNOLD, M., *Luther on Christ's person and work*, in: R. KOLB, I. DINGEL, L. BATKA (eds.), *The Oxford Handbook of Martin Luther's Theology*, 274-293, Oxford University Press, Oxford 2014
BALTHASAR, H.U. VON, *Karl Barth: Darstellung Und Deutung Seiner Theologie*, Hegner, Köln, 1962
BATKA, L., *Luther's teaching on sin and evil*, in: R. KOLB, I. DINGEL, L. BATKA (eds.), *The Oxford Handbook of Martin Luther's Theology*, 233-253, Oxford University Press, Oxford 2014
BEEKE, J.R., *Calvin on piety*, in: MCKIM, D. K., *The Cambridge Companion to John Calvin*, 125-145, Cambridge University Press, Cambridge 2004
BLANCO, P., *El ministerio en Lutero, Trento y el Vaticano II. Un recorrido histórico-dogmático*, «Scripta Theologica» 40 (2008/3), 733-776
BLAUMEISER, H., *Martin Luther's Kreuzestheologie: Schlüssel zu einer Deutung von Mensch und Wirklichkeit; eine Untersuchung anhand der Operationes in Psalmos (1519-1521)*, Bonifatius, Paderborn 1995
BORNKAMM, H., *Luther's geistige Welt*, Gütersloh 1960
BORNKAMM, K., *Christus – König und Priester. Das Amt Christi bei Luther im Verhältnis zur Vor- und Nachgeschichte*, Mohr Siebeck, Tübingen 1998

CALABRESE, *Comunione*, in: G. CALABRESE, P. GOYRET, O. PIAZZA (eds), *Dizionario di Ecclesiologia*, Città Nuova, Roma 2010, 268-288
CASTELLUCCI, E., *Sacerdozio*, in: G. CALABRESE, P. GOYRET, O. PIAZZA, O. (eds.), *Dizionario di Ecclesiologia*, Città Nuova, Roma 2010, 1229-42
COTTRET, B., *Calvin: A Biography*, Eerdmans Grand Rapids, Michigan 2000
ESCRIVÁ DE BALAGUER, J.M., *Christ is passing by*, Four Courts Scepter, Dublin 1982
---------------------------------------, *Furrow*, Scepter, London New York 1987
---------------------------------------, *the Forge*, Scepter, London New York 1988
FREIWALD, J., *Das Verhältnis von Allgemeinen Priestertum und besonderem Amt bei Luther*, Ruprecht-Karls-Universität, Heidelberg 1993
GANOCZY, A., *Calvin's life*, in: MCKIM, D. K., *The Cambridge Companion to John Calvin*, 3-24, Cambridge University Press, Cambridge 2004
GARCIA, M.A., *Life in Christ. Union with Christ and Twofold Grace in Calvin's Theology*, Paternoster, Milton Keynes 2008
GARCÍA IBÁÑEZ, A., *L'Eucharistia, dono e mistero, trattato storico-dogmatico sul mistero eucarístico*, Edizioni Università della Santa Croce, Roma 2006
GARCÍA VILLOSLADA, R., *Martin Lutero Vol 1-2*, Biblioteca de Autores Cristianos, Madrid 1976
GARUTI, A., *Primacy of the Bishop of Rome and Ecumenical Dialogue*, Ignatius press, San Francisco 2004
GIRALDO, R., SGROI, P., VETRALI, T. (eds.), *Ecumenismo come conversione*, Istituto di studi ecumenici San Bernardino, Venezia 2007
GREEF, W. DE, *Calvin's writings*, in: MCKIM, D. K., *The Cambridge Companion to John Calvin*, 41-75, Cambridge University Press, Cambridge 2004
HAAS, G.H., *Calvin's ethics*, in: MCKIM, D. K., *The Cambridge Companion to John Calvin*, 93-105, Cambridge University Press, Cambridge 2004
HACKER, P., *Das Ich im Glauben bei Martin Luther*, Styria, Graz 1966
HAMM, B., *Martin Luther's Revolutionary Theology of Pure Gift without Reciprocation*, «Lutheran Quarterly», XXIX (2015) 125-161
HERING, W., *Zwischen Gott und Welt. Anmerkungen zum Priestertum aller Gläubigen*, Deutschen Pfarrerblatt, 1 (2009) 1-4
HESSELINK, J., *Calvin's theology*, in: MCKIM, D. K., *The Cambridge Companion to John Calvin*, Cambridge University Press, Cambridge 2004, 74-92
HILDEBRAND, D. VON, *Fundamental Moral Attitudes*, trans. A. M. Jourdain, Longmans, Green and Co., New York 1950

——————————————, *Christian Ethics*, D. McKay Company, New York 1953

——————————————, *Gesammelte Werke IV, Metaphysik der Gemeinschaft, Untersuchungen über Wesen und Wert der Gemeinschaft*, Verlag Josef Habbel Regensburg, 1975

HUNSINGER, G., *A Tale of Two Simultaneities: Justification and Sanctification in Calvin and Barth*, «Zeitschrift für Dialektische Theologie» 18 (2002) 316-338

HUIZINGA, J., *The Waning of the Middle Ages*, Doubleday, New York 1954

IAMMARRONE, G., *Il dialogo sulla giustificazione: La formula 'simul iustus et peccator' in Lutero, nel Concilio di Trento e nel confronto ecumenico attuale*, Edizioni Messaggero, Padova 2002

ILLANES, J.L., *On the Theology of Work*, Scepter, Dublin and Chicago 1968

——————————, *La santificación del trabajo*, Palabra, Madrid 2001

ISERLOH, E., *Martin Luther und der Aufbruch der Reformation (1517-1525)*, in: H. JEDIN (ed.), *Handbuch der Kirchengeschichte, Bd. 4, Reformation, katholische Reform und Gegenreformation*, Herder, Freiburg 1979

KARKKAINEN, V-M., *"By the Washing of Regeneration and Renewal in the Holy Spirit": Towards a Pneumatological Theology of Justification*, 317, in: H. MARSHALL, V. RABENS, C. BENNEMA (eds.), *The Spirit and Christ in the New Testament and Christian Theology*, 303-322, W. B. Eerdmans, Grand Rapids, Michigan/Cambridge 2012

KINNEGING, A.A.M., *Realist Phenomenology and the foundations of natural law: the vindication of the moral order in the works of Scheler, Hartmann and Hildebrand*, «American Journal of Jurisprudence» 46 (2001) 257-276

KOLB, R., *Luther's hermeneutics of distinctions*, in: R. KOLB, I. DINGEL, L. BATKA (eds.), *The Oxford Handbook of Martin Luther's Theology*, Oxford University Press, Oxford 2014, 168-184

KUYPER, A., *Calvinism*, Sovereign Grace Union, London 1937

LIEBELT, M., *Allgemeines Priestertum, Charisma und Struktur. Grundlagen für ein biblisch-theologisches Verständnis geistlicher Leitung*, Brockhaus, Wuppertal 2000

LINDER, R.D., *The Reformation Era*, Greenwood Press, Westport (Connecticut), London 2008

LOCHER, G.W., *Sign of the Advent: A Study in Protestant Ecclesiology* Academic Press, Fribourg 2004

LORTZ, J., *Geschichte der Kirche in ideengeschichtlicher Betrachtung / Bd. II, Die Neuzeit*, Aschendorff, Münster 1964

LUTHERAN–ROMAN CATHOLIC COMMISSION, Report *From Conflict to Communion*, Joint Lutheran – Roman Catholic Commemoration of the reformation in 2017, published in 2013

MACINTYRE, A., *Edith Stein, A philosophical Prologue,* Continuum, London, New York 2006

MADSEN, D.P., *Das geistliche Priestertum der Christen,* Bertelsmann 1882

MARTÍN GÓMEZ, J., *Sacerdocio común-sacerdocio ministerial, Presupuestos teologicos y consecuencias pastorales: discurso de apertura del curso 2007-2008,* Instituto Superior de Estudios Teológicos San Ildefonso, Toledo 2008

MATTES, M., *Luther on justification as forensic and effective,* in: R. KOLB, I. DINGEL, L. BATKA (eds.), *The Oxford Handbook of Martin Luther's Theology,* , Oxford University Press, Oxford 2014, 264-273

METHUEN, C., *Luther's life,* in: R. KOLB, I. DINGEL, L. BATKA (eds.), *The Oxford Handbook of Martin Luther's Theology,* Oxford University Press, Oxford 2014, 7-27

MILNER, B.C., *Calvin's doctrine of the Church,* Brill, Leiden 1970

MÖHLER, J.A., *Symbolik oder Darstellung der dogmatischen Gegensätze der Katholiken und Protestanten nach ihren öffentliche Bekenntnisschriften,* Manz, Regensburg 1913

MOLTMANN, J., *God for a Secular Society: The Public Relevance of Theology,* Fortress Press, Minneapolis 1999

MÜHLHAUPT, E., *Allgemeines Priestertum oder Klerikalismus?,* Calwer Hefte 65, Stuttgart 1963

MUTHIAH, R., *Christian Practices, Congregational Leadership and the Priesthood,* «Journal of Religious Leadership» 2 (2003) 167-203

------------------, *The Priesthood of all Believers in the 21st Century,* Pickwick, Eugene 2009

NIESEL, W., *The Theology of Calvin,* Grand Rapids Baker Book House, Michigan 1980

O'CALLAGHAN, P., *God and Mediation, Retrospective Appraisal of Luther the Reformer,* Fortress Press, Minneapolis 2017

--------------------------, *Luther and 'sola gratia': The Rapport between Grace. Human Freedom, Good Works and Moral Life,* «Scripta Theologica» 49 (2017) 193-212

O'COLLINS, G., KEENAN JONES, M., *Jesus Our Priest, A Christian Approach to the Priesthood of Christ,* Oxford University Press, Oxford 2010

PARKER, T.H.L., *Calvin: An Introduction to His Thought,* Geoffrey Chapman, London 1995

PIRENNE, H., *Histoire de l'Europe des invasions au XVIe siècle,* Nouvelle Société D'Éditions, Bruxelles 1939

RADE, M., *Das Königliche Priestertum der Gläubigen und seine Forderung an die Evangelischer Kirche unserer Zeit*, Mohr Siebeck, Tübingen 1918

RAHNER, K., *Gerecht und Sünder zugleich*, «Schriften zur Theologie» 6 (1965), 262-276; in English: *Justified and sinner at the same time*, «Theological Investigations» 6 (1969), 218-230

RATZINGER, J., *Pilgrim Fellowship of Faith, the Church as Communion*, Ignatius Press, San Francisco 2005

RODRÍGUEZ, P., *Sacerdocio ministerial y sacerdocio común en la estructura fundamental de la Iglesia*, «Romana» 4 (1987), 162-176

ROHLS, J., *Das geistliche Ambt in der reformatorischen theologie*, «Kerygma und Dogma, Zeitschrift für theologische Forschung und kirchliche Lehre» 31 (1985) 135-161

SAARINEN, R., *Justification by faith. The view of the Mannermaa School*, in: R. KOLB, I. DINGEL, L. BATKA (eds.), *The Oxford Handbook of Martin Luther's Theology*, Oxford University Press, Oxford 2014, 254-322

SCHWANKE, J., *Luther's theology of creation*, in: R. KOLB, I. DINGEL, L. BATKA (eds.), *The Oxford Handbook of Martin Luther's Theology*, Oxford University Press, Oxford 2014, 201-211

SILCOCK, J.G., *Luther on the Holy Spirit and his use of God's Word*, in: R. KOLB, I. DINGEL, L. BATKA (eds.), *The Oxford Handbook of Martin Luther's Theology*, Oxford University Press, Oxford 2014, 294-309

SLENCZKA, N., *Luther's anthropology*, in: R. KOLB, I. DINGEL, L. BATKA (eds.), *The Oxford Handbook of Martin Luther's Theology*, Oxford University Press, Oxford 2014, 212-232

STROHL, J.E., *Luther's eschatology*, in: R. KOLB, I. DINGEL, L. BATKA (eds.), *The Oxford Handbook of Martin Luther's Theology*, Oxford University Press, Oxford 2014, 353-362

TAYLOR, C., *A Secular Age*, The Belknap Press of Harvard University Press, Cambridge, Massachusetts, London 2007

TORI, M.T., *Luther and Cajetan on the Sacrifice of the Mass*, «Logia» IX (2000) 29-36

TROCHU, C.F., *le curé d'Ars, Jean-Marie-Baptise Vianney (1786-1859)*, Librairie Catholique Emmanuel Vitte, Lyon-Paris 1925

VANHOYE, A., *Sacerdotes antiguos, sacerdote nuevo según el Nuevo Testamento*, Ediciones Sígueme, Salamanca 2002

VOLTAIRE, *The works of Voltaire: Volume xxvii, Ancient and Modern History, vol. iv, Charles V., 1512—Philip II, 1584*, E.R. Dumont, Paris 1901

WENGERT, T.J., *Priesthood, Pastors, Bishops: Public Ministry for the Reformation and Today*, Fortress Press, Minneapolis 2008

YODER, J.H., *The Royal Priesthood. Essays Ecclesiological and Ecumenical*, Grand Rapids, Michigan 1994

INDEX

Abyss	35-39, 51, 52, 60, 80, 91, 101
Access, Direct access	35, 40-41, 45, 48-49, 55, 59-60, 63, 67, 76, 95, 107-108, 125-133, 137, 143-144, 146-148, 153, 159-166, 168, 177, 179, 185, 196, 199-201, 204
Admirabile commercium	40
Advocate	51, 64-65, 69, 71, 125-126, 192, 205
Anabaptists	54, 56, 81, 91, 110, 142
Analogy	33, 40, 82, 173, 182, 186, 203
Anamnesis	38, 139
Anarchy	142-143, 199
Anthropology	163-165
Ascension	104-105, 107, 125, 153, 160, 178-179, 188, 192, 204
Attribution, imputation	39, 53, 61-62, 80, 102, 104, 106-107, 109, 121, 128, 137, 145, 147, 163-164, 168, 177
Authority	24-27, 56, 59, 61, 63, 69, 83, 88, 90-92, 111-112, 136, 200, 202
Autonomy	176-177
Baptism	25-26, 32, 40, 51, 55, 59, 65-68, 70-71, 80-81, 83-84, 89, 112, 138, 149, 152, 162-163, 168, 183-187, 193, 200, 205
Benefits (spiritual)	18, 35, 39-41, 46, 48-51, 55, 57-58, 60, 79, 82, 95, 101-102, 127-128, 132, 138, 145-147, 159, 202
Calling, vocation	25, 26, 28, 56, 59, 68, 81, 84, 88, 92, 108, 110, 112-113, 120, 123, 128-129, 138, 143, 149, 152, 200
Capax Dei	37, 175
Certainty	30, 35-36, 40-41, 45, 47-51, 55, 60-63, 92, 101, 142-143, 146, 148, 151-152, 160-163, 165, 168, 190, 194, 197, 199, 201
Clergy	315, 24-32, 46, 56, 68, 80, 83-84, 112, 143, 149, 156, 200
Communion, community	46-47, 51, 53, 57, 60, 89, 92-93, 95, 102-109, 113, 121, 145-147, 151, 164, 166, 168-169, 172, 179-197, 201, 204-206

Confession	24, 30, 70, 72, 80, 83, 90, 112, 136, 145
Confidence	21, 42, 75, 79, 90, 100-101, 107, 130, 190, 197
Confusion	25, 55, 100, 103, 159-161, 167, 201
Congregation of believers	38, 55, 57, 81, 136, 166
Consacratio mundi	26
Continuity (principle of)	117, 172-173, 193, 200, 203-204
Contrition	39, 101, 165, 175-176, 192, 196, 201, 205
Conversion	30, 49, 88, 116, 150, 175, 189
Cooperation	52-54, 61, 108, 113-114, 138, 157, 166, 187, 191, 194, 206
Coram Deo	58-59
Counsels of perfection	26, 56
Creation	24, 36, 42, 47, 52, 60, 90, 95, 97-98, 104-105, 109, 116, 144, 150, 154, 157, 164-165, 172, 175-176, 178, 187-189, 192, 194, 203-205
ex nihilo	46, 49, 51-53, 64, 146-147, 161, 164-165, 172, 182
Creature(s)	35, 46-47, 52, 60, 90, 109, 113, 128, 144, 157, 176, 183-184, 187-188
Cross-bearing	108, 116-117, 133, 155
Death	38, 46, 53, 91, 100, 104, 106-108, 110, 116-119, 125, 132-134, 139, 149, 174
Decalogue, Law	26, 29-30, 36-39, 42, 61, 70, 100-101, 113-121, 124-127, 142-148, 150, 152, 155, 157, 166, 199, 201
Deification	103, 164
Devil, Satan	39, 54, 91, 155
Dialectics	20, 39, 46
Direct access, see Access	
Discipline	25, 28, 31, 70, 89, 92, 112-113, 120, 135-136, 143
Divine filiation	102, 109, 128, 146, 163, 182-186, 189, 204-205
Dualism	45, 52-53, 56, 168, 191
Ecclesiology	16, 35, 55, 89, 92, 143, 159, 160, 166-168, 181
Ecumenical dialogue	11-12, 16, 171, 197, 199
Elect, godly	90, 98-99, 103-106, 109-111, 114-121, 126-139, 145

Equality (radical)	15, 55-56, 89, 142-143, 146-150, 160, 183-186, 199-200, 204
Eschatological	
Access	45, 48, 55, 91, 107, 143-144, 147-148, 161, 168, 199
Benefits	35, 46, 48-50, 55, 58-60, 95, 159-162, 177, 201
Certainty	30, 35, 55, 63, 163, 165, 197
Confusion	55, 159-161, 167, 201
Destiny	26, 50, 60, 142, 146, 167, 178-179, 190, 192, 194, 199, 204-205
Estates, Orders	23-26, 33, 56-57
Eternal life	40, 50-51, 53, 65, 100, 102, 114, 116, 120, 129, 136, 159, 162
Eucharist	60, 101, 174, 179, 180, 188, 193-194, 203-204
Existential theology	17-18, 151-152
Ex opere operato	27-28, 167
Experience	
of certainty	42-43, 45
of paradox	19, 45
of salvation	29-30, 37, 40, 45
of sin	35-37
Expiation	77, 124, 132
Fall (Adam's)	36, 95, 97, 109, 119, 164, 172, 176, 184, 190, 204
Faith	
and Certainty	35, 41-43, 47-51, 58, 61, 142, 148, 152, 199, 201
and Despair	38-39, 41-42, 51, 100-101, 142, 145, 160
and Dualism	20-21, 45-46, 48-50, 60-61, 145, 153, 160, 165, 168, 174, 181
Experience, Act of faith	28, 30-32, 37, 40, 42-43, 46-49, 52, 55, 57-62, 65, 68, 70-72, 75-77, 79-80, 82, 85, 89, 91-92, 99, 101-102, 105, 107-108, 110, 114, 116, 134, 142, 145-148, 150, 152-153, 159-163, 167, 169, 172-173, 176, 182, 184, 189, 196, 199-203
and Identification	51, 102-103, 105, 108-109, 112, 145, 181
and Justification	17-18, 30-32, 35-36, 40-41, 58, 79, 85, 98-99, 120, 142, 145, 147, 155, 161, 167, 190, 202

Objective faith	25, 28, 64, 67-68, 70, 88-89, 97-101, 113-114, 116, 125, 127-128, 134, 142, 145, 162-164, 166, 168, 171-172, 174, 176, 181, 184, 186, 188, 190, 194
and Reason	20-21, 37-38, 42-43, 46, 161
Family	367, 84, 117, 133, 138, 171, 174, 180-187, 190, 193, 196-197, 204-205
Favour (*Favor Dei*)	81, 115, 124, 126-128, 132-133, 138, 151, 161-162, 199
Filiation (Divine)	102, 109, 128, 146, 163, 182, 184-186, 189, 204-205
Forgiveness	17, 40, 50-51, 65, 70, 101, 115, 151, 163, 176, 205
Freedom	36, 40, 46, 50, 58, 92, 95, 111, 114-115, 121, 146-148, 151, 160, 162-165, 173, 175-176, 187-192, 194-197, 199, 201-206
Fröhliche Wechsel	40, 84
Gap, see Abyss	
Gift	30, 41, 47, 52, 56, 59, 83-85, 103, 109, 147, 151, 154, 165, 186-189, 194, 200
Glory, Majesty	35-36, 46, 48, 52-53, 64, 72, 90-92, 95-98, 100, 103, 108-109, 113, 116-118, 120-121, 128, 130-131, 136, 144, 147-150, 152, 165, 176-178, 194, 199, 202, 206
Gospel	20, 24, 27-28, 30, 32-33, 37-38, 40, 50, 54-55, 57, 66-67, 69, 80, 83, 88, 90, 99-101, 108-109, 114-115, 127-128, 134-138, 143, 145, 152, 165, 174
Grace	21, 27-28, 32-33, 36, 39, 47, 51, 55, 57-58, 61-62, 66, 70, 77, 95, 98, 101, 105, 110, 113-114, 116, 125-128, 135, 149, 155, 163, 166-168, 172, 174, 176, 180, 182, 186-188, 191-192, 195, 200, 202, 205-206
Gratitude	77, 128, 138, 155, 157, 176, 189
Greatness	59, 72, 84, 95, 149, 152, 159, 177, 196-197, 200
Heart	30, 36-38, 45, 72-73, 77, 79, 95-96, 99-100, 114, 116, 119, 137, 146-147, 161, 165, 168, 172, 175-176, 179-180, 188, 192, 203
Hermeneutical key	17, 19, 35, 160
Hierarchy	24-25, 27, 56, 180-183

Holiness	35-38, 40, 42, 46-53, 55-59, 97, 102-107, 109-110, 111, 114-116, 120-121, 124-129, 137, 146-149, 156-157, 160, 165, 167, 177, 190, 196, 200, 202
Human nature	19, 35-37, 39, 42, 48-49, 51, 53, 55, 61, 64, 70, 82, 84, 95-100, 103-106, 110, 117-120, 144, 146, 155, 164, 167, 176, 178, 181, 184, 204
Humility	51-52, 100, 150-152, 155, 164, 186, 190, 195-196, 202,
Identification (spiritual)	35, 39-40-42, 49, 51, 55, 60, 77-79, 84, 108, 116, 133, 162, 175, 181-184
Imitation of Christ	59-60, 78, 116-117, 133, 154-155, 177
Imputation, see attribution	
Incarnation	38, 45, 104, 162, 173-174, 178, 181, 184, 188, 193, 203-204
Indulgences (selling of)	29, 31-32
Intention	18, 31, 36, 38, 45, 54, 58-59, 118, 120, 188-189
Intercession	42, 65, 76, 79, 84, 108, 125-126, 130, 144, 147, 188, 196, 202, 206
In statu viae	46, 48, 50, 52, 95, 108, 167, 179, 182, 184, 190
See also Pilgrims	
Joy	3117, 141, 176
Joyous exchange	40, 67-68, 84, 102, 145, 151
Judgement (particular)	48, 50, 98-99, 108, 119, 159-160, 165
Justification	17-18, 32, 50, 58, 61, 68-69, 77, 98-99, 102, 109, 114, 119, 145, 159, 162-163, 202
Kingdom	28, 55, 63, 66, 90, 92, 99, 107-109, 113, 119-120, 125, 146, 156, 194
Knowledge of God	19, 21, 35-39, 45, 48, 55, 90, 95-96, 98-99, 114, 120, 144, 161, 188
Laity, laymen	15, 25-27, 55-56, 59, 124, 136, 143, 149, 156
Law, see Decalogue	
Layered structure	178-179, 183, 196-197, 204
Liturgy	327-28, 57, 90, 92, 120, 148, 168, 179, 203-204
Love	347, 105, 109-110, 131, 145, 155, 183, 192
for God	97, 100, 109-110, 119, 176, 189-193, 206

God's love	42, 51, 67-68, 119, 151-152, 172-174, 190-192, 195, 206
of neighbour	56, 58-59, 71, 78-80, 83, 151-152, 176, 202
of self	39, 97, 116
Self-giving	61, 78, 82, 103, 147, 152, 154-157, 179, 193-195, 201-206
Magisterium	46, 111
Majesty, see Glory	
Mass	324, 28, 30-31, 65, 72-80, 133, 191
Mediation	57, 75, 79, 82-83, 111, 129, 137, 149, 166-169, 202
Merit	323, 32, 41-42, 62, 65, 78, 85, 98, 101-104, 106, 109, 114
Mind (human)	38-39, 42, 46, 52, 57, 92, 96-97, 100, 114, 118, 120, 146-147, 161-162, 165, 168, 172, 176
Ministerial priesthood	12, 15-16, 22, 26-27, 32, 56, 72, 85, 110, 141, 168, 171, 186, 193-194, 199, 201, 205-206
Ministries, ministry	28, 56, 59, 70, 81, 84, 89, 111-112, 123, 135-136, 144, 174, 194, 200
Morality	61, 175
Mortification	30, 61, 117-118, 155, 157
Mystery	177, 181, 188, 196
See also Paschal Mystery	
Neighbour (doctrine of)	50, 55-56, 58-59, 71, 78-79, 83-84, 97, 109-110, 129, 151, 155, 157, 160, 163, 165, 168, 176, 179, 202
Nothingness	38-39, 53, 72, 77, 100, 105, 145, 151, 154-155, 201
Obedience	26, 92, 100-101, 106-108, 113-118, 121, 143, 148, 157, 176
Offering	58, 65, 72-79, 84-85, 125, 130-132, 134, 137-138, 152-153, 162, 177, 179-180, 185, 193-195, 200, 203, 205-206
Ontology of relations	175, 183-184
Orders, see Estates	
Paradox	19-20, 37, 46, 52, 54, 92, 145, 160-161, 172-173, 203
Parallel	346, 52-53, 104-107, 119, 121, 146, 163, 181, 203
Parousia	160, 179, 204

Paschal Mystery	149, 172, 178, 188, 192, 193, 195, 204
Penance, Penitence	29-31, 61, 77, 155
Perfection	25-27, 50, 53, 64, 96, 100, 103, 107, 109, 111, 135, 142, 157, 184, 193
Perseverance	50, 114
Phenomenology (realist)	19
Pilgrims	46, 100, 104, 108-110, 134, 145, 177, 190
See also *in statu viae*	
Power of the keys, see Confession	
Praise	362, 68, 72-79, 83, 90, 128, 130, 134, 137-139, 147, 152-157, 192, 202
Prayer	48, 51, 64-66, 70-79, 82, 84, 88, 107-108, 114, 128-130, 137-138, 148, 150, 152, 155, 169, 179, 195, 202, 204
Preaching	25, 27-28, 32-33, 38, 54, 57, 61, 69-71, 81-84, 90, 112, 123, 134, 137-138, 143, 150, 152, 161, 169, 193, 202
Predestination (double)	92, 108, 119, 160
Presence	41, 58, 60, 72, 87, 100-101, 104-108, 125, 127, 129, 133-135, 151, 163, 167, 171, 179, 180, 193, 202, 204
Promise	20-21, 31, 33, 39, 41-42, 48, 50-51, 58, 65, 70, 72, 75-80, 82, 99, 100-101, 104, 107, 109, 112, 151, 154, 160, 165-166, 169, 190
Qualitas, quality	106, 121, 175-176, 205
Reality	18-21, 27, 32, 36, 39-40, 43, 45-50, 53, 58, 62, 100, 115, 127, 146, 153, 160-167, 172, 174, 177, 180-181, 190, 192, 195-196, 203-204
Reconciliation	70, 177
Redemption	18, 42, 47-49, 51-52, 77, 80, 82, 98, 104, 132-133, 138, 146-147, 150-151, 157, 159-162, 169, 172, 174, 176, 178, 182, 187, 199, 202, 204
Reductionism	46, 173, 202
Regeneration	50-51, 68, 92, 108-110, 113-114, 120, 134, 146, 148, 182, 200
See also Sanctification	
Religious	24-28, 32, 55-56, 149, 156-157, 194
Repentance	70, 110, 114
Replication principle	116

Respect	88, 114, 175, 177, 187-188, 194, 203-204, 206
Resurrection	38, 50, 104, 106, 118, 134, 149, 173-174, 178
Revelation	19-20, 32, 37, 81, 99, 127, 171, 173, 175, 203
Righteousness	29-32, 40, 46, 49, 51, 65, 70, 91, 97, 101-121, 125, 128, 136, 146, 152, 163, 191
Roman Catholic Church	25, 31-33, 54, 57, 61, 88, 90-91, 110, 142, 155
Sacrament(s)	24-28, 32, 36, 54, 57, 60, 73-77, 81-82, 84, 89-91, 101, 104, 110-112, 134, 143-144, 149, 165, 168, 179, 181, 188
Sacramental economy	60, 180, 186, 204
Sacrifice	
Christ's	23, 30-32, 36, 42, 51, 62, 64-65, 67, 69-70, 72-79, 84-85, 87, 98, 124-125-126, 138, 147, 153-156, 160-162, 177, 179, 191-196, 201-206
Believers'	23, 58, 68-69-70, 72-79, 82-85, 87, 118, 124, 128-134, 137-139, 147, 149, 152-157, 167, 169, 182, 193-196, 200-206
Saints	11, 19, 31, 55, 57, 64, 67, 84, 116, 130, 135, 179, 188, 191, 195-196, 204
Sanctification	49-53, 56, 92, 103-104, 106, 111-114, 128, 132, 134, 161, 163, 172,
see also Regeneration	177-178, 188, 194-195, 204, 206
Scripture	17, 32, 64, 66, 81, 90, 99, 111-112, 135-136, 142, 145, 150, 161, 182
Second Vatican Council	12, 16, 22, 149-150, 171
Secular, secularisation	25-27, 56, 108, 119-120, 136
Self-denial	61-62, 116-117, 129, 137-138, 152, 154-157, 195-196, 202
Self-giving	61, 78, 82, 103, 147, 152, 154-157, 179, 193-195, 201-206
Self-righteousness	29-32, 73, 90, 101, 152, 191
Service	23, 31, 56, 58-59, 68-69, 78, 81, 84, 108, 115, 118-119, 131, 136-138, 155-157, 168-169, 179, 194-195, 200, 202
Simul iustus et peccator	48-49, 61, 160
Sola Dei Gloria	35, 120

Solidarity	77, 85, 113, 130, 138, 152, 154
Soul	340, 53, 56, 64, 95, 100-101, 106, 109, 127, 132, 151, 176
Sovereignty	35, 92, 95, 97-98, 104, 111, 123, 143, 146-148, 150, 161, 163-164, 176, 199
Sphere	
Spiritual	41, 45-52, 57-62, 67, 70, 76, 82-83, 153, 159-160, 165-168, 171-172, 196, 201
Temporal-earthly	20-21, 36, 40-42, 45-62, 64, 67-68, 70, 77, 79-85, 91, 95, 101, 105, 107-108, 113, 120-121, 137, 144-147, 152-156, 159-172, 174-175, 179-182, 184, 187-188, 190, 192-197, 200-206
Strict liability	98, 121
Suffering	20, 38, 70, 77-78, 85, 116-117, 133, 155, 194
Supper	370, 80-81, 84, 89, 112, 131, 133-134, 138-139
Task	324, 27, 32, 37, 80, 90, 143, 153-157, 177, 187, 189, 194, 202
Thanksgiving	41, 57, 72-79, 83, 130, 132, 134, 137-138, 155, 196, 202
Theandric actions	191
Theology of the Cross (*theologia crucis*)	19-21, 37-42, 50-51, 60-61, 104, 145, 173
Throne (of God)	41, 48-52, 55, 108, 125, 136, 148, 152-153, 156-160, 179, 196, 206
Time and space	41, 48, 52, 60, 111, 145, 159-160, 165, 171-172, 176-180, 188, 193-194, 199, 204, 206
Trust, Distrust	19-21, 30-31, 36-39, 42, 49, 51, 57, 81, 91, 101, 127, 154, 162, 165-166, 173, 192, 199
Truth	54, 57, 63, 90, 96, 178, 188, 190
Union, communion	40, 46, 47, 51, 53, 60-61, 89, 92-93, 95, 102-109, 113, 116, 120-121, 128, 130, 144-147, 151, 164-169, 172, 178-197, 201, 204-206
Universal call to holiness	55, 59, 149
Value	56, 58, 73, 77, 80, 83, 85, 104, 108, 113, 118, 121, 133, 154, 157, 175, 194, 201
Vocation, see calling	
Vows	326, 29

Will
God's 24, 30, 70, 78, 92, 100, 105-106, 114-119, 133, 135, 143, 145, 147, 152, 155-156, 162, 184
Human's 37, 41, 47, 78, 95, 113-117, 121, 175-176, 179, 188, 192, 203
Works 17, 23, 29-32, 36-37, 41, 46, 53, 58, 61, 68-73, 78, 83-84, 91, 96-97, 101-108, 113-116, 118, 121, 131-132, 134, 137-138, 146-147, 152-156, 163, 168, 176, 191, 196
Worship 29, 70, 72, 83, 88, 91, 111, 115, 131-132, 137-138, 148, 179, 184